A Member of
a Distinguished Family

GENERATIONS

A History of Canada's Peoples

A Member of
a Distinguished Family

The Polish Group in Canada

Henry Radecki
with Benedykt Heydenkorn

Published by McClelland and Stewart in association with
the Multiculturalism Program, Department
of the Secretary of State of Canada and the
Publishing Centre, Supply and Services Canada.

The Canadian Publishers
McClelland and Stewart
25 Hollinger Road
Toronto, Ontario

Printed and bound in Canada
   by John Deyell Company

DEDICATION

This monograph is dedicated to the thousands of anonymous Polish immigrants whose life in Canada was without heroic deeds but full of courage, perseverance and suffering, crowned by later achievements, satisfaction and even happiness.

Contents

Preface

People of Polish descent at present comprise about 2 per cent of the population of Canada. Yet among this small percentage is a very large number of engineers, university lecturers, researchers, doctors and lawyers, a number highly out of proportion to their small segment of the population. In these particular areas, among many others, the Polish group has made a significant contribution to the social and economic life of Canada.

This was not always so, for the patterns of Polish immigration to Canada and the individuals that did immigrate initially, did not allow for rapid upward mobility in Canadian society. The first immigrants to arrive in Canada came as the result of political persecution in their homeland, and even though they were among the better educated classes, their contributions were not significant due to their small numbers. But after the late 1850s many Polish famers came to Canada, at first to the Renfrew County area of Ontario, and later to the West after Clifford Sifton began promoting settlement in the area.

After World War II, many skilled Poles began arriving in Canada, and large numbers of them settled in urban areas, They established their own churches, newspapers, and social organizations. By this time as well the second generation Poles, whose parents had been the early farmers, were moving into the urban areas and were becoming integrated into all aspects of Canadian life.

During all phases of their arrival in Canada, the Polish group has made significant contributions to agriculture and industry. Much of the farming area of the West, in particular in Manitoba and Alberta, was developed by the Poles. The skilled labourers of the post-World War II era added a great deal to the economic and manufacturing potential of the country. But their contributions go far beyond these areas. Polish poets, painters, educators, politicians and publishers are now prominent.

The impact of Polish settlement in Canada is far from over. Be they immigrant or native-born, the Poles in Canada today have shown a strong desire to offer their particular skills and talents to the development of the country, and unquestionably they will continue to thrive in the multicultural environment which Canada offers to all people.

Dr Stanley Haidasz

Editor's Introduction

Canadians, like many other people, have recently been changing their attitude towards the ethnic dimension in society. Instead of thinking of the many distinctive heritages and identities to be found among them as constituting a problem, though one that time would solve, they have begun to recognize the ethnic diversity of their country as a rich resource. They have begun to take pride in the fact that people have come and are coming here from all parts of the world, bringing with them varied outlooks, knowledge, skills and traditions, to the great benefit of all.

It is for this reason that Book IV of the *Report of the Royal Commission on Bilingualism and Biculturalism* dealt with the cultural contributions of the ethnic groups other than the British, the French and the Native Peoples to Canada, and that the federal government in its response to Book IV announced that the Citizenship Branch of the Department of the Secretary of State would commission "histories specifically directed to the background, contributions and problems of various cultural groups in Canada." This series presents the histories that have resulted from that mandate. Although commissioned by the Government, they are not intended as definitive or official, but rather as the efforts of scholars to bring together much of what is known about the ethnic groups studied, to indicate what remains to be learned, and thus to stimulate further research concerning the ethnic dimension in Canadian society. The histories are to be objective, analytical, and readable, and directed towards the general reading public, as well as students at the senior high school and the college and university levels, and teachers in the elementary schools.

Most Canadians belong to an ethnic group, since to do so is simply to have "a sense of identity rooted in a common origin . . . whether this common origin is real or imaginary."[1] The Native Peoples, the British and French (referred to as charter groups because they were the first Europeans to take possession of the land), the groups such as the Germans and Dutch who have been established in Canada for over a hundred years and those who began to arrive only yesterday all have traditions and values that they cherish and that now are part of the cultural riches that Canadians share. The groups vary widely in numbers, geographical location and distribution and degree of social and economic power. The stories of their struggles, failures and triumphs will be told in this series.

As the Royal Commission on Bilingualism and Biculturalism pointed out, this sense of ethnic origin or identity "is much keener in certain individuals than in others."[2] In contemporary Canadian society, with the increasing number of intermarriages across ethnic lines, and hence the growing diversity of people's ancestors, many are coming to identify themselves as simple Canadian, without reference to their ancestral origins. In focusing on the ethnic dimension of Canadian society, past and present, the series does not assume that everyone should be categorized into one particular group, or that ethnicity is always the most important dimension of people's lives. It is, however, one dimension that needs examination if we are to understand fully the contours and nature of Canadian society and identity.

Professional Canadian historians have in the past emphasized political and economic history, and since the country's economic and political institutions have been controlled largely by people of British and French origin, the role of those of other origins in the development of Canada has been neglected. Also, Canadian historians in the past have been almost exclusively of British and French origin, and have lacked the interest and the linguistic skills necessary to explore the history of other ethnic groups. Indeed, there has rarely ever been an examination of the part played by specifically British – or, better, specifically English, Irish, Scottish and Welsh – traditions and values in Canadian development, because of the lack of recognition of pluralism in the society. The part played by French traditions and values, and particular varieties of French traditions and values, has for a number of reasons been more carefully scrutinized.

This series is an indication of growing interest in Canadian social history, which includes immigration and ethnic history. This may particularly be a reflection of an increasing number of scholars whose origins and ethnic identities are other than British or French. Because such trends are recent, many of the authors of the histories in this series have not had a large body of published writing to work from. It is true that some histories have already been written of particular groups other than the British and French; but these have often been characterized by filio pietism, a narrow perspective and a dearth of scholarly analysis.

Despite the scarcity of secondary sources, the authors have been asked to be as comprehensive as possible, and to give balanced coverage to a number of themes: historical background, settlement patterns, ethnic identity and assimilation, ethnic associations, population trends, religion, values, occupations and social class, the family, the ethnic press, language patterns, political behaviour, education, interethnic relations, the arts and recreation. They have also been asked to give a sense of the way the group differs in various parts of the country. Finally, they have been asked to give, as much as possibile, an insider's view of what the immigrant and ethnic experiences were like at different periods of time, but yet at the same time to be as objective as possible, and not simply to present the group as it sees itself, or as it would like to be seen.

The authors have thus been faced with a herculean task. To the extent that they have succeeded, they provide us with new glimpses into many aspects of Canadian society of the past and the present. To the extent that they have fallen short of their goal, they challenge other historians, sociologists and social anthropologists to continue the work begun here.

Jean Burnet
Howard Palmer

[1] *Report of the Royal Commission on Bilingualism and Biculturalism.* General Introduction, paragraph 7.
[2] Ibid, paragraph 8.

Authors' Preface

For some decades now Canada has been referred to as a 'Mosaic of cultures'. The Polish ethnic group is one of the larger segments which form this Multicultural Society. The census of 1971 found 316,430 Canadians of Polish origin. They are contributing in all fields, helping shape Canada's cultural and economic life, enjoying the benefits which Canada offers to all its citizens. This monograph is devoted to the historical portrayal of the Polish immigrants and their descendants who have chosen Canada as their new home.

It is hoped that the monograph will serve to acquaint all interested Canadians with the Polish ethnic group and that it will allow Canadian-born descendants of Polish immigrants to acquire a broader and deeper awareness of the history and development of their ethnic group under often difficult conditions. Lastly, the monograph will serve to illustrate the existing gaps in knowledge about this group, and spur scholars and others to further research in this area.

Through the co-operation of various Polish organizations, especially the Canadian-Polish Research Institute in Toronto, Federal and Provincial bodies, and many individuals, the writers were able to accumulate a wide but far from complete range of data, articles, memoirs, and documents dealing with some aspect of the Polish presence in Canada. No one topic has been dealt with in depth. A number of issues are considered in some detail, others are touched on but briefly. We have thought widely and as rigorously as our resources permitted, but do not claim to have presented a total or fully accurate portrayal of the Polish group, its development and its present life in Canada.

We have not attempted to provide detailed information relating to the experiences of particular individuals or groups, the establishment of particular institutions, organizations, or voluntary associations, or to the qualities or achievements of numerous outstanding Polish individuals. We have consciously attempted to avoid those topics, focusing rather on the group and their general experiences. By the emphasis on the general patterns and broad developments of the Polish immigrants to Canada we hope to inform and impress on those raised and on those born in Canada the need for awareness of their heritage and history.

There are a number of topics of some interest that have not been raised in this monograph. The contribution of the Poles to arts and letters in the Canadian society has received adequate attention in a number of sources and we deem that no further elaboration is necessary. No attention was given to the participation of the Polish ethnic group in the political life of Canada; details in other areas such as occupational and status mobility, Polish group social stratification and leisure patterns, geographical and residential mobility and residential concentration, all await further research. Should this monograph allow for a better understanding of the culture, values, traditions, and dynamics that characterize and distinguish the Polish people from other ethno-cultural groups in this society, despite the recognizable gaps of information, we will be satisfied with this effort.

We wish to acknowledge the role of the Federal Department of the Secretary of State in initiating and supporting this study generously through advice and financial aid. We are deeply grateful for the patience and understanding shown by our wives during the long process of data gathering and writing. Our thanks go to the many individuals who shared with us their knowledge and experiences. We would especially like to acknowledge contributions made by the Director of the Canadian-Polish Research Institute in Toronto, Mr. R.K. Kogler. Our gratitude to Professors W.W. Isajiw of the University of Toronto, and H. Palmer of the University of Calgary, for reading, comments and expert criticism of the first drafts. We are especially indebted to Professor Jean Burnet of Glendon College, York University for her invaluable suggestions and advice throughout all the phases of rewriting the monograph. Her involvement in this effort is sincerely appreciated. We alone, of course, are responsible for the monograph's failings.

Henry Radecki
Benedykt Heydenkorn

ONE

Overview

The first Polish immigrant is known to have come to Canada in 1752,[1] but in the next hundred years only a few other Poles followed his example. It is likely that larger numbers of Polish immigrants have made Canada their new home every year since Confederation than in the entire preceding century. The Canadian censuses of 1850-51,[2] 1860-61, 1870-71, and 1880-81 suggest that the number of Poles in Canada was slowly increasing. Difficulty in establishing exact numbers lies in the fact that the data are incorporated under the census categories of Russian-Polish or Russian and Polish. Without further research it is not possible to determine how many of the people listed under this category were Russian and how many Polish.

It is quite likely that the classification of Poles as a distinct category applied only to those immigrants originating from the Congress Kingdom, an area which included the Russian domain of partitioned Poland. There was at least one other large group of Polish people already in Canada in 1870 whose numbers are not recorded within the Polish category, those being the Kashubs in the Renfrew-Barry's Bay area of Ontario. The census data to 1901 are inadequate and require further research.

Statistics are available which provide the number of new Polish arrivals beginning in 1900, but once again the figures do not correspond to the Canadian decennial census and require further clarification.

The Canadian census for 1901 shows 6,285 people of Polish origin in Canada. Between the years 1900 to 1914 the Department of Manpower and Immigration registered 109,613 Polish immigrants arriving in Canada, yet the 1921 Canadian census found only 53,403 individuals of the Polish ethnic group. Even without allowing for the natural increase, incongruity is obvious.

There are a number of factors which could possibly throw some light on

1

TABLE 1

ORIGIN OF PEOPLE – RUSSIA AND POLAND

Census-Classification	New Bruns.	Nova Scotia	Prince Edward Island	QUEBEC			ONTARIO			Manitoba	B.C.	Territories
				Montreal	Quebec	Other	Toronto	Hamilton	Other			
Russia and Poland 1860–1861				20	21	18	23	12	126	no data	no data	no data
TOTALS					59			161				
Russia and Poland 1870–1871	1	28	–	28	29	129	81	31	280	no data	no data	no data
TOTALS	1	28	–		186			392				
Russia and Poland 1880–1881	26	Halifax 14	1	220	?		132	38	–	Winnipeg 6	48	no data
TOTALS	26	30			300			787		24	48	
Russia and Poland 1885–1886										293 (Birth-place, 5,724)		17 (Birth-place, 97)
1890–1891 Polish as a separate category	1	9		176	4		97	17		31	New Wstm.29 Vanc. 3 Vict. 5	Alta. 10 Assinb. E.177 Assinb. W. 4
TOTALS					236			187		31	40	191

Sources: *Census of the Canadas, 1860-1861. Census of Canada, 1870-71; 1880-81; 1890-91. Census of Manitoba, 1885-6.*

2

TABLE 2
NUMBER OF POLISH IMMIGRANTS ARRIVING IN CANADA
1900 - 1974*

Year	No.	Year	No.	Year	No.	Year	No.
1900/1	4,702	1920	3,544	1940	19	1960	3,182
1902/2	6,550	1921	2,853	1941	16	1961	2,753
1902/3	8,656	1922	2,758	1942	5	1962	1,956
1903/4	8,398	1923	4,157	1943	6	1963	1,866
1904/5	7,671	1924	2,908	1944	32	1964	2,399
1905/6	6,381	1925	1,952	1945	249	1965	2,566
1906/7	2,685	1926	5,359	1946	565	1966	1,678
1907/8	15,861	1927	8,248	1947	2,610	1967	1,470
1908	7,346	1928	8,319	1948	13,799	1968	1,092
1909	4,098	1929	6,197	1949	12,233	1969	859
1910	5,454	1930	4,968	1950	6,612	1970	723
1911	6,028	1931	560	1951	12,938	1971	1,132
1912	10,077	1932	379	1952	5,485	1972	1,321
1913	13,339	1933	360	1953	3,176	1973	1,261
1914	2,373	1934	392	1954	2,274	1974	945
1915	7	1935	405	1955	1,886		
1916	15	1936	378	1956	2,269		
1917		1937	632	1957	2,909		
1918	2	1938	570	1958	2,996		
1919	24	1939	381	1959	3,733		

* In the years 1900 to 1965, Polish was defined by ethnic origin. Since 1966, Polish category is based on the country of former residence.

Source: *The Report of the Royal Commission* (1970; Table A-1; 238-245), and immigration statistics for years 1966-1974.

this puzzle. Before 1918 Poland was partitioned among three neighbouring states: Russia, Austria and Germany. Immigrants required passports, exit permits or other documents which had to be obtained from the official authorities in their communities. The Canadian officials, who were perhaps unaware or unconcerned with ethnic distinctions, applied the criterion of citizenship based on the immigrants' documents for purposes of census statistics. Usually not fluent in English, the immigrants were unable to provide the correct information even if they wished to do so.

Another important factor relates to identity. The vast majority from among this phase of Polish immigration had an extremely weak or underdeveloped sense of national identity. First, they saw themselves as subjects of one of the emperors – Austrian, Prussian, or Russian. This identity was imposed on them throughout their lives and over generations. It was evident in conscription to military service, payment of taxes, and the presence of the official representatives of the emperors – soldiers, policemen, and petty bureaucrats. Officially, they were the subjects of

3

whichever power ruled over them. They also referred to themselves as Poles from Galicia (Austrian Poland), or from the Congress Kingdom (Russian Poland) or from "Poznańskie" or "Śląsk" (Prussian Poland). But most clearly and distinctly they identified themselves as members of a particular community with its immediate surroundings. As Balch[3] put it, "Each little village was a tiny world in itself, with its own traditions and ways, its own dress, perhaps even its own dialect. The neighbour from the next town . . . is an outsider."

This was to change for the Polish immigrants following the events of the World War I, but the initial absence of clear ethnic identity resulted in great confusion for the Canadian authorities; large numbers of Poles were classified or identified themselves as Austrians, Germans or Russians. When Poland regained its independence in 1918 the new nation contained a number of ethnic minorities who identified themselves or were classified as Polish. This resulted in further confusion, which, according to some writers, has not been fully resolved and has led to what may be termed an 'ethnic numbers game,' in which some groups claim members in other ethnic groups.[4]

The two factors may explain a proportion of the statistical incongruity of the numbers of Polish people in Canada in the period between 1900 and 1921, but two other factors need to be considered as well. Many immigrants from Poland did not come with the intention of remaining permanently in Canada but expected to work for a period of time, earn funds and return to reclaim their mortgaged land or to purchase farms. While no statistical data are available on the returning immigrants (Canada has never kept statistics on this movement) some writers claim that between 10% and 15% of Polish immigrants did in fact return. It is likely that those figures should be revised and the figure of 35-45% returnees accepted as a more realistic one. Prior to 1921, entrance to the United States was comparatively easy for all Europeans. No data are at present available concerning the numbers of Polish immigrants who arrived in Canada and were registered as landed immigrants but moved eventually to the United States.

A final consideration revolves around the total assimilation of Polish immigrants and especially their descendants into one of the dominant groups – the French and the Anglo-Saxons – or into another minority, usually the Ukrainians. Primarily, the assimilation followed marriage with a non-Polish spouse. Statistical data show that there was a preponderance of males in the Polish ethnic group.[5] Many brought over their fiancés or prospective brides from Poland, when practical. Others resorted to easier solutions and married those with whom they were in closest contact. For the scattered and isolated individuals the choice fell on the French, Anglo-Saxons and other ethnic groups. These factors could explain the obvious incongruities of the two sets of data, but their precise role remains to be tested.

As Table 2 shows, only in 1917 is there no record of Polish immigration to Canada. Despite this seemingly unbroken movement of people, there are in fact five discernible periods. These can be distinguished by societal conditions in Poland and in Canada, and by the kinds of people arriving: their socio-economic characteristics, their motives for emigration, their numbers, and their last place of residence before coming to Canada.

During the first and the longest phase, which lasted until 1895, a relatively small number of individuals and groups came to Canada for a variety of reasons. The next phase saw thousands of people arriving in search of work and land, predominantly from Austrian Poland, an area known as Galicia. This mass movement of people culminated in the year 1907 with the arrival of 15,861 Polish immigrants and ceased in 1914. The third phase began in 1920. Again, there was a mass movement of people coming in search of work and land, this time from the already independent state and not overwhelmingly from Galicia. Restrictions introduced by an order-in-council in 1930 put a virtual stop to immigration and fewer than 4,000 Polish immigrants came to Canada between 1932 and 1939, before the outbreak of World War II stopped all movement. The fourth phase began in 1945, and in the next eleven years another 63,845 immigrants arrived in Canada, this time not directly from Poland, but from Italy, Great Britain, various parts of continental Europe, and other parts of the world. They were the veterans of the Polish armed forces, ex-prisoners of war, concentration camp inmates, and slave labourers in Germany, liberated by one of the Western Allies: political refugees who did not wish to live under a Communist socio-political system. The final and ongoing phase, beginning in 1957, is numerically smaller than the three preceding ones, originating more and more directly from Poland.

This study will elaborate further on each of these phases through a broad characterization of the people belonging to them and of their motives for emigrating to Canada, but it may be useful to introduce the Polish people by providing a brief overview of the structure of the country of the origin.

THE CONTEXT OF POLAND

The year 966, when the ruler of the largest independent princedom was baptized, is generally accepted as the beginning of the history of Poland. The tribal history of the Polish people goes back much further, but there is a dearth of accurate and trustworthy sources in this respect. Scholars base their findings on the brief remarks of a few chroniclers and travellers. Thus it seems more valid to begin the outline of Poland's history with the above date, especially since Prince Mieszko constructed the framework of the Polish state. He consistently strove for the creation of a homogeneous state with a monarch to whom the feudal princes would be required to pay allegiance as the central authority. By marrying a Czech princess, Mieszko opened the Christian era in his geographical and national territories.

The history of the Polish nation is full of turmoil, drama, successes, and failures. Mieszko's son, Bolesław, managed to free himself from paying tribute to the Roman-German Holy Empire and to crown himself as king, but the new state faced serious problems following his death. Throughout Poland's entire history, a tendency to expand eastward has always been characteristic of her foreign policy. In some ways Boleslaw was the initiator of this policy, as he conquered territory as far east as Kiev. Several centuries passed, however, before Poland was again in a position to fulfil her ambitious political goals. Eastward expansion was a result of objective circumstances since the political situation in these areas was fluid, the organization of states was still in its infancy and took the form of struggles and battles between various feudal lords, whereas in the west the situation was more stable. The eastward expansion culminated in the Union of Lublin in 1569, when Lithuania merged with the Polish Kingdom.

It is remarkable that while Poland from the fifteenth century on enlarged her territory in the easterly direction, she was able to establish only superficial cultural roots there. Poland was not a colonizing nation and managed only to assimilate some members of the Lithuanian, Byelorussian and Ukrainian higher classes; the middle and lower classes were left untouched by Polish influences. During the Renaissance, her most glorious period, Poland was the most tolerant nation in Europe. The burning of heretics, religious wars, and the persecution of religious minorities, so prevalent in other European nations at the time, were all largely absent in Poland. When Jews were persecuted in Western Europe and had to flee from or were driven out of Spain, Portugal, England, and the German principalities, Poland not only gave them shelter but also offered them self-government in religious matters. Naturally, religious tolerance was neither unlimited nor permanent, but even during the most intense period of counter-reformation activities, Polish dissidents – the Arians – did not perish at the stake but left the country.

Until her loss of independence in 1795, Poland was a monarchy in which the ruling class was the nobility or the "szlachta." Kings were elected, but their power was dependent upon their prevailing political position among a few powerful magnate families. The principle of unanimity of the Diet's decisions prevented both the magnates and the king from achieving absolute power. "Liberum veto" – that is, one vote of opposition with the power to negate all discussion and to make the passing of certain statutes impossible – was simultaneously an instrument of factiousness and a manifestation of true democracy, pushed to its limits. Its destructive effects were, however, more pronounced than the constructive.

Only the nobility and the clergy enjoyed full citizens' rights and all the resulting privileges. Just before the loss of independence, the Polish society was divided into the categories that appear in Table 3, p. 7.

Frederick the Great, the King of Prussia, engineered the first partition of Poland in 1772, where one-third of the territory and about half of the

TABLE 3

POLISH SOCIETY – 1791

Nobility	700,000
Clergy	50,000
Townspeople	600,000
Jews	900,000
Villagers	6,500,000
Others (Armenians, Tartars Old Believers, etc.)	250,000
Total Population of Poland	9,000,000

Source: Tazibr and Rostworowski (1968:344).

population was taken over by Austria, Prussia, and Russia. The second partition of Poland among her neighbours followed in 1793 and Poland disappeared from the map of Europe in 1795. Numerous problems in the partitioned Poland's social and economic structure played an important role in shaping the emigration movement.[6] Political issues, such as unwillingness to serve in one of the conquerors' armies, were an additional factor, as well as the nationalistic feelings which were most pronounced in the Prussian sector, where the Poles were subject to Germanization pressures and ousted from their land for non-compliance. But the overriding consideration was the lack of arable land and of work which motivated many to seek those things abroad.[7]

Poland regained her independence in November, 1918, as the outcome of many varied actions and manoeuvres in the political arena and of the armed Polish nation's efforts during World War I. Reborn Poland's boundaries were neither those of her historical period of glory nor those that she had before losing her independence. In November, 1918, the frontiers of Poland were fluid, part of the territory was still under German administration, and another part was engulfed by military activities.

The Polish state immediately found itself beset by economic, political, and military difficulties; the country was in ruins after the war, politically divided into a number of camps and already threatened in its independence. Battles with the Ukrainians were being fought in southeastern Poland, the Czechs had managed to occupy part of the Cieszyn area of Silesia, and Upper Silesia was in German hands. The war with the USSR in 1920 was the most severe trial for the new state. After several campaigns, in which the two sides were alternately successful, peace was signed in Riga in March, 1921, which established the frontier between Poland and the USSR. The western boundaries were established after a plebiscite in Upper Silesia, which led to the area being divided into two parts, with the larger falling to Germany's lot, and Poland's frontiers were finally confirmed in 1923.

In 1921, the first census in independent Poland found a population of

7

27,400,000 persons in an area of 388,634 square kilometers. The territory of Poland increased slightly in 1938, as a result of acquiring parts of the Cieszyn area of Silesia and parts of Slovakia, to 389,720 square kilometers. According to the census of 1931, the population was 32,348,000 persons, and towards the end of 1938, according to the Bureau of Statistics' estimates 34,875,000 persons.

The new Poland had a considerable number of national and religious minorities within her boundaries. [8] The heterogeneous composition of her population began with the acquisition of territories through conquest, especially in the east, through political agreements as with the Lithuanians, or through mergers of territories following marriages of the ruling royal houses. A large number of German settlers played an important role in the growth of Polish towns but, maintaining their religions, they were largely assimilated to the Polish society. The Jewish population, which began to settle in large numbers in the first half of the fourteenth century, the Byelorussians, the Ruthenians and the Ukrainians, all remained culturally and religiously distinct over the centuries under the Polish rule.

The new Polish state assured other concerned nations that all religious and national minorities within her political boundaries enjoyed full rights of citizenship, guaranteed under the Polish Constitution of 1920. Further official assurances of the rights of minorities were given by Poland in the League of Nations in 1934, but in fact Polish authorities devised various means of absorbing and eventually assimilating the minorities and implemented certain measures against those opposed. For example, the Polish Constitution assured full privileges of education in their own language for all minorities, but did not provide such schools with adequate state funds, facilities, or other necessary resources. Polish national and religious minorities were seldom accepted for government posts and were discriminated against in all levels of public service and in land distribution. The resentment, stemming from the perceived injustice and discrimination, combined with nationalistic and independence movements among some groups, was general and took the form of armed conflict by the Ukrainians in the years 1918-1919. The Ukrainians were defeated by the Polish forces but continued in their opposition to the Polish state through assassinations and sabotage up to the outbreak of World War II. The independence movements of the Lithuanians and the Byelorussians were never well developed while the German minority remained quiescent but hostile to the Polish state. The Jewish population was equally discriminated against but had no champions to defend it.

The Polish government's attitude towards the minorities was not always consistent. The period 1926-1930 was characterized by liberal policies which were replaced by a strong Polish nationalism after that date. The degree of discrimination varied among the minorities; the Germans and the Russians, for example, received more consideration than the Ukrainians and the Jews.

TABLE 4

MOTHER TONGUE AND RELIGION – POLAND – 1931

Religion	Totals (in '000s)	Mother Tongue							
		Polish	Ukrainian	Ruthenian	Byelo-Russian	Russian	German	Jewish and Hebrew	Other And not Given
Totals (in '000)	31,915.8	21,993.4	3,222.0	1,319.6	989.9	138.7	741.0	2,732.6	878.6
Roman Catholic	20,670.1	20,333.3	12.6	12.9	77.8	1.9	118.5	–	113.1
Greek Catholic	3,336.2	487.0	1,676.8	1,163.8	2.3	0.9	0.3	–	5.1
Greek Orthodox	3,762.5	497.3	1,501.3	38.7	903.6	99.6	0.1	–	721.9
Evangelical	835.2	219.0	6.7	0.5	0.5	0.7	598.9	–	8.9
Other Christian	145.4	55.1	23.2	2.7	4.2	35.0	15.9	–	9.3
Judaic	3,113.9	371.9	0.2	0.3	0.2	0.4	6.8	2,731.4	2.7
Other Non-Christian	6.8	4.4	0.1	0.1	1.0	0.1	0.0	–	1.1
Unknown and Not Given	45.7	25.4	1.1	0.6	0.3	0.1	0.5	1.2	16.5

Source: *Mały Rocznik Statystyczny*, 1939.

The policies and plans for absorption and assimilation were largely unsuccessful, but the conditions of the Polish minorities in Poland in the years 1918-1939 had an important bearing on the growth and development of the Polish aggregate in Canada. It is likely that their condition motivated many to emigrate from Poland and large numbers of Ukrainians, Byelorussians, Lithuanians, Germans, and Jews found their way to Canada.[9] Born in Poland, they left as Polish-speaking citizens of Poland but on arrival to Canada claimed membership in an ethnic group other than Polish, or redefined their nationality or ethnicity in one of the decennial Canadian censuses.[10]

In May, 1926, a military coup was staged by Marshall Józef Piłsudski, one of the chief architects and defenders of the new Polish state, which overthrew the parliamentary system and replaced it with a partial dictatorship. The Communist party and its various affiliates had been declared illegal in 1919, and following the military coup political opposition parties faced the arrest and imprisonment of leaders and influential activists, and certain basic citizen's rights were considerably limited. However, no political opposition party ever lost its legal status, however bitterly opposed it may have been to the system introduced by Piłsudski. The press organs representing the opposition remained free to publish, and trade unions continued to carry on their activities openly, maintaining the right to free recruitment, demonstrations and confrontations.

In the international arena Poland was allied with France and, as far as her neighbours were concerned, above all with Romania. As a result of a dispute concerning part of the Cieszyn area of Silesia, relations with Czechoslovakia were strained. Polish-German relations were continually tense until 1933, when Hitler skilfully managed to take advantage of France's lack of interest in Polish suggestions for preventive war, and offered Poland a mutual non-aggression pact, which was broken in September, 1939. Poland also had a mutual non-aggression pact with the USSR, which was broken by Moscow on September 17, 1939, when the Soviet forces marched into Polish territory in accord with secret Soviet-German agreements of August, 1939.

Poland was an agricultural country in 1939 and according to the available statistical data,[11] 60.9% of the population supported itself from agriculture.[12] Considerable changes had occurred, however, in the agricultural structure during the two decades between the two world wars. Poland become a country of small, independent agricultural enterprises. During the years 1919-1937, 2,536,000 hectares were parcelled out and, in addition, easements totalling 589,000 hectares were liquidated. Thus, the peasants' land increased during this period by more than 3,100,000 hectares which gave them, together with the parcelling carried out in 1938 and 1939, more than 3,400,000 hectares of land.

In 1939, farms larger than 50 hectares constituted about 15% of the arable land; that is, about 3,600,00 hectares, and of this about 10% of the arable land, that is, about 2,500,000 hectares, was in the hands of large landowners. Of all the land parcelled out, both by the state and by private persons, 2,538,000 hectares (54%) were used to create new peasant farms, 38% to increase the size of very small farms, and 7% for gardens and plots. These transformations increased agricultural employment by 1,880,000 persons. Still, according to some calculations, the number of superfluous agricultural workers was anywhere from 5 to 8 million.[13]

On September 1, 1939, the German armed forces invaded Poland and World War II began. The strength of the Polish and German forces was so disproportionate that the outcome of the campaign was inevitable. Catastrophe struck sooner than expected, however, because the USSR broke its non-aggression pact and entered the war on the German side. The Soviet army marched into Poland on September 17, 1939. The USSR and Germany established the division and thus Poland found herself under the occupation of two of her neighbours.

The Poles did not, however, lay down their arms. An underground political and military organization commenced activities throughout Polish territory literally on the day of Warsaw's capture by the Germans. At the same time the formation of Polish armies was begun in France. The Polish navy and air force managed to get through to the West, and later many soldiers, who had escaped from occupied Poland and had been interned in camps in Romania and Hungary, found their way to France and England. In addition, Poles living in France were drafted there for the Polish army. A new government, headed by General Władysław Sikorski, was formed in Paris. This government also directed the political and military activities in the occupied country. Polish soldiers fought literally on all fronts in the West. The great and courageous Home Army sprang up in Poland, and its members carried out a whole series of extremely daring operations. Not only did the Home Army effect many acts of sabotage, but also supplied the Western Allies with much military intelligence and a V-1 rocket together with very precise information regarding the location of the weapon's production.[14]

On the strength of the agreement of August, 1941, diplomatic relations between Poland the USSR, which had been broken on September 17, 1939, were renewed. A Polish army was formed in the USSR from among the soldiers who found themselves in prisoner of war camps or as deportees to Siberia and elsewhere in the Soviet Union. Various difficulties and misunderstandings resulted in the evacuation of the Polish armed forces from the USSR in the summer of 1942, and after the Katyń crime[15] was revealed in April, 1943, diplomatic relations were again broken off. Recruitment for the Polish army in the USSR continued under the leadership of Colonel Zygmunt Berling, Chief of Staff of the Polish Infantry Division in the USSR, a unit subordinated to Soviet command. The entire organizational apparatus consisted of Polish Communists, while the officers and instructors were delegated from the Soviet army, part of them being of Polish origin, but the majority native Russians. Many of them remained in the Polish service until the end of 1956, when they were recalled on the demand of Władysław Gomułka, the new first secretary of the Central Committee of the Polish United Worker's Party.

Poland's political future was already decided by agreements in Teheran and was given the final rubber stamp in Yalta in February, 1945. The Western Powers recognized Poland as being within the USSR's sphere of influence, and were satisfied by some empty promises Stalin made. A communist political and administrative apparatus, formed in the USSR, assumed authority in liberated Poland. At first Moscow acted through the National Liberation Committee, later transformed into the interim government, which was recognized by most countries, including the Western Allies, in July, 1945.

After the Potsdam Conference in 1945, there followed a rapid period of Sovietization in Poland. An agricultural reform was carried out, although it did not greatly affect private ownership in those territories that were a part of pre-war Poland. Rebuilding after the terrible destruction of war was commenced, and at the same time a new socio-economic model was implemented through which Poland ceased to be an agricultural country and became industrialized.

After the Yalta and Potsdam Agreements, Poland shifted territorially to the West, and the makeup of her population changed radically. In the areas taken over by the USSR were the largest numbers of the Ukrainian and Byelorussian ethnic minorities. The German minority, both in previously-held and in newly acquired areas, was earmarked for repatriation, and the vast majority of the Jewish population had been murdered by the German occupants. Those who had survived left Poland in several waves. Ethnically, Poland is almost perfectly homogeneous. The political system brought about changes both in the occupational composition of the population and in the national economy. Ruined by war, the country was rebuilt through enormous effort and sacrifice of the population. During the initial period of development, or more precisely until the end of 1956, agriculture was subjected to the process of collectivization as had been the case in the USSR, but when Gomułka returned to power in October, 1956, he immediately ended enforced collectivization and returned private property to agriculture. Poland has remained the only state in the Soviet bloc with private enterprise in agriculture.

Following the initial relaxation, marked by greater liberties, even for the Roman Catholic Church, Gomułka began systematically to narrow the margin of freedom. The worsening economic situation inevitably drew various signs of protest from the population and led to the return of a police state. The 1960s were characterized by power struggles at the higher party levels. In 1967 there were widespread youth demonstrations and in June of that year, taking advantage of the Arab-Israeli war, Gomułka officially inaugurated an anti-semitic wave, disguising it as "anti-Zionism." Anti-Zionism took a greater impetus after the students' demonstration in March, 1968. This and the participation of the Polish army in the invasion of Czechoslovakia in 1968 saved Gomułka at the Party

Congress in October, 1968, but his victory was short-lived. Economic conditions in Poland worsened inexorably and the dissatisfaction of most of the population increased further. To cope with these economic difficulties the Polish government issued a decree raising prices of all consumer goods on December 12, 1970. The reaction was immediate. Two days later the Gdańsk shipyard workers went on a strike which later spread to Gdynia, Elbląg and Szczecin. Gomułka interpreted the workers' actions as a counter-revolution and ordered it to be put down. The police and the army ruthlessly attempted to suppress the strike, while the workers destroyed a number of party buildings and fought in the streets. The Party authorities in Warsaw concealed the events from Gomułka for two days, but an internal party power struggle soon ensued. Moscow, it would seem, expressed a desire for political calm, which meant changing the party leadership and removing those most responsible, and Edward Gierek assumed power on December 20, 1970.

Emigration from post-war Poland was minimal, and for a certain period of time it did not exist at all. Between 1945 and 1956 those who arrived from Poland were mainly refugees and a few people rejoining their families which had been split up by the war. From 1957 on, the Polish emigration regulations were modified or relaxed, and in the years 1960-1963 annual immigration to Canada reached a peak of about 3,000 persons, after which there was another decline. In the last few years, the number of immigrants from Poland has not surpassed 1,000 persons annually.

THE CANADIAN CONTEXT

Canadian immigration policies provided the context and terms under which the Polish people came to Canada. Before 1910 Canada did not have an immigration policy.[16] A number of acts or orders-in-council were introduced following Confederation but they did little more than prohibit three classes of immigrants: mentally or physically defective and diseased persons; a variety of categories of criminals; and persons considered morally or socially undesirable, including those likely to become public charges. Unofficially public opinion was reflected in three different levels of encouragement and financial aid to immigrants and in different numbers of recruiting officers in various nations. The 'preferred' categories included first and foremost people from the British Isles, white Americans, especially farmers, and Western and Northern Europeans. The 'non-preferred' category was made up of other Europeans, including Poles, and immigrants in this category, while never strongly encouraged to migrate to Canada, were allowed to enter once the general rules of admissibility were met. The 'undesirable' category referred primarily to non-Europeans. The majority of the acts and the orders-in-council were aimed specifically at the last category and did not affect Polish immigrants to any extent. Prior to 1915, Polish immigrants arriving at a Canadian port of entry had to possess a small sum of money ($25.00 per family), be in good health and be without a criminal record. The rates of refusal of admission for the Polish group were much below the average.[17]

In the early 1920s somewhat more stringent health inspections met the prospective Polish immigrants. One inspection took place in Poland; the second, in Gdańsk (or Danzig), the port of exit, included a disinfection unit. With the establishment of Canadian consular offices in Warsaw in the early 1920s prospective emigrants required an entry visa for Canada. In the granting of visas farmers and farm workers were given preference and others discouraged, but basically anyone not falling into the three prohibited categories was eventually granted an entry visa.

Canada was among many nations severely affected by the Great Depression. Significant numbers of its labour force were unemployed and to prevent increases in their numbers further immigration was stopped by an order-in-council in 1930. Only families of husbands already residing in Canada and others with sufficient funds to establish a farm and begin producing on a farm were allowed landed immigrant status. The regulation applied to all Europeans.

There were no further changes in the Canadian immigration policy until 1947, at which time Prime Minister King outlined a new approach towards immigration to Canada. The new policy was based on the position that large scale immigration should not alter the character of the Canadian population. The policy was designed to give preference to those nationalities which were numerically dominant in Canada and was to attract permanent settlers, not transients. It was also planned to facilitate economic absorption of the newcomers. The Polish people (and other Slavs) were low on the scale of desirable categories under this policy. The Canadian government agreed to accept a number of Polish veterans and refugees but with certain stipulations. The selected individuals had to agree to work for a length of time (one or two years) as farm hands, in the textile industry, and at other menial jobs. The labour commissioners who were sent to Europe recruited those considered most suitable for the Canadian economy at the time. Even without the 'welcome mat' thousands of Poles would have undoubtedly emigrated to Canada from a war-torn and impoverished country, but the Iron Curtain has effectively sealed off Poland, and the Polish government was totally opposed to further losses of population through emigration.

The selective and restrictive measures of the new immigration policy were in time relaxed on compassionate or humanitarian grounds, with respect to post-war refugees and political exiles. Special consideration was given to the Polish veterans who served with the Allies during World War II. The majority of the Poles who came in the years 1945 to 1956 were affected by these considerations. In addition, provisions whereby a landed immigrant could sponsor relatives as immigrants were utilized by Polish landed immigrants to bring their relatives from various parts of the world, and after 1956 directly from Poland.

New immigration regulations were introduced in 1962 which no longer discriminated on the grounds of race, ethnicity, or place of origin but retained provisions for the exclusion of certain unsponsored nationals from societies "where normal security screening cannot be carried out."[18] Those societies fell within the so-called Communist Bloc and included Poland. Following the modification of the regulations in 1967 to allow application for landed immigrant status from within Canada, many Polish visitors resorted to this opportunity with mixed success. Since November of 1972 no one can apply for landed immigrant status from within Canada and once again only sponsored individuals from countries such as Poland are considered for a permanent stay in Canada.

NOTES

1. See William Makowski, *History and Integration of Poles in Canada* (Niagara Peninsula, 1967), and B.J. Zubrzycki, *Polacy w Kanadzie 1759-1946* (Toronto, 1947).
2. There were 188 Russians or Poles in Upper Canada and 8 in Lower Canada at that time.
3. Emily Balch, *Our Slavic Fellow Citizens* (New York, 1910), p. 34.
4. For further elaboration on this and related issues see N.J. Hunchak, *Population: Ukrainians of Canadian Origin, Series No. 1* (Winnipeg, 1945); V.J. Kaye, "Problems of Research Connected with the Dictionary of Ukrainian-Canadian Biography, 1891-1900," in Cornelius J. Jaenen, ed., *Slavs in Canada,* Vol. III (Toronto, 1971); N.B. Ryder, "The Interpretation of Origin Statistics," *The Canadian Journal of Economics and Political Science*, XXI (1955), 466-79; Victor Turek, *Poles in Manitoba* (Toronto, 1967).
5. For a demographic portrayal of the Polish community including the male/female ratio see R.K. Kogler, "A Demographic Profile of the Polish Community in Canada," T.W. Krychowski, ed., *Polish Canadians: Profile and Image* (Toronto, 1969).
6. For socio-economic and political conditions in the period of partitions see S. Estreicher, "Galicia in the Period of Autonomy and Self-Government, 1849-1914," in W.F. Reddaway *et al.*, eds., *The Cambridge History of Poland*, II (Cambridge, 1941), and W.J. Rose, "Russian Poland in the Late Nineteenth Century" and "Prussian Poland, 1850-1914," in Reddaway, *ibid.*
7. See Graph 1, Appendix 1.
8. See Graph 2, Appendix 1.
9. In the period 1927 to 1939, of the 100,000 Polish citizens who emigrated to Canada, 35,000 were Greek Catholics (predominantly Ruthenians), 10,500 Greek Orthodox (overwhelmingly Ukrainians), 6,000 Evange-

lists (predominantly Germans) and 13,500 Jews. It is likely that over 65% of the emigrants from Poland to Canada during this period were Polish national and religious minorities. *Mały Rocznik Statystyczny* 1939.

10. This is illustrated by the change that took place between 1961 and 1971 in relation to the Jewish, Greek Catholic and Greek Orthodox members of the Polish ethnic group in Canada. Personal contacts, close and frequently friendly relations were at times maintained, especially between the Ukrainian and Polish people, but on the whole the Polish minorities had few formal contacts and did not identify with the interests of the Polish aggregate in Canada. Taking this into consideration, this study will not discuss to any extent the Polish religious and national minorities in Canada.

11. *Mały Rocznik Statystyczny*, 1939.

12. See Graph 3, Appendix 1.

13. Interested readers may consult the following for further elaboration on this subject: Lidia Ciołkoszowa and Barabara Wysocka, *Informator Polski* (London, 1945); Tadeusz Mincer, *The Agrarian Problem in Poland* (London, 1944); Stanisław Rak, *Agricultural Reform in Poland* (London, 1946); Janusz Rakowski, *Wczoraj i Dziś Reformy Rolnej (Fryburg, Switzerland, 1946); Mały Rocznik Statystyczny.* 1939.

14. As a result of this, Peenemuende was bombed and sections of the V-1 factories, together with its scientific and production personnel, was destroyed, considerably delaying the Germans in using this weapon.

15. In which over 10,000 Polish officers and non-commissioned officers were shot by the Russians, probably in 1940.

16. See Mabel F. Timlin, "Canada's Immigration Policy, 1896-1910," *The Canadian Journal of Economics and Political Science*, XXVI (1960), pp. 517-32. A number of sources provide a more detailed discussion of Canadian immigration policies. See, for example, Freda Hawkins, *Canada and Immigration, Public Policy and Public Concern* (Montreal, 1972); Benedykt Heydenkorn, "The Immigration Policy of Canada," in J.M. Kirschbaum *et al.*, eds., *Twenty Years of the Ethnic Press Association of Ontario* (Toronto, 1971); W.E. Kalbach, *The Impact of Immigration on Canada's Population* (Ottawa, 1970); and Anthony H. Richmond, *Post-War Immigrants in Canada* (Toronto, 1967).

17. According to Smith, between January 1, 1903, and March 31, 1909, there were 2,303 British, 49 Galicians, 20 Austrians, and 5 Poles deported. (W.G. Smith, *A Study in Canadian Immigration* (Toronto, 1920), p. 78.) According to the *Statistical Year Book, 1915*, Table 39, for the years 1903-1915 inclusive, a total of 76 Poles were deported. The ratio for deportation for selected groups is as follows:
West Indian – 1 in every 30   Polish – 1 in every 471
British – 1 in every 168   Greek (lowest) – 1 in every 477
Average 1 in every 255

18. "Canadian Immigration Policy," *White Paper on Immigration* (Ottawa, 1966/37), Para. 96.

TWO

Arrival

There have been those who have come to stay because of peace and stability. Some are refugees tired of running and waiting. Others want no further part of Europe in her destruction and suffering. Some come because of a spirit of adventure.

R. Helling

NOTABLES, KASHUBS, AND OTHERS – THE FIRST PHASE

The vast, rich, and beautiful land of Canada attracted a variety of peoples from the earliest stages of its development. The French came first to settle, trade, and trap; they were soon joined by British businessmen, administrators, colonizers, and indentured workers. There were fishermen and sailors from the Iberian and Scandinavian peninsulas and from Italy who decided to settle permanently in Canada. Soldiers of fortune, adventurers, fugitives from justice or oppression came from various European nations.

Before Confederation groups and individuals came every year. Scottish Highlanders began to settle in Nova Scotia in 1621; by 1763 there were approximately 10,000 German settlers in Lunenburg and vicinity. The years 1783-1787 saw the arrival of Loyalists from the United States, strengthening the English composition in Upper Canada and the Maritimes. Entire communities of Mennonites from the United States settled in the present county of Waterloo in 1799. The Irish potato famine in the 1840s resulted in thousands of Irishmen settling in various parts of what are now Ontario and Quebec. Following the end of Napoleonic Wars in 1815, increasingly larger numbers of immigrants from the United Kingdom began to settle, predominantly in Upper Canada. The Maritimes, and the present provinces of Quebec and Ontario, were being populated by the new arrivals, but vast stretches of land remained the domain of hunters, trappers, and traders.[1]

The first Canadian census of 1870-71 found a population of over three

18

million, but with a composition clearly illustrating the ethnic heterogeneity that was increasingly to characterize this nation to the present time. In 1871, the largest ethnic group in Canada was the French, followed by the Irish, English, and Scotish.[2] There were over 200,000 Germans, and smaller numbers of Dutch, Scandinavians, and Italians. Other Europeans were undifferentiated by the census for lack of sufficient numbers. There were also the Canadian native people and Negroes.

Among the Europeans were Polish immigrants and their descendants. Information which would substantiate their presence and numbers is still largely hidden in municipal and parish records, shipping companies lists, and government archives, but we know about a number of Polish individuals who stand out because of their achievements and influence in Canadian society.[3] Among the more noteworthy is August F. Globenski who came to Canada with the Hesse-Heynau Regiment in 1776. Following the conclusion of the Treaty of 1783, Globenski left the regiment, married a French Canadian and practised medicine in St. Eustache, Quebec. His three sons served with distinction in the Canadian militia during the War of 1812, and one of them, Maximillian, played a prominent part during the Rebellion of 1837. A grandson, Charles Augustus Maximillian Globenski, born in 1830, became the seigneur of Mille Iles and was elected to the House of Commons in 1875. The second Polish immigrant to be elected to the House of Commons, in 1867, was Aleksander Edward Kierzkowski, who arrived in Canada in 1841, settling in St. Hyacinthe, Quebec.

Perhaps the outstanding individual among the earlier Polish immigrants to Canada was Sir Casimir Gzowski. Having taken part in the 1831 insurrection in Poland, Gzowski arrived in Canada in 1842 via the United States, and soon became involved in political, industrial, educational, and military affairs and developments of Canadian society. He served as an honorary aide-de-camp to Queen Victoria and was knighted. He also acted as lieutenant-governor of Ontario. For twenty years he was a member of the Senate of the University of Toronto and president of Wycliffe College. He was closely involved with the Dominion Rifle Association and the Royal Military College, and had a rank of Colonel in the Canadian militia. His greatest fame rests on the various engineering projects he either initiated or carried out: the laying out of Yonge Street between Toronto and Simcoe; the building of bridges, canals, roads, and railways; the planning of the Niagara park, and the building of the International Bridge crossing the Niagara River from Fort Erie to Buffalo.[4]

Another prominent Polish immigrant was Edwin Brokowski. His activities and interests ranged from teaching school in Ontario to journalism, civil service, and service in the Canadian militia during the Fenian Raids of 1870. Moving to Winnipeg, Brokowski became the editor of the *Manitoba Gazette* and later its owner. In 1881 he was appointed Dominion land agent for Saskatchewan, a position he held until his death in 1916.

19

These and other individuals such as Bishop Hellmuth, Brother Kowalc-zyk, Debartzch, Łucki, Mazell, Blaskowitz, and Czerwiński of the first phase of Polish immigration to Canada were career soldiers, emigrés, and political exiles, many of whom had travelled or lived in various European capitals or in the United States before arriving in Canada. It is doubtful if many of them chose Canada initially as a country in which to settle permanently, but since they were well-educated, already speaking French or English, they were readily accepted and given full opportunity to participate in all aspects of this society.

Their numbers were small[5] and the roles that some played in the development of Canadian society had little effect on other Polish immigrants. They did not provide leadership or maintain contacts with others, or with Poland. They did not seemingly wish to retain their ethnic identity. Many intermarried, adopted Canadian citizenship, language and values, and all became absorbed by the larger society. Of some there is now no trace; descendants of others carry the names of their forefathers but do not themselves identify with the Polish ethnic group.[6]

The de Meuron Soldiers

Apart from these prominent individuals, there were several groups of less well-known Poles in Canada before the year 1895. Chronologically, the first of these were the so-called de Meuron soldiers. Poland, having lost its independence in 1795, saw a possibility of regaining it through the efforts of Napoleon Bonaparte. Many individuals joined the Polish Legion which fought in various theatres of war under French command. In 1807 the Polish Legion came in contact with British forces in Spain. A number of Poles were captured and imprisoned under extremely adverse conditions. Some took the opportunity to improve their situation by serving under the British flag and were placed in two mercenary Swiss regiments led by Colonels de Meuron and de Watteville. According to one source[7] there were eleven Poles serving in the de Meuron Regiment and 529 in that of de Watteville. Eventually the two regiments were sent to Canada to take part in the War of 1812. The de Watteville Regiment saw action around Fort Erie, Ontario, where it was noted that many Polish soldiers deserted to the American side. With the cessation of hostilities the de Watteville Regiment joined the de Meuron Regiment which was by then stationed near Kingston, Ontario. It is not certain how many Poles remained in the two regiments after 1815. The Crown granted a parcel of land to soldiers wishing to remain and settle in Canada and it is possible that some of the Polish ex-legionnaires accepted this offer.[8]

When Lord Selkirk planned his expeditions to Manitoba in 1815 and 1817 to protect the Red River settlers, he recruited, among others, twelve Poles. They were simple soldiers of peasant background, uneducated and all bachelors. With one possible exception[9] the Poles did not remain in the Red River colony permanently. Some died, others moved elsewhere in Canada or to the United States.[10]

The Kashubs

Another group of Poles arrived in Quebec in 1858 from the German port of Bremen after about eleven weeks at sea in an overcrowded ship, suffering from typhus and hunger. Having been told by a shipping company agent that each family would receive 100 acres of land in Canada, they sold their few acres and cottages and landed here paupers, without as much as the price of a loaf of bread amongst them.[11] There were 16 families, 76 people, in this group. As a result of the concern of the Canadian immigration agent over their plight, the group was transported to the Renfrew area and located with established residents there. The agent proudly noted that "they were considered a burthen on their arrival but in one year they have already elicited honorable mention from the Ottawa Agency."[12]

These people were the Kashubs, a distinct minority but closely related to the Poles, who left their homes[13] not only to escape attempts of Prussian authorities to Germanize them but also to improve their economic conditions. They were allocated land and within a few years other families joined them, settling in the townships of Hogarty, Richards, Sherwood, Jones and Burns. Others followed and by 1864 there were about 500 Kashubs in the area, according to personal recollections of the oldest living residents.[14] The land that the Kashubs settled on was full of stones, "enough to build many walls of China."[15] It is possible that better farm land was available but the Kashubs themselves chose certain areas since they reminded them of their homeland.[16]

Some men did not settle on land[17] but worked in lumber camps or on road-building, including most likely the building of the historic Opeongo Road. Others hired out as labourers, thus competing with the Irish immigrants; there were frequent confrontations, even fights between the two groups. With time economic conditions stabilized, the CNR line was built through Wilno in 1894, the main road was completed in 1905, improving social and economic life generally, and good relationships began to be enjoyed among all residents of the area.

The mid-1890s saw a renewal of Kashub immigration, and another 250 families arrived within a period of four years, recruited in Poland by the Wilno parish priest. Another 40 families came from the United States, where they had been since the 1860s but where they had had difficulties with language and suffered from local economic depressions. The new families settled in Barry's Bay and other nearby communities.

Today the community of Barry's Bay has a population of about 1,400, over 75% of whom are of Polish origin. The community of Wilno, a short distance from Barry's Bay, remains secluded and ethnically distinct. It has a population of about 700, all of them Kashubs and their descendants. Other groups of Polish immigrants and their descendants are in Combermere, Whitney, Brudnell, and Killaloe, in all about 2,000 people.

The Kashubs were and remain deeply religious people. Before 1875 they walked to the nearest Roman Catholic church in Brudnell, for most a distance of 10 miles. There, they were served by an Irish priest.[18] The distance and the incomprehensible service were not satisfactory for the Kashubs, and letters of complaint were written to bishops in Poland. A few priests from Poland did arrive, but never stayed long. Around 1870 a Polish priest came and remained for six months, establishing a Polish parish in Wilno.[19]

In 1875 another priest arrived from Poland and the following year a chapel was built. Since that year the Wilno parish has had its own Polish priests. In 1880 a wooden church was begun which was finally finished in 1895. The same year another wooden church was built in Barry's Bay to serve the growing Polish community in that town. A third Polish church was erected in Round Lake Center in 1910. The Wilno church burned down in 1936 and was replaced in the same year by a fine brick edifice. Building a new church at the height of the Great Depression demanded many financial sacrifices. The Kashubs donated their time and labour, some giving 150 days of work free, and there were usually 60 volunteers working on the project each working day.[20]

The primary concern of the Kashubs focused on religious life and was reflected in the establishment of parish organizations. Since 1890 the Wilno parish has had a church choir and in 1901 two other religious organizations became active – the Holy Rosary Society and the Brotherhood of the Holy Scapular. At the same time the Kashubs were concerned with education for their children, building a schoolhouse in 1894, which provided two grades of elementary education and offered twice-weekly instruction in the Polish language, reading, writing and history.[21]

The Kashubs are a cohesive group. Parish records of Barry's Bay and Wilno show that only about 3% intermarry with other groups, yet apart from their language they are not easily distinguishable in lifestyle or in activities from their non-Polish neighbours. They "do not emphasize their heritage by performing Polish folk dances or maintaining old-world customs."[22]

Relationships with other Polish groups in Ontario and elsewhere were not maintained until recently by the Kashubs and there was little interest shown by the Polish immigrants in these early settlers. The geographical isolation of the Wilno-Barry's Bay area from other centres where Polish immigrants lived retarded the development of contacts. Also, while the Kashubs claim Polish identity and background, they speak with a distinct dialect not easily understood by other Poles. Some contacts were established through participation in religious festivals in the 1950s, and since that time various events have strengthened the relationships between Kashubs and other Polish Canadians. The ex-political prisoners deposited the ashes of the dead of Oświęcim (Auschwitz) in the Wilno church and gather there annually to commemorate their death. Barry's Bay is now frequently chosen for conferences, discussions, and seminars by various Polish-Canadian associations. The Polish Boy and Girl Scouts have their summer camps nearby. Extensive and friendly contacts have been established by Polish Canadians who have summer cottages in the area built by the Kashubs on land purchased from them.

These developments may lead the Kashubs of the Wilno-Barry's Bay area to enter fully into the life of Polish-Canadian communities in Canada. However, both Wilno and Barry's Bay have little industry and few prospects for the future. As in many other rural areas the youth are leaving for larger centres where opportunities are greater.

Other Pioneers

The Kashubs were followed by another small group who came to Canada in 1862. Since many of these people spoke German, they were directed to Berlin (now Kitchener, Ontario) where there were already large numbers of German immigrants. By 1872, there were nearly fifty Polish families in Berlin.[23] They worked at whatever was available. From 1861 to 1865 they had their own chapel in an old school building and were visited regularly by Polish Redemptionist Fathers from the United States. They also established their own mutual aid society which began to function, with the bishop's permission, in 1872 and received a provincial charter in 1886. The original numbers were strengthened by later immigrants and Kitchener Poles maintain a viable community with its own church and a number of organizations.[24]

With time, news of opportunities available in North America seeped to other parts of partitioned Poland, and it is likely that while the United States attracted the 'lion's share' of the hopeful migrants, some found their way to Canada as well. Among others, Gibbon[25] noted the presence of "large settlements" of Polish immigrants in sub-marginal lands east of Winnipeg between 1890 and 1900. The first Polish settlers came to Assiniboia, NWT (now Saskatchewan), in the years 1886 and 1888,[26] and about a half-dozen families settled in the district of Bolognie, all originating from the same village of Onufry in Bukovina.[27]

Before 1895 Polish immigrants also came to Canada via the United States. Immigration to the United States from the Russian part of partitioned Poland and from the Prussian Polish provinces began in 1854[28] and within the next three decades assumed significant size.[29] For the vast majority of Polish emigrants, the United States was seen as the land of unequalled opportunities, flowing with milk and honey, with city streets paved with gold, whereas before 1895 they knew little of Canada except, perhaps, as a cold and inhospitable land. Hundreds of thousands streamed into the 'promised land' in search of riches and happiness, and today they constitute a group several million strong. Overwhelmingly they were poor farmers and farm workers and other labourers. Only small numbers of intellectuals and professionals followed the masses. Most settled in towns and cities close to the Canadian border accepting any available work. But the American streets were not paved with gold, and frequent economic stagnation forced the new arrivals to seek work elsewhere. Canada in the

1880s was engaged in extensive railroad construction and other capital works. Contractors hired the cheapest and most available labour, primarily from among the new immigrants, including Italians, Slovaks, Hungarians, and Poles.[30] It is not certain how many of the labourers who came to work on road-building, canals, and railway construction or went to lumber camps[31] remained in Canada permanently, but immigrant memoirs[32] and other sources suggest that some settled here on completion of their contracts.[33] Others who initially settled in Buffalo, New York, Chicago, or other American cities came to Hamilton and other Ontario or Quebec cities. The first few Polish immigrants settling in Montreal came via the United States in 1894 and a year later "another twenty-five Polish families, also from the United States, joined them."[34] By 1897 there were about two hundred Polish immigrants working for various industries in Montreal. Records of the City of Hamilton show that there were Polish people listed as taxpayers as early as 1878.[35] Yet others travelled west to claim their homesteads. *Czas*[36] reports a number of Polish settlers in Manitoba in 1879; Turek[37] discussed a Polish settlement in Brookland, Manitoba, in 1882; and there was a "whole stock of American Poles, all from Buffalo, New York, who first immigrated into the United States and were later induced to seek land in the Hunn's Valley District."[38] According to another source the Hunn's Valley settlers included "an admixture of Poles"[39] who "soon outnumbered the Slovak settlers, so that the settlement became for three decades or so [1890-1920] strictly a Polish colony."[40]

Other settlements have been mentioned by various writers[41] and the number of Polish immigrants in Canada before 1895 is undoubtedly greater than has been documented thus far. Many individuals disappeared in the vast expanses of the Canadian territory leaving few traces.

Summary – The First Phase

Members of the first phase of Polish immigration to Canada originated from various parts of partitioned Poland and emigrated for political, economic, and ideological reasons. It is likely that the majority were illiterate or poorly educated and entered into the lowest socio-economic rungs in the new setting. Some, like the Kashubs, retained their old identity over many generations but generally over time all adapted successfully to the new environment and were, in turn, fully accepted by other Canadians. A small segment of the professionals and highly educated entered readily, and were accepted in all spheres of Canadian life.

Numerically, this phase of Polish immigration was small; the size cannot be ascertained with any certainty at present because of lack of adequate information, ambiguous criteria utilized for their identification by the Canadian authorities, and dispersion over great distances. The *Census of Canada 1890-91*, providing a distinct category for the Polish group for the first time, found them in all provinces and territories. There were 40 people of Polish origin in British Columbia, 29 of them in New Westminster; 31 in Manitoba; 187 in Ontario, with 97 in Toronto; 236 in Quebec, with 176 in Montreal; 191 in the Territories and a few in Nova Scotia and New Brunswick. Obviously these numbers are incorrect if the size of the Kashub group alone is considered, but they illustrate the presence and the dispersion of Polish migrants in Canada. Their presence and experiences did not in any way affect the masses of new Polish immigrants who, on Clifford Sifton's invitation, began to arrive after 1895 to fill the newly opened prairie lands.

THE GALICIANS AND OTHERS – THE SECOND PHASE

Towards the close of the last century Canada was a viable nation. It was rich in natural resources, enjoyed a "livable" climate and had hopes of becoming a great nation. The transcontinental railway was completed in 1885, linking the provinces together, allowing easy movement of goods and people, solidifying Canadian sovereignty over the Prairie provinces, and opening vast new areas of previously inaccessible fertile land. It was hoped that the Dominion Act of 1872 would assure settlement through offers of free homesteads.[42] The resources were there and waiting, economic conditions were favourable, but the crucial factor necessary for further development was missing – the people to populate and work the land. Despite strenuous campaigns to recruit Canadians for the West, the hoped-for numbers of Canadian settlers did not take advantage of free land and other incentives being offered. The Canadian government of the time realized that it could acquire the needed settlers only by actively and vigorously promoting immigration. To this end numerous recruitment offices were established in Great Britain, Western and Northern Europe, and the United States.

At first, the Canadian "immigration net" aimed exclusively at nations whose people were already known to Canadians and possessed similar cultural traits, mainly Great Britain, the United States and Western Europe. But at this time Canada was only one of several receiving societies, or 'shoppers for human material': the United States remained the most attractive place to settle or to seek work, and other societies, such as Australia, also actively sought British immigrants. The recruitment campaign saw the arrival of 1,250,000 immigrants from the United Kingdom, almost one million from the United States and another 800,000 from northwestern Europe in the years 1896-1914.[43] Though the numbers of arrivals from the United States, Great Britain, and Western Europe were large, they were considered by the Canadian government inadequate to settle the prairies.

The Canadian government expected a much larger number of settlers from the United States but many of the American farmers were sceptical of potentialities and opportunities being offered in the seemingly hostile northern environment despite all assurances and evidence to the contrary,

25

and land for homesteads was still available in the United States. In addition, it is likely that a significant proportion of the American farmers who came to the Canadian West returned to the United States,[44] after finding that the best land was already taken. Immigrants coming from the United Kingdom were not always experienced farmers,[45] and many remained in the towns and cities.

One man was undaunted by the results of the extensive and costly recruitment campaigns[46] – the Laurier Government's Minister of the Interior, Clifford Sifton, who was responsible, among others, for the Department of Immigration.[47] Realizing that conventional and preferred sources were not meeting Canadian demands, Sifton instructed the North Atlantic Trading Company to search Central and Eastern Europe, the home of Polish and other Slavic peoples, for additional people to fill the waiting prairie lands. A great number of shipping company agents[48] began to recruit settlers and found them in abundance, especially in the Austrian Polish provinces known as Galicia.[49] Canada was portrayed by those agents as a place of plentiful and remunerative jobs, with land and free homesteads for all willing to settle on them, a country of unlimited opportunities. This image was further strengthened by the earlier emigrants who had settled successfully and wrote encouraging letters, inviting friends and relatives to join them. Others were attracted by advertising in the press or had heard wonderful tales from travelling beggars or from those able to read Canadian immigration pamphlets in German, all extolling the opportunities found in Canada.[50]

Polish immigration to Canada began as a trickle in the mid-1890s, but the numbers steadily increased, forming a large movement of anxious and willing people ready to fulfill their obligations and expectations and to enjoy the benefits offered all newcomers to this land. In 1907, 15,861 Poles arrived who had left their homes, families, and communities in search of earnings, land, and a better life. In all there were 115,895 Poles admitted to Canada by the year 1915.[51] Following the outbreak of World War I, emigration from Poland ceased and in the years 1915 to 1918 only 24 Poles found their way to Canada, probably as re-migrants from the United States.

At present there is little authoritative information about the geographical origin of these people. It is likely that most who settled in the Prairie provinces before 1914 came from the area known as Galicia.[52] Others came from the Congress Kingdom either directly (after being smuggled across the Russian-Prussian borders) or via the United States. There were also smaller numbers of immigrants from the Prussian provinces of Poland.[53]

Immigrants of this phase were not a cross-section of the Polish population as a whole, nor even of the rural population. Few farmers who had their own land emigrated. The bulk of the newcomers were cotters, non-inheriting farmers, farm labourers, or farmers' sons, sent over to earn money in order to increase the size of land already owned, or to pay off

TABLE 5

NUMBER OF ARRIVALS IN INLAND AND OCEAN PORTS IN CANADA
FISCAL YEARS 1908-1915

	1908	1909	1910	1911	1912	1913	1914	1915
Bukowinians	2145	1546	725	700	328	687	1549	72
Galicians	14268	6644	3368	3553	1594	497	1698	36
Hebrew (Polish)	46	2	28	85	52	26	22	6
Polish Austrian	586	42	483	1065	2773	4462	4310	1272
Polish German	16	3	12	43	21	29	46	7
Polish Russian	736	255	738	800	1624	4488	4507	544
Polish N.E.S.	255	76	174	269	642	966	930	153

Source: *Canada Year Book, 1915.*

debts incurred in bad years. Occasionally fathers alone went for this purpose.[54]

After 1870 few intellectuals, professionals, politicians, or social leaders emigrated from Poland. The numerically small middle classes and tradesmen had little reason to leave the country since the economy and social conditions under all partitioning powers assured them of employment, whereas in North America they had little chance of a career in their own occupation or profession.[55] Only a few priests followed the Polish migrants to Canada, never enough to provide the services demanded by the scattered settlers.

The petty farmers and farm workers had little to lose. Many had been migrating for seasonal work to Prussia,[56] and going to America was a logical extension of this pattern. There were greater opportunities there. Since the vast majority were extremely poor, all their worldly possessions were sold to pay for passage over. Frequently this was insufficient and money was borrowed from richer relatives or from money lenders.[57] On arrival in Canada the immigrants were not only poor but strangers to each other, since they came singly and independently. Rates of illiteracy among them were high[58] but they were unconcerned about this. Their education, derived from the 'school of life,' was sufficiently broad to allow them to meet most of the problems in the new setting. They differed sharply from the Canadians in lifestyle, behaviour, attitudes, and values, but they were hard working, honest, and frugal.

Sifton's policy of settling the West called for strong backs and willing hands. The Polish people who came before 1915 were well suited to clear the bush or forests for cultivation or to struggle with the virgin soil, climate, and natural or man-made calamities. Others dug ditches, bored for coal or other minerals, cut lumber, built roads, or sought other jobs requiring stamina but little training.

Motives for Emigration

Those who are aware of the feelings and attachment that peasants have for the land and their communities can understand the importance of the decision to uproot themselves from all that was familiar. Yet thousands embarked on a journey to an unknown place which was only vaguely visualized but offered great promise for the future.[59]

Of the three parts of partitioned Poland, Galicia was the area most severely impoverished, both economically and culturally. It had little industry and a growing surplus population. Families were large; infant mortality was dropping sharply and the farmers did not have enough land to distribute among their maturing sons. The prospect of earning money for land purchase was minimal in the traditional agricultural society. Those who were forced to work for wages (a lowering of social status in itself) were rarely able to save enough to buy land, even after many years of hard work and the exercise of great frugality. One mistake, one bad year wiped out all their savings. Only migration, seasonal or more permanent, could possibly break this seemingly hopeless situation. The peasants came with hopes of acquiring the treasured land and were happy to remain in Canada, the country in which their dreams came true.[60]

It is likely that many more landless peasants or farm workers would have come to Canada, but for the high material[61] and emotional cost. Only the most adventurous, daring, or despondent took this step. There were many others who emigrated to escape compulsory military service in the Austrian, Prussian, or Russian armies.[62]

This period of immigration is characterized by two streams: one more permanent, made up of families and individuals in search of land or permanent work, the other composed of people who came only to find work, save, and return.[63] It is probable that the majority of Polish immigrants to Canada of this phase came with intentions of returning once sufficient money was saved to pay off accrued debts, to purchase land, or both.

The Polish immigrants who came via the United States were attracted by the Canadian immigration agents and other recruiters,[64] and encouraged by their own organizations to seek land in Canada.[65] Others found employment opportunities in the American cities inadequate and sought better chances in the burgeoning Canadian economy.

First Impressions and Experiences

Coming to Canada from Europe for the first time was a strange and often dreaded experience; for those who had lived in one community all their lives, venturing out to the nearest town only on market days, the thought of the ocean, large ships, and days or weeks of travel, was unimaginable. A number of writers portray the journeys across the Atlantic;[66] perhaps the most vivid portrayals are to be found in memoirs[67] or novels.[68]

Prior to embarking on a ship that would take them over to Halifax or Quebec City, Polish immigrants were subjected to conditions, demands,

28

and situations which were totally strange or alien. Documentation, strange customs and border checks, large cities and different languages all confronted them for the first time in their lives. The physically or mentally deficient died during the passage over, or were rejected by the immigration officials in Canada. Only the healthy of mind and body could survive.[69]

When the ship arrived, the dazed and bewildered immigrants faced a world with a new language, new dress, and new customs. Possession of money was demanded of them as proof of solvency; a paltry $25.00 per family was enough, but not many had such a sum. Friends, countrymen, or land agents came to their rescue and 'lent' the necessary sum so that the newcomers could disembark.

Those Polish immigrants destined for the prairies were herded into waiting sheds in preparation for the train. There were no welcoming committees, no organizations, no government representatives to inform them or make them welcome. They were expected to purchase food parcels to serve them on their train journey. Much of the food was canned and people sometimes discarded it not knowing what it was.

The trains were comfortable by their standards and frequently there was an interpreter and adviser or a land agent who could speak their language, but they were not allowed to leave the trains before their stipulated destination. The railway police were constantly checking for violations of this rule.

Finding themselves in Winnipeg and points west, petty farmers, farmers' sons, cotters and farm labourers were not all clamouring for their free homesteads, anxious to settle on land or work on the land for another farmer. Many remained in towns and cities to seek unskilled labouring jobs. By 1889 Winnipeg had 1,000 Poles out of a total population of 30,000,[70] and every little town in the West had its Polish community.[71] Soon many ventured to Ontario and Quebec in search of non-agricultural employment, where jobs were more plentiful and the pay higher. These were the temporary migrants, working, saving, and thinking of returning to Poland.

But there were many others whose one goal and reason for coming was the land. Land was plentiful at this time but often the best land was already taken, or the Polish immigrants were directed to the less desirable areas, or they themselves chose unwisely, motivated by sentiment perhaps, but unaware of different conditions of Canadian agriculture. Immigrant memoirs refer to the fact that many settlers were not able to succeed and abandoned their homesteads and took up other work.

The Canadian government did not encourage block settlements but some ethnic concentration took place nevertheless. Polish immigrants wanted to live near other Poles or at least people familiar to them; if there were no Poles, Ukrainians were chosen as neighbours. The land developers and the CPR promoted settlement regardless of people's ethnicity, and once an area contained a number of Polish families a chapel or even a church was erected and this in turn attracted other Poles to settle nearby.

A number of primarily Polish 'colonies' are known to have emerged in all three western provinces, some with clearly identifiable names such as Wisla, Kopernik, Vilno, and Krakow, but thus far the information is incomplete.[72] It is most probable that Polish rural concentrations were a small segment of the overall pattern of Polish settlement which took the form of wide dispersal or some concentration with the numerically larger Ukrainian communities.

The Polish pioneers established patterns and structures which affected all later phases of Polish immigration to Canada. They left their homes with only vague notions of what was awaiting them in Canada. There was no Polish government to protect them and the Canadian authorities took minimal interest in the 'non-preferred' immigrants. They came independently, with the awareness that they had to 'sink or swim,' to succeed or perish on their own. Isolation and loneliness were common. There were no voluntary associations to ease the difficulties of their initial adjustment. They soon saw the need for creating associations and those coming later were able to reap the benefits. They also bore the brunt of discrimination, prejudice, and ill feeling shown to foreign peasants in the first two decades of this century. The ill feelings turned to hostility during the war. As nominal Austrian or German nationals, the Poles were labelled enemy aliens, some were sent to internment camps and others placed under close surveillance by the police. Later arrivals from Poland owe much to their predecessors who built churches and halls, established organizations and newspapers, and most importantly gained valuable experience in working conditions, social relations and techniques of survival in the new setting, all of which they shared with new Polish arrivals.

THE POLES – THE THIRD PHASE

Poland became an independent state once again in 1918. The country was an arena of many great battles between the Russians and the Central Powers. Polish men, conscripted to serve in one army or another, frequently fought against each other. The war did not stop in Poland in 1918. Armed struggles continued with the Ukrainians, Lithuanians and Czechs, and with the new Soviet state. The country was devastated economically and physically.

The task of rebuilding required all available skilled, trained, and professional people. They were encouraged and urged to remain and not to emigrate. Very few did not heed this call, in particular those who could not reconcile themselves to the Polish government and a handful of others who sought economic opportunities or new challenges in North America. Not many of them found their way to Canada, for after all Canada did not really want them. Once again, Canada wanted farmers and farm workers of good health and morals. The newly established Canadian consular personnel implemented this policy through selection of applicants who appeared to be farmers or farm workers, and who passed close medical examinations.[73]

There were thousands of applicants. Despite war losses of manpower and agricultural reforms, there was still not enough land for all peasants or farm workers in Poland, nor was there enough other work for all able-bodied men in a fledgling Polish industry. Emigration appeared to be the only solution for many, and North America was still the promised land. But the United States could no longer be relied upon, for its quota system, introduced in 1921 and revised in 1924, allowed only 6,524 Poles as immigrants each year. (In 1932 this was reduced to 2,000 yearly.) Canada kept its doors open and the migration stream resumed once again. The numbers were not as great as in the pre-war period but fewer came as temporary migrants. Between 1919 and 1931, 51,847 Polish immigrants came to Canada, with 8,248 arriving in 1927 and 8,319 in 1928.

Migration slowed down at the onset of the Great Depression. Between 1932 and 1939 only 3,497 Polish immigrants arrived in Canada. The majority of immigrants in this phase were of rural background, but there was also a substantial segment of urban proletarians passing themselves off as farm workers. There were families going together but also fathers leaving alone, hoping to bring their families later. There were now many single men who saw other parts of Poland and Europe during World War I, who received some training and education in the service, who were exposed to different people and cultures, and who were no longer satisfied to remain in small, isolated, perhaps stultifying villages.

The immigrants originated from various parts of the now-independent Poland and not predominantly from villages. The rates of illiteracy were dropping following the compulsory educational laws, and many of the new immigrants had some organizational experience acquired in the services or during the reorganization of the new Republic.

Processes associated with migration were now better organized. The Polish government provided information for the prospective migrants,[74] and other publications were available.[75] A colonization society was established in Warsaw in 1927 and a delegate, Baron de Logo,[76] was sent to Canada in 1929 to seek areas suitable for Polish settlement. Shipping companies had many years of experience in transporting millions of migrants to the New World; the reception centres were now better prepared to deal with thousands of strange and bewildered new arrivals. The Polish Emigration Office (Urząd Emigracyjny) had for some years co-operated with both Canadian railway companies in the recruitment of families for specific areas or projects.[77] Still, the majority of emigrants went independently without sponsorship of organizations and without preconceived plans.

A distinct aspect of this phase was that a great many migrants who had travelled to North America in the years 1895 to 1914 and returned before or after the war re-migrated to Canada (or to the United States). Memoirs illustrate the ambivalence experienced by these people. In Canada they sorely missed their relatives and community, familiar customs and countryside, and longed to return home, but once in Poland, they were no longer able to adjust either economically or socially in the still largely traditional society.

Polish arrivals were still encouraged to travel west and undertake work on farms. Some marginal land was also available for homesteads but the majority sought work in towns and cities, in the mines, railroad or road construction, lumber camps and anything else available. More than half of the new arrivals chose Ontario and Quebec and many others, previously living and working in the Prairie provinces, began to drift east in the 1930s in search of better conditions.

THE POST-WAR REFUGEES AND EXILES – THE FOURTH PHASE

With the outbreak of World War II direct immigration from Poland to Canada ceased again, not to be resumed until 1957.[78] In 1939, Poland was conquered and partitioned between the Soviet Union and Germany. By 1940 masses of Poles were relocated or resettled (as the Soviet authorities euphemistically referred to this deportation) in Siberia and other parts of the Soviet Union.[79] During the German occupation millions[80] of Poles were sent to Germany as forced labour to join the prisoners of war captured in 1939.[81] While millions of Polish people were sent to die in German concentration camps on Polish territory, thousands found themselves in other concentration camps in Germany itself.

Polish people never gave up the struggle against the occupier and while most remained to fight in the Polish underground thousands of others escaped to volunteer to serve and fight on the side of the Allies.[82] In the years 1941 and 1942 nearly one thousand technicians, engineers and skilled workers arrived to contribute to the Canadian war effort. They were not considered immigrants at the time but temporary residents.[83] A number of Polish pilots and airmen came to Canada for training. They engaged in ferrying planes from Canada to various theatres of war.[84]

Following the defeat of Germany, military prisoners, inmates of concentration camps, and forced labourers freed by the Western Allies had the choice[85] of returning to their homes or remaining as refugees or displaced persons. The majority of Poles who found themselves outside Polish borders in 1945 did in fact return: of the Polish armed services abroad 94,000 were repatriated, and of the millions of forced labourers only approximately 380,000 remained as refugees or stateless persons.[86]

Great Britain assumed responsibility for Polish military personnel and their dependents who did not wish to be repatriated. The choice was to remain in Great Britain or emigrate elsewhere[87] under an assisted passage plan. The majority of those wishing to emigrate chose the United States or Australia, but in time Canada became a popular choice. Between the years 1945 and 1956 another 64,096 Poles came under a variety of programmes and outside of the existing immigration laws of Canada. They came not directly from Poland but from other European states and other parts of the world, from refugee camps, military bases, liberated concentration camps and prisons.

The Polish community in Canada was concerned about the fate of these people. Representations were made by the Canadian Polish Congress and others[88] to the Senate Standing Committee on Immigration in June of 1946 that Canada could receive 500,000 suitable immigrants from among the Polish refugees and veterans. Their admittance was opposed by another Polish organization,[89] claiming that these people were unproductive, dissident and unsuitable material for Canada.

To what extent the representations influenced policies and decisions of Canadian immigration leaders is not certain but in the summer of 1946 a commission of agricultural experts was sent to Italy to recruit 5,000 agricultural workers from among the members of the Polish 2nd Corps,[90] to be admitted by a special order-in-council. They were the first large group to arrive as immigrants after World War II.

The Canadian government adopted a humanitarian approach with respect to the refugees, but was also influenced by other considerations. In the immediate post-war years Canada was suffering from a shortage of manpower in farm labour and other low skilled occupations. Polish veterans and refugees undoubtedly were suited to relieving this shortage. Many were of agricultural background, healthy and strong, and willing to work in certain occupations or to undertake other obligations in exchange for being admitted to Canada.

In all, 4,247 men were recruited to work on farms under a two-year agreement after which they would be considered for permanent residence. There were 2,800 from Italy and the rest from England, the main concentration of Polish soldiers. Those recruited from Italy arrived in Canada in November, 1946, and after two weeks rest began to work on farms, primarily in Ontario. Those from Great Britain joined them the following year.[91] There was no further recruitment of the veterans but many came in groups or individually, assisted by the British government.

Polish refugees in various European camps were under the auspices of the International Refugee Organization. Canada sent a number of recruiting bodies from the Department of Labour to select suitable individuals for certain industries, mines and lumbering, railway gangs and construction. Women were recruited for factory or hospital work and as domestics. These refugees began to arrive in 1947, destined for towns and cities in various Canadian provinces. The year 1948 was the apex of this phase and 13,799 Poles were admitted to Canada. The two programmes – recruitment for specific occupations and sponsorship by the British government – were responsible for the bulk of Polish immigration to Canada before 1955.[92] In addition, some immigrants came through a sponsorship system introduced in the 1952 Immigration Act, and others came independently through various and sometimes devious means.[93]

The immigrants of this period differed greatly from those of other phases. For the first time a significant proportion were highly educated,

many with specialized trades or qualifications; there were academics, lawyers, engineers, architects, and a great many professional military officers.
Their average age was between 30 and 35 years, and there were three
times as many men as women. The veterans came with savings, clothing,
and some knowledge of the English language and customs. The refugees
arrived penniless, and less aware of Canada and the opportunities being
offered them.

They approximated closely the structure of the pre-war Polish society,
originating from every area of Poland, from villages, towns, and cities, but
were also the products of six years of military or prison discipline, abnormal stresses, separation from families, and constant mobility.

It is doubtful if many of the Poles of this phase of immigration saw
Canada as a permanent place of residence, especially those that served in
one of the branches of the Polish armed forces, hoping to return to a
liberated Poland. In Canada they found organizational structures created
by their predecessors, easing their initial period of transition. Various
levels of Canadian government and private organizations informed the
newcomers of the conditions and resources available to them.[94]

THE LATEST NEWCOMERS – THE FIFTH PHASE

In the years 1957-1971, there were 31,320 Polish arrivals to Canada. The
number declined from a high of 3,733 immigrants in 1959 to a low of 723
in 1970. The year 1957 is chosen somewhat arbitrarily as the beginning of
a new and ongoing phase of Polish immigration to Canada, but the division of the whole post-war period into two parts is dictated by a number
of factors. It was in 1957 that direct emigration from Poland, albeit on a
small scale, resumed with the passing of a Stalinist government and the
temporary return of more liberal leadership under Gomułka. A number of
regulations were relaxed allowing for some categories of relatives of permanent residents abroad to leave. Families could be reunited after a separation that may have lasted fifteen years or more.

The changes taking place in Poland attracted many Polish Canadians as
visitors, among them single men in search of wives. Such 'shopping trips'
resulted frequently in the arrival of a bride-to-be to join her future husband. Marriages with Polish women were also arranged through the press
and by mail. Between 1967 and 1972, a number of visitors from Poland
asked for landed immigrant status and remained in Canada.

While allowing relatives to depart and permitting or encouraging others to emigrate, Poland does not consider open and free emigration per-
missible. The laws of Poland do not allow individuals to choose to leave
the society permanently and at will. It is claimed that the growing economy requires all available manpower and not only is there no unemployment, but there are shortages in some sectors, and emigration would put a
further strain on the already serious situation.

It is not likely that these conditions will change in the near future. Even if they were to change, the existing immigration laws of Canada do not provide for unsponsored immigration from Poland, since normal security screening cannot be carried out.[95] It must be concluded that immigration from Poland will remain low in the forseeable future.

Within this last phase there are also two other categories of Polish newcomers to Canada. The first are the remnants of post-war refugees who were admitted between 1957 and 1960 and a small number of newcomers, ship-jumpers, for example, who left Poland by various means to claim refugee status in Canada. The second category are the post-war refugees and veterans who settled in Holland, Germany, Great Britain, Australia, Argentina and elsewhere for a number of years but now see Canada as a land of better opportunities and prospects for the future. Others re-emigrate to join their relatives and friends who came here earlier. Many of these immigrants are sponsored and others come independently. At the beginning of this phase their numbers constituted the bulk of Polish newcomers, but since the mid-1960s they make up only about 10% of the total.

The composition of this phase is varied in age, socio-economic background and in motive for emigration. There are incomplete families as well as individuals coming over to join their relatives. A number of women come to marry. Many sponsored families arrive from Poland and elsewhere in search of improvement in economic, social or political conditions. Most are well educated with significant numbers of professionals and technicians. There are no illiterates while many arrive with university, even post-graduate studies behind them. English (or French) -language training courses are widely available and occupational retraining programmes are offered to all Canadians including landed immigrants.[96] There are now also a number of public departments and private voluntary organizations whose main task is the care and welfare of all newcomers to Canada.[97]

The majority of the Polish newcomers settle in Ontario, with Quebec, especially Montreal, as a second choice. About half of all newcomers join the labour force in Canada. Many find it relatively easy to enter into their old occupations: teaching at universities, or working in various fields of technology and industry. Of course a prerequisite is the knowledge of one of the official languages. There are relatively few unskilled or semi-skilled immigrants. It is likely that these Polish immigrants are fully accepted by other Canadians and find few difficulties in adjusting to the new environment.

NOTES

1. Department of the Secretary of State, *Our History* (Ottawa, 1970). See also Arthur R.M. Lower, *Colony To Nation* (Toronto, 1971); Edgar McInnis, *Canada: A Political and Social History* (Toronto, 1969); Report of the Royal Commission on Bilingualism and Biculturalism, Book IV, *The Cultural Contribution of Other Ethnic Groups* (Ottawa, 1970).

2. *Census of Canada, 1870-71.*

3. There are numerous sources that the reader can consult for further references to individual Polish immigrants who were in Canada before the turn of the twentieth century. The following have references to one or more individuals: Henry Archacki, "America's Polish Gift to Canada," 24th Annual Meeting of the Polish-American Historical Association, Toronto, December 28, 1967; O.E. Breton, *Kowal Boży* (London, 1961); A.H. Crowfoot, *Life of Isaac Hellmuth, This Dreamer* (Toronto, 1963); J. Murray Gibbon, *Canadian Mosaic* (Toronto, 1938); Edward M. Hubicz, *Father Joe – A Manitoba Missionary* (London, 1958); V.J. Kaye, "Sir Casimir Stanislaus Gzowski, a Great Canadian" (1813-1898), *Revue de l'Université d'Ottawa*, 25 (4), 457-64; L. Kos-Rabcewicz-Zubkowski, *The Poles in Canada* (Toronto, 1968); L. Kos-Rabcewicz-Zubkowski, and W.E. Greening, *Sir Casimir Gzowski* (Toronto, 1959); Bolesław Makowski, *Polska Emigracja w Kanadzie* (Linz-Salzburg, 1951) and *History and Integration, op. cit.*; H.J. Morgan, ed., *Canadian Men and Women of the Time* (Toronto, 1912); Victor Turek, "Jeszcze o Polonii Kanadyjskiej," *Kultura* (Paris, 1957) 122, 85-94; Turek, *Sir Casimir Gzowski (1813-1898)* (Toronto, 1957); Turek, ed., *The Polish Past in Canada* (Toronto, 1960); Turek, *Poles in Manitoba*; A. Wołodkiewicz, *Polish Contribution to Arts and Sciences in Canada* (London, 1969); B.J. Zubrzycki, *op. cit.*

4. This brief reference cannot possibly do justice to the myriad of interests and activities of this one individual. There are two biographies, one in English and one in Polish, that the interested reader can consult for further details. See L. Kos-Rabcewicz-Żubkowski and Greening, *op. cit.*, Turek, *op. cit.*, and a personal account of a meeting in 1873 in Skorzewski (1888).

5. According to A.J. Staniewski, "Do Wokandy Historyka – z Życia Polonii Toronto," *Związkowiec* (Toronto), Jubilee Issue, April, 1935, and others, one group of Polish exiles of the 1863 insurrection found themselves in Canada in the late 1860s or early 1870s. Their passage was arranged by the English Association of the Friends of Poland. They settled primarily in Toronto where they founded as association called the Slavic Club which was later renamed the Polish Citizens Club. The club functioned between 1880 and 1890 and thus could have the distinction of being the first lay organization formed by the Polish group in Canada. Staniewski's information is based on second-hand accounts and by 1905 he found no traces of this group, speculating that they moved to the United States or

became fully assimilated and no longer recognizable as Polish.

6. For example, Peter Gzowski, author, journalist, and well-known radio personality, is the great-great-grandson of Sir Casimir. He retains the name and the awareness of his background, but has very little in common with the Polish ethnic community in Canada. Peter's father and grandfather as well as other members of the family participated in the World War II activities of the Polish group (generally in honourary positions), with the aim of aiding Poland in its war effort.

7. Mieczysław Haiman, *Ślady Polskie w Ameryce* (Chicago, 1938), provides names of all Polish members of the two regiments.

8. Robert England, "Disbanded and Discharged Soldiers in Canada Prior to 1914," *The Canadian Historical Review*, XXVII (I), 1-18, found that members of the "Foreign Legion" of the British-American War were granted lands in the townships of Oxford, Montague, Wolford, and Malborough, all in Ontario.

9. L.S. Garczyński, "Od Atlantyku Po Ocean Spokojny," *Księga Pamiątkowa Z.P.w.K. 1906-1946* (Toronto, 1946).

10. Victor Turek, "Poles Among the De Meuron Soldiers," *Historical and Scientific Society of Manitoba*, Series III (9), 53-68, claims that "the first Polish pioneers in Western Canada were persevering colonists and valuable settlers."

11. "Report of the Select Committee on Emigration, 1860," *Journal of the Legal Association*, XVIII, Appendix 4.

12. *Ibid.*

13. J.L. Perkowski, "Folkways of the Canadian Kashubs," in Cornelius J. Jaenen, ed., *Slavs in Canada*, Vol. III (Toronto, 1971), p 332, notes that they "come from a region east of Bytowo." S.K. Głęborzecki, "Kanadyskie Wilno," *Związkowiec*, Nos. 23, 25, 27 (Toronto, 1957), lists about 15 localities in Poland from which the Kashubs originated.

14. Bolesław Makowski, *History and Integration.*

15. Głęborzecki, p. 25.

16. *Kalendarz Czasu Na 1951 Rok; Czas* (1951).

17. The census of 1870-71 found 18 families, 77 persons, in the village of Renfrew whose occupation was that of labourer. From Makowski, *History and Integration.*

18. The priest made an effort to communicate with the Kashubs at least for the purpose of hearing their confessions and managed to learn some Polish, according to Głęborzecki, who derived his information from chronicles, parish records, and the oral traditions of the oldest residents.

19. The date of the parish is very likely 1873, since there are no further records of Kashubs in the Brudnell church after 1872.

20. Głęborzecki, *op. cit.*

21. Pieprzycki (1974) provides other details of the religious and socio-cultural life of the Wilno parish from its inception to the present.

22. Brenda B. Lee-Whiting, "First Polish Settlement in Canada," *Canadian*

Geographical Journal, LXXV (1967), 108-12. However, Perkowski found that the Kashubs still maintain some old traditions such as "dyngus" and special church rituals. They also retain beliefs in supernatural beings and practise some "folk medicine." Głęborzecki points out that there are all-night vigils over the dead, called "pusta noc" or empty night, and weddings, while no longer three-day affairs, have a special ceremony related to the removal of the bridal veil. Traditional dances are also retained for weddings and deaths.

23. John Iwicki, C.R., *The First One Hundred Years* (Rome, 1966).
24. S. Kinastowski, "Dzieje Polonii w Kitchener," *Głos Polski*, No. 24, June 14, 1973.
25. Gibbon, *op. cit.*
26. Kaye, *op. cit.*
27. This group is unusual in two respects: (a) Polish emigration from Galicia, of which Bukovina formed an administrative part, according to most sources did not start until 1894, and this group would constitute an exception to the rule; (b) Writers dealing with the subject accepted the position that it was only in rare instances (Kashubs, the Berlin group) that more than one family left simultaneously from the same village and settled in close proximity in Canada. The authors are grateful to Professor Kaye for this information.
28. Joseph A. Wytrwal, *America's Polish Heritage: A Social History of the Poles in America* (Detroit, 1961).
29. According to Theresita Polzin, *The Polish Americans: Whence and Whither* (Pulaski, Wisc., 1973), by 1860 there were 30,000 Polish immigrants in the United States; their numbers rose to 50,000 by 1870, to 500,000 by 1880, and to 1,000,000 in 1890. See also M. Haiman, *op. cit.*; Wacław Kruszka, *Historya Polska w Ameryce* (Milwaukee, 1905); R.A. Schermerhorn, *These Our People* (Boston, 1949); Wytrwal, *op. cit.* See also Graph 4, Appendix 1.
30. The influx of labour from the United States in large numbers resulted in the Alien Labour Act of 1897, designed primarily to curb the entry of foreign railway workers. See Timlin, *op. cit.*
31. J. Kage, "From 'Bohunk' to 'New Canadian,'" *Social Worker* 29 (4), 1, found that "all the bush camps in those days were full of 'Bohunks' [a derisive name for Poles and other Slavs] and no one liked them very much."
32. *Pamiętniki Emigrantów: KANADA* (Warsaw, 1971).
33. According to L.W. Luke, "Citizenship and Immigration," *28th Annual Meeting of the Canadian Chamber of Commerce*, Victoria, B.C., October 3, 1957, p. 5, Sudbury was founded in 1883 when the CPR was built through Northern Ontario and the "Italians, Poles and others who pushed the steel across Canada were the first families."
34. Makowski, *History and Integration*, p. 115.
35. *Czterdziestoletni Jubileusz* (1952).
36. *Czas* (1959).

37. Turek, *Poles in Manitoba*. He also mentions two Polish groceries in Winnipeg which were known to exist in the 1870s.
38. *Northwest Review* (45th Anniversary Issue), Winnipeg, 1930, p. 119.
39. Joseph M. Kirschbaum, *Slovaks in Canada* (Toronto, 1967), p. 224.
40. *Ibid.*, p. 66.
41. See especially C.A. Dawson, "Group Settlement: Ethnic Communities in Western Canada," in W.A. Mackintosh and W.L.G. Jones, eds., *Canadian Frontiers of Settlement*, Vol. VII (Toronto, 1936); C.A. Dawson and R.W. Murchie, "The Settlement of the Peace River Country," in Mackintosh, *op. cit.*; C.A. Dawson and Eva R. Younge, "Pioneering in the Prairie Provinces," in Mackintosh, Vol. VIII, 1940.
42. See David C. Corbett, *Canada's Immigration Policy: A Critique* (Toronto, 1957), and Duncan M. McDougal "Immigration into Canada, 1851-1920," *Canadian Journal of Economics and Political Science*, XXVII (1961), 162-175, for an in-depth study of these conditions.
43. *Report of the Royal Commission.*
44. Nathan Keyfitz, "The Growth of the Canadian Population," *Population Studies* (IV), June, 1950; Ryder, *op. cit.*
45. Hugh Emerson, *The Sowing* (Winnipeg, 1909); James S. Woodsworth, *Strangers Within Our Gates* (n.p., 1909).
46. Woodsworth, *Ibid.*, notes that 2,703,646 pamphlets and other material in English, German, Dutch, Norwegian, Swedish and French were distributed in Europe after Sifton's instructions. Smith found that the cost of propaganda between 1898 and 1908 was $2,500,432 for Canada, $1,936,000 spent in the United States, $1,643,000 in the United Kingdom, and only $700,000 in Central Europe. See his Table 4, p. 59.
47. See J.W. Dafoe, *Clifford Sifton in Relation to his Times* (Toronto, 1931).
48. Sifton's recruitment policy included payment of bonuses to steamship agents who sent immigrants to Canada rather than elsewhere. The bonuses were considerable: £1 ($4.86) was paid for each person 18 years of age and over and half that amount for younger recruits. This policy was initially applicable to British subjects only from within certain occupational categories (agriculture and general labour) but was quickly extended to include other Europeans and eventually Slavic peoples as well.
49. The Canadian immigration office took some precautions in determining the 'suitability' of the Galicians by sending the inspector of immigration in Europe, W.T.R. Preston, to visit villages and other communities there. The inspector found much favourable to comment on: cleanliness, sobriety, thrift, and good farming practices. See "Sessional Papers No. 10, Vol. XXXIV, Part II, Immigration," *Department of the Interior Sessional Papers 13, No. 2*, Report of W.T.R. Preston, Inspector of Agencies in Europe (London, December 23, 1899), 12-19.
50. The *Statistical Year Books* (1885-1904) illustrated the effects of promotion through rising immigration figures. Galicians arriving in Canada in

5,509; 1899:6,700; 1900 (1st six months): 4,992.

51. The number includes 6,285 of Polish origin found in the 1901 census. *Report of the Royal Commission, op. cit.*

52. This is the position taken by Turek, *Poles in Manitoba*, in his very thoroughly researched monograph.

53. J.T.M. Anderson, *The Education of the New Canadians* (Toronto, 1918).

54. E.K. Francis, "Variables in the Formation of So-Called 'Minority Groups,'" *The American Journal of Sociology*, 60, 6-14.

55. Some urban workers and political activists did come to Canada following the unsuccessful revolution of 1905, a Russian revolution which encompassed a number of Polish industrial centres in the Congress Kingdom.

56. See especially Roman Mazurkiewicz, *Polskie Wychodźctwo i Osadnictwo w Kanadzie* (Warsaw, 1930); Turek, *Poles in Manitoba*; J. Zubrzycki, *Polish Immigrants in Britain* (The Hague, 1956).

57. Examples are found in *Pamiętniki Emigrantów*, and Melchior Wańkowicz, *Tworzywo* (Warsaw, 1970).

58. According to Turek, *Poles in Manitoba*, over 40% of the male population from Galicia emigrating to Canada could not read or write.

59. The motives for emigrating are an integral part of any study of population movement and, according to Oscar Handlin, *The Uprooted* (New York, 1951), p. 16, to understand the character of adjustment in the new setting it is "necessary to know about circumstances under which the newcomers departed from their land."

60. Wańkowicz provides a factual portrayal of one such family who decided to leave their existence as cotters (or komornicy) and embark on a new venture in Canada, with most satisfactory results.

61. Steerage fees between 1870 and 1880 were $17-$18, but in the late 1880s and 1890 they rose to an average of $38 from a German port to Quebec City, a large sum for the average Polish cotter.

62. Balch talks about coming across many individuals in the United States who were there for the sole purpose of escaping conscription of themselves or their sons for lengthy periods in the "Emperors' Armies."

63. See Y.W. Lozowchuk and H. Radecki, "Slavs in Canada," a paper presented to the Symposium on Race and Ethnic Relations at the Annual American Anthropological Association Meeting, Toronto, November 30-December 2, 1972.

64. Count Esterhazy's work is discussed in Kirschbaum, *op. cit.*

65. Kennedy's concern was expressed in this regard: "I hear of a Polish Committee in Chicago who contemplates transplanting 50,000 families of their countrymen to Canada [the object in this case is philanthropic rather than commercial]. If the scheme is carried out, I hope the Poles will be well scattered over the prairie where the fresh air can blow every taint of Chicago out of them." H.A. Kennedy, *New Canada and the New Canadians* (Toronto, 1907), pp. 56-7.

66. Edith Abbott, *Historical Aspects of the Immigration Problem* (Chicago, 1926); H.A. Citoren, *European Immigration Overseas, Past and Future*

(The Hague, 1951); Handlin, *op. cit.*
67. *Pamiętniki Emigrantów.*
68. Wańkowicz, *op. cit.*
69. Many travelled on ships which brought a cargo of cattle from North America to Europe and not much effort was made to clean and refit these ships so that they would be fit for human cargo.
70. Edward M. Hubicz, *Polish Churches in Manitoba* (London, 1960).
71. Stewart W. Wallace, ed., "The Polish Group," *The Encyclopedia of Canada*, Vol. 5 (Toronto, 1937), 131; Kate A. Foster, *Our Canadian Mosaic* (Toronto, 1926).
72. There are references to specific concentrations of Polish settlers in the following sources: Rev. A.J. Gocki, *Historia Osiedli Polskiej w Candiac, Saskatchewan* (Regina, 1924); Edward M. Hubicz, "Early Polish Priests in Manitoba," in Victor Turek, ed., *The Polish Past in Canada* (Toronto, 1960); W. Makowski, *History and Integration, op. cit.*; Howard Palmer, *Land of the Second Chance* (A History of Ethnic Groups in Southern Alberta), (Lethbridge, 1972); Turek, *Poles in Manitoba*, and other commemorative publications of various Polish organizations.
73. *Pamiętniki Emigrantów.*
74. *Wskazówki dla Wychodzców do Kanady* (Warszawa, 1927).
75. *Kalendarz Rolnika Polskiego Na Rok 1929* (Toruń, Poland, 1929); Jan Bargiel, *Amerykańska Pula; Organizacja Zbytu Amerykanskich Rolników* (Warsaw, 1937); L.S. Garczyński, *Co To Jest Kanada?* (Warsaw, 1930); Jósef Lubicz *Kanada – Kraj i Ludność* (Toledo, Ohio, 1929).
76. The attempts never went beyond the discussion stage. See Turek, *Poles in Manitoba*, pp. 87 ff.
77. About 150 families were required for settlement in an experimental station near La Ferme and Barrant, Quebec, run by the CNR. It was stipulated that the applicants be farmers with knowledge of woodcutting and in possession of $250 per family, and agree to work in forests and on road construction, in exchange for which they were to receive a three-room house and all the necessary equipment at easy rates of repayment. The settlements were to be made up of at least ten families each. The scheme was judged "laudatory" (*Czas*), but the soil proved to be "famous poor clay." No other information is available on the fate of this scheme.
78. A few individuals were able to escape from behind the Iron Curtain and a few others were reunited with their families through the intercession of the International Red Cross between 1945 and 1956.
79. Some estimates have placed their numbers between 1,000,000 and 1,500,000.
80. Jacques Vernant, *The Refugee in the Post-War World* (London, 1953), claims that 2,500,000 were deported to Germany.
81. About 150,000 were liberated by the Western Allies alone.
82. In 1946, the stated strength of Polish forces in Western Europe was 228,000 officers and other ranks, according to Vernant, *ibid.*, pp. 74-5.
83. Benedykt Heydenkorn, "Emigracja Polska w Kanadzie," *Kultura*, 54

(Paris, 1952), 79-93. Only a few of these individuals returned to Poland at the end of the war. The majority applied for landed immigrant status and remain in Canada to the present day.

84. *Złoty Jubileusz Towarzystwa Białego Orła w Montrealu, 1902-1952* (Toronto, 1952).

85. The new Polish government demanded that the Allies repatriate all Polish citizens under their jurisdiction, by force if necessary.

86. For a fuller discussion of this development see Vernant, pp. 73-8.

87. With the agreement of the receiving society. Canada agreed to this plan but it is not certain if conditions were stipulated.

88. *Stowarzyszenie Polaków w Kanadzie* and Mr. Victor Podoski, a pre-war Polish consul-general, who became First Polish Minister for Canada in 1943.

89. The Democratic Committee of the Aid to Poland, represented by Mr. W. Dutkiewicz. It is likely that this organization represented the wishes of the Polish government for the return to Poland of all refugees and those serving in the armed forces abroad. See The Senate of Canada, *Proceedings of the Standing Committee on Immigration and Labour*, No. 12, June 18, 1947.

90. This corps fought in the Italian Campaign with the British Eighth Army and remained as an occupying force until 1946.

91. Of the total, 4,112 were granted permanent admission.

92. From April, 1947, to December, 1951, there were 36,549 Polish refugees admitted to Canada.

93. Three small fishing boats manned by Baltic people and a number of Poles arrived from Scandinavia in August and December, 1948. The crews were allowed to remain in Canada. Unsponsored Polish immigrants were admitted as well on the condition that they had at least $2,000 in their possession and agreed to buy a farm. An unknown but probably small number of Polish immigrants fell into this category.

94. "Guide for New Canadians," *The Toronto Telegram*, n.d.

95. "Canadian Immigration Policy," 1966, p. 37.

96. While enrolled in these courses the 'student' receives a sum of money which assures financial independence for him and his family for the duration of the course.

97. See Hawkins for further elaboration, especially Part V.

THREE

Adjustment

When I speak of quality . . . I think a stalwart peasant in a sheep-skin coat, born on the soil, whose forefathers had been farmers for generations, with a stout wife and half-a-dozen children, is good quality.

Clifford Sifton

The people of Canada do not wish, as a result of mass immigration, to make a fundamental alteration in the character of our population.

Rt. Hon. W.L. MacKenzie King

The recruitment campaigns, advertising, and glowing reports sent by relatives and friends in Canada all helped to create favourable image of possibilities and opportunities offered newcomers.

Polish emigrants left with high expectations. Land was given away in large parcels and employers were begging people to work. With such opportunities they were going to conquer the world if only health would allow it. They came to Canada full of hope and trust that this rich country would result in rapid economic and social improvement in their lives. They were determined to overcome all odds and hardships, cope with all adversities. Eventually most succeeded, but at a much greater cost than they originally envisaged.

The difficulties and problems facing the Polish newcomers to Canada were legion and there was little understanding of the difficulties that an immigrant from a totally different and strange culture was forced to cope with in a new setting. The problems fall into three broad categories: the attitudes of the receiving society, which strongly affected the life chances of immigrants and their descendants; the specific problems of the agricultural communities; and the problems of the industrial and urban communities.[1]

THE STRANGERS

The Polish culture is sharply distinct from the dominant cultures in Canada. The Polish language has no affinity to either of Canada's official languages and the absence of a means of communication became a real barrier to mutual adjustment. It is likely that the majority of Polish immigrants of the earlier phases were unaware of the necessity of adapting to certain Canadian norms and values related to work, education, public behaviour, hygiene and language; it is possible that they were unconcerned with establishing closer contact with their hosts, since most expected or hoped to return to Poland after a few years.

There were few agencies or organizations interested in helping the immigrant to adjust. There were no Polish government representatives to help immigrants in time of trouble.[2] The Canadian government's concerns were limited primarily to admitting and settling the newcomers. The *laissez-faire* attitude expressed itself in an immigrant's having to sink or swim on his own.

On arrival immigrants were met by officials who directed them to specific areas in Canada.[3] They were also met by religious orders of nuns, distributing literature exhorting them not to foresake their faith. Later, Protestant missionaries were concerned with their 'low' morals or 'wrong' religion and attempted to convert them. Some social activists expressed concern about their children, and they were of great concern to police forces when accused of drunkenness, brawling, political radicalism, or vagrancy.[4]

Most significantly, they quickly became of great concern to numerous vocal and influential spokesmen who saw in them all that was undesirable for Canada. The first arrivals, the precursors of the mass Polish immigration of the 1896-1914 period, were received with all the curiosity and interest aroused by any people who came dressed in 'outlandish' garb, speaking an incomprehensible language, and exhibiting 'peculiar' customs.[5] Within a few years, with growing numbers of new arrivals,[6] curiosity turned to anxiety, and then to alarm. The newcomers were *too* strange! Their illiteracy and backwardness would retard the development of Canadian society. Their customs and traditions made them unsuitable and unlikely subjects for Canadian citizenship. Their concern with making money was a threat not only to Canadian culture but also to the native worker. Immigrants accepted low wages, thus threatening the livelihood of Canadians.

Groups and individuals began to agitate at meetings, in the press, and in other publications to curtail admissions of Poles and other Slavs. In support of their arguments voices expounded the negative traits of the Slavs, their shortcomings and inadequacies. A few 'voices of doom' predicted the rapid demise of Canadian civilization under the flood of "men in sheepskin coats." Sifton was berated and accused of bringing the "scum of Europe" to Canada, and his policies were sharply criticized for years, even after his resignation in 1905.[7]

There are a number of articles, books, speeches, and other reports which contain references to the feeling prevailing at the time in Canada, with suggestions or demands for changes in Canadian immigration policies. Only a few will be used for purposes of illustration. Woodsworth quoted Whelpley:

> It is extremely undesirable that thousands of foreigners of questionable value from a mental, moral, and physical point of view should be allowed to freely invade well-governed and prosperous communities. They underbid the market, raise important and vexatious municipal questions, strain charitable resources to the utmost, increase the cost of government, expose a healthy people to contagious diseases common to the poorer classes of Europe, corrupt the body politic.[8]

He also quoted P.F. Hall, "Emphatically too many people are coming over here; too many of undesirable sort."[9] "The welcome of Eastern Europeans will test severely or endanger our British ideals and those things we love."[10] "Poles and police courts seem to be invariably connected in this country and it is difficult for us to think of the people of this nationality other than in the vague class of undesirable citizens,"[11] and "they are peasants, the majority are superstitious, some of them bigoted fanatics, some of them poor, dumb, driven cattle, some intensely patriotic."[12] They are "ignorant parents,"[13] and "they are not desirable, not wanted, oppressed, handicapped. They would be happier to return back where they came from."[14] Some advocated the introduction of a quota system similar to that of the United States and considered that Slavs and Southern Europeans were undesirable elements for Canadian immigration needs.[15]

Many stereotypes and misconceptions arose at the time which have persisted tenaciously over years and generations, images of a general negative kind. The public opinion and the images created the greatest problems of adjustment and survived with lasting effects on the reception, experiences, and development of later Polish immigrants and on the lives of Canadian-born descendants of the earlier Polish arrivals.

The Poles (and other Slavs) were depicted as ignorant and cruel, a dirty, uncivilized people frequently giving vent to lawless outbursts which strained the existing agencies to the utmost. The customs and traditions in which they had taken pride were regarded with contempt, even despised. It was believed that they were only suitable for the most menial work in farming, building roads, digging for coal and similar tasks, under the supervision or direction of a Canadian. Their women, in time, could become satisfactory domestic servants, but Canada did not need masses of this type of immigrants.

Calmer voices[16] reservedly defended the newcomers. It was argued that they were needed for many jobs which the Canadians left vacant. It was pointed out that some managed to establish themselves quickly and with some success on homesteads. It was stressed that the children would certainly be socialized into the "Canadian way of life" sooner or later.[17] Such voices were few and almost drowned in the sea of opposition.

The defence was weak. The Polish people themselves were unable to deny the charges, accusations and stereotypes for lack of knowledge of the English language or conditions and expectations, or means of voicing their protest. They had few champions. It is understandable that Canadians developed and maintained such an image of Polish and other Slavic immigrants. Ontario and the Prairie provinces were fast becoming industrialized and modernized, exposed to the dynamic developments of the United States. Contact and confrontation with large numbers of people from strongly traditional, economically undeveloped, and educationally backward societies seemed a threat to many of their values.

The negative images which were well developed by the first decade of this century gave way to open hostility during World War I, for the Poles were now enemies of Canada. As was already noted, Poland did not exist as a political state at the time of this phase of immigration. Those coming with intentions of returning saw no reason to acquire Canadian citizenship; others were unaware of benefits and advantages of such a change. Thus the majority of the Polish group were legally classified as Austrians, Germans, or Russians at the outbreak of the war.

During World War I Polish immigrants in Canada were faced with a cruel paradox. Those from the Congress Kingdom or the Russian part of partitioned Poland were friends and allies of Canada. The Austrian and German nationals were despised enemies. While many volunteered to serve in the Canadian[18] or Polish[19] armies to fight the Central Powers, their fellow Poles were interned with the Austrians and Germans.

A number of organizations and associations actively supported the Canadian war effort; others were banned or closed on suspicion of aiding the enemy cause. Individuals not interned were issued identity cards that had to be produced when purchasing food or applying for work and were ordered to report regularly to the police or the post office.[20] The police frequently checked strangers in smaller communities for possession of such cards. The feelings of the general population against Poles intensified. Many were dismissed from jobs and told to go back to Austria and "ask Franz Joseph for work."[21] The intensification of struggles in Europe saw corresponding intensification of ill feeling towards the 'enemy aliens.' The mass deportation of the undesirable foreigners was advocated.[22] Hostile feelings abated somewhat with the cessation of the war, only to be rekindled in 1919 with the Winnipeg General Strike. The spectre of Bolshevism arrived in Canada, and were not the Slavs progenitors of this vile ideology?

By 1920, public opinion and attitudes towards Polish immigrants clearly reflected their position as a "non-preferred" category. The renewal of immigration from Poland in the years 1920-1939 affected little the image of the group as a whole. All came now with an "entrance status,"[23] deemed suitable to occupy only the lowest socio-economic position in Canadian society. Concern was raised once again at the possibility of detrimental and long-lasting effects on Canada through the influx of these undesirables.

Opposition to the renewed post-war influx of the "non-preferred" immigrants was raised from various sources; trade unions claimed that the new arrivals lowered the wages of Canadians by underbidding existing pay scales;[24] George Exton Lloyd, the Anglican bishop of Saskatchewan, was alarmed that Canada was turning into a "Little Balkans" and advocated limiting immigration to 100,000 yearly, of which 75% would be British, 10% Scandinavians, 5% French, and 10% all others. This concern was expressed in a pastoral letter which appealed to all parishioners to protest the arrival of "dirty, stupid, reeking of garlic, undesirable Contintental Europeans."[25]

Objection to 'strangeness,' poverty, dietary habits and other customs was also voiced by concerned citizens, groups, and newspapers. The Canadian living standards, held to be sacred,[26] were being threatened. The Canadian government was urged to introduce immigrant quotas, similar to those which came into effect in the United States in 1921 and 1924. It was claimed[27] that such a restrictive policy would lower the crime rates and illiteracy, and would facilitate speedier assimilation of the 'preferred' types of immigrants.

THE CRISIS PERIOD

For as long as economic conditions required a pool of unskilled and cheap labour, Polish immigrants generally managed not only to survive various negative opinions and discriminatory treatment but in time to establish themselves. The hope was always present that conditions would be better next year. This changed drastically in 1929.

The Great Depression was a time of hardship for millions of people in many societies. Thousands of Canadians waited for work at each large factory or mine across Canada, and few immigrants escaped unemployment, deprivation and insecurity. It is generally agreed that the established farmers could survive the economic crisis somewhat more easily than others since they had shelter and food. The urban workers, especially the immigrants who came from Poland in the years 1927 and 1928,[28] were deeply affected. Lack of skills or training, in combination with an inability to communicate in English, had limited them to the most menial and hardest jobs. They had had little opportunity to accumulate savings. Many had had only seasonal or temporary work.

During the Great Depression even this type of work was no longer easily available and Canadian citizens or residents had the first right to it. The single men[29] were most affected; for them there was no welfare and little other help. Most dared not apply for public relief, for threats of deportation hung over those considered a burden to society. Some were lucky and found themselves in "Bennett's work camps" where at least they received food, shelter, some clothing and 20¢ daily. Others found work in exchange for which they received food and living quarters. Many became regular users of "soup kitchens," some even resorted to begging. Yet others lived, in summer and fall, on potatoes dug from the fields, fish (often caught illegally), mushrooms and berries.[30] If friends, neighbours or acquaintances were located, at least shelter and some food were assured.

The married men who had left their families behind expecting to bring them to Canada later were not in a position to help them. The families in Poland depended on the good will of relatives, friends or neighbours. The mental anguish of fathers and husbands is easily imaginable. Even if they wished to return and take their chances with their families in Poland, there was no money for passage back. In despondency, some individuals committed suicide.[31]

Undoubtedly, the economic turmoil and hardship was blamed by all Canadians on the government and its policies. But this body and its representatives were in Ottawa or inaccessible in various offices, and there was another element that was starkly visible and which was blamed for aggravating the economic conditions: the 'strange' immigrants who underbid for wages and took work away from Canadians.[32] They were the Eastern Europeans, generally Polish immigrants. The term "Bohunk" achieved prominence at this time and flourished for some years, to denote the "dirty, stupid, uncivilized people" who added to the problems facing other Canadians.

The early 1930s marked the final period of widespread and vocal negative opinion against Polish immigrants and other Slavs. Common and widespread misery proved to be a great leveller, and there were few new Polish immigrants after 1931. Those already present began to adapt, cope, and gradually blend into the undistinguishable masses of farmers, workers, or unemployed. Public outcries began to be less frequent and were replaced, gradually, by a hesitant re-evaluation of the newcomers to Canada. Some writers began to paint a picture entirely different from that previously held. They spoke of a rich cultural heritage that Polish immigrants and other Eastern Europeans brought with them which could only enrich and add to the Canadian society.[33]

Canada declared war on Germany on September 10, 1939, thus becoming an ally of fighting Poland. The Canadian mass media eulogized the heroic deeds and struggles of the Polish army and fighting Polish people. The Canadian public began to express sympathy to Canadian Poles on their loss of a nation, sufferings, and atrocities at the hands of the German and Russian occupiers. Derision and discrimination against Poles were no longer popular. Poles and Canadians were joined in an effort to defeat a common enemy.[34]

NEW ATMOSPHERE AND CONDITIONS

It took over forty years for the Polish group in Canada to shed its strongly negative image; its position was strengthened through further immigration as well as through the entrance of Canadian-born individuals into various spheres of society. By 1946, the attitudes of the Canadian population as well as those of various governments marked an increasing concern towards the arrival of masses of new immigrants. Efforts were made to welcome the newcomers and help them to adjust to the new environment. Free English (or French) classes were provided, information and literature were available. Voluntary organizations, both native Canadian and specifically ethnic, were helping the newcomers in the initial process of adjustment. Mass unemployment was in the past and Canadian industry and agriculture welcomed all new arrivals.

This was not to say that problems, especially for the Polish immigrants, disappeared. Rather, for many they were intensified. As was noted, the post-war immigration included the veterans of the Polish armed forces and refugees, those liberated from German concentration camps or slave labour. Basically political exiles, they experienced a set of unique problems. Most had inadequate or erroneous images of Canada, its lifestyles, culture, and government, and they often came with exaggerated or wrong expectations of their own potentialities for the future.

Advice on conditions in Canada was often rejected. Letters from relatives or friends in Canada, sent to the prospective Polish immigrants from among veterans of the Polish armed forces in Great Britain and refugees in various parts of Europe, were not believed. Reports by a correspondent[35] in Canada, published in the Polish-language daily in London, England, in the years 1950-1952, warned of difficulties in finding suitable work, of seasonal unemployment, and other difficulties, but those determined to come to Canada retained their own images of what the society was like.

The veterans and hereos of Narvik, Tobruk, the Battle of Britain or the Atlantic, conquerors of Monte Cassino, liberators of Breda, and participants of various other battles, had to face the harsh reality of contract labour on farms or in industry. Many who had spent years in prisons, labour camps, or enforced work situations were once again subjected to the discipline of communal life in barracks, subjected to orders and demands of exacting employers. Without a working knowledge of the English language, skilled mechanics, clerks, professional officers, teachers and professors began as farm hands or lumberjacks, or in other menial labour.[36] Then as now, people with specialized qualifications could not find employment in their own professions or use their skills because they did not have a command of the English language or because their qualifications were not recognized by professional organizations or trade unions.

There were exceptions. Polish engineers generally found quick acceptance into their professional field in Canada. The doctors and dentists who

49

had practised with the Polish armed forces during the war or those trained in England were welcomed in some provinces. A number of teachers also found employment on Indian reservations.

The political refugees and ex-political prisoners suffered from other handicaps. Years of abnormal existence, constant threats of death, flight from perceived oppressors, and a sense of insecurity about their future all contributed to mental and physical breakdowns. This was further aggravated by anxieties about families scattered or left behind in Poland, and an inability to apply for protection for them from the Canadian government. Solutions to these problems were hampered by language difficulties even when sympathetic officials and social workers were available. For these people adjustment was difficult and long for, as one writer puts it, they were "conditioned by fear, possessed by suspicion and often predisposed to think happiness dwells in the place where they are not."[37] But in time problems of adjustment diminished and for most disappeared, aided by a more tolerant or encouraging attitude of both the public and official bodies.[38]

Those who have arrived during the last phase of Polish immigration to Canada are exposed to problems of adjustment as well. Their knowledge and awareness of Canada and of the Polish-Canadian group here are minimal. They also come with false or erroneous attitudes, impressions and expectations, resulting in initial disappointments or bitterness after facing reality. Those coming directly from Poland are products of long years of cultural and ideological turmoil, and have distinctive attitudes towards the legal, political, and economic systems. While the problems are real there is now at their disposal a full range of public and private resources dedicated or willing to help with advice, re-education, training or through other means. Unlike their predecessors, the new Polish arrivals are received and accepted with dignity.

PROBLEMS ON THE LAND

The opening of the West and Sifton's policy of recruitment and settlement of the prairies attracted many land-hungry peasants and farmers from Europe and from the United States. Only the American farmers were familiar with the frontier conditions and methods of farming. More importantly, they also possessed funds for the purchase of necessary equipment and livestock, or brought these indispensables with them.

A vast majority of the Europeans settlers arrived without savings, often in debt, and they faced a "New World." For them, pioneer life was a constant struggle for survival, divided between the hard toil of breaking the virgin land and heavy labour on railroad construction, lumber camps, or road-building. There was no time for rest; funds had to be acquired for the necessary purchases.

50

Land was widely available for a fee of $10 per 160 acres, but the European newcomers lacked both capital and knowledge of Canadian conditions. The amount of capital necessary varied. The Canadian government considered $1,500 sufficient to start farming, but experienced farmers claimed that $5,000 would be more accurate. Knowledge of conditions and techniques could be acquired only by working for someone else or through trial and error.

The struggles and difficulties of the pioneers are dealt within a number of sources.[39] The problems experienced by the Polish settlers were similar to those of many others. At the same time there were some characteristics and societal conditions that set this group apart. The Polish settlers were hardy people, inured to harsh physical conditions by decades, even centuries of struggle for their livelihood. They were able to survive on the simplest of diets of potatoes and bread and milk; meat for most was a luxury reserved for special holidays. This background served them in good stead during the first years on their homesteads in Canada since few managed to plant crops or vegetables, or acquire poultry or livestock for their first long winter.

Those in dire need depended on the generosity of their neighbours or shopkeepers who shared their surpluses or gave the necessary items on credit.[40] The harsh climate, poverty, and difficulties with language and customs did not discourage the Polish settlers. The ownership or possession of so much land provided hope and incentive for remaining to cope with any difficulties.

Arriving from a strongly traditional and agriculturally unsophisticated society, they had much to learn: soil conditions, types of suitable seed, seasonal and weather peculiarities, marketing conditions and other characteristics of the prairie farming. They also had to acquaint themselves with modern farm implements and their use. Most acquired the necessary knowledge by working for an established farmer or receiving advice from others who came before them. Others learned by their mistakes. But they were farmers and were able with relatively little difficulty to integrate the knowledge they had brought with the new methods, techniques and conditions. Underlying many of the initial problems of adjustment was their inability to converse in English. Lack of communication with the established English-speaking settlers prevented many from taking full advantage of the opportunities available[41] and thus from improving their conditions sooner. These and many other problems facing the pioneers were drawbacks, but they were overcome in time. All that was required was perseverance, strength, endurance and liberal amounts of hope. But social, spiritual and psychological needs were harder to satisfy.

For a variety of reasons Poland had been largely unaffected by socio-economic changes which took place in other parts of Europe. The country remained isolated, economically underdeveloped and agriculturally backward.[42] The people, uneducated, were steeped in traditions and customs which ruled all aspects of their lives. Relationships with the manor, with

51

the priest and other members of the community, exchange of goods and services, property holding and distribution among family members, land use, distribution of produce, farming techniques, types of tools, methods of fertilization and others aspects of farm life – all were regulated by traditions and customs. They provided clear guidelines for a person's beliefs and behaviour in the daily interaction with family, kin, community, and 'outsiders.' They provided a framework known and observed by all, a well-established set of rules and expectations for each individual. Together with a few formal laws, introduced from time to time by outside authorities, the customs and traditions constituted the total reality and concreteness for the Polish villagers.

This was invariably shattered on arrival in Canada. Almost immediate attempts were made to re-establish, at least in part, what was missing by forming Polish parishes and organizations, but the immigrants succeeded only infrequently and to a limited degree. The vast majority of Polish immigrants, both the settlers on the homesteads and those remaining in towns and cities, were faced with long periods of isolation from their families, friends, and community, in an alien environment, where their interpretation of reality was inapplicable, incomprehensible and useless.

They saw a new world where people acted, spoke, dressed, even worshipped 'strangely.' The cities and towns looked as though they were built only yesterday and the vast and empty expanses of land alarmed people who had lived in close proximity to other villages all their lives. There were no familiar (if disliked) uniforms: officials were dressed in civilian clothing. No one told them what to do, no one prohibited them from doing anything. The customs were strange. In purchasing goods a previously established price had to be paid without any bargaining. There were no visible lines of hierarchy, a situation which pleased many, disquieted others. They were unaware of their position, rights and obligations.

The adjustment, acquisition of new values, modification of old ones – all was a slow process and such a period of transition may well have been the greatest burden that the Polish immigrants of the 1895-1914 phase faced in Canada. Not the demands of heavy work, economic deprivation, sickness or natural calamities nor the indifference, exploitation, and occasional hostility that they were exposed to, but the absence of all that was familiar, the absence of relatives and friends, and the loss of the established personal identity or place in the community weighed heavily. The Polish immigrant was no longer a member of his village, not yet a member of a new society; he was a man in a social and psychological vacuum.

PROBLEMS OF THE WORKERS

Not all Polish immigrants settled on the land. A great many came expressly to work, save and return home with funds to pay off debts or to purchase land. Others, who had been attracted by the free land, decided that the problems and difficulties were insurmountable without the help of the rest of their families whom they had left behind. For still others any kind of work and remuneration seemed a vast improvement over their previous condition. After 1920, homesteads were available only in the Peace River districts of Alberta and British Columbia,[43] and not many Polish immigrants ventured to stake their claims there.

Arriving penniless, the newcomers had to get work immediately, any kind of work, under any conditions. Many became "a ready prey for exploiting employers, swindling fellow countrymen, greedy money lenders."[44] In the first two decades work was plentiful in the North American continent. Help was wanted on railroads, in factories, mines, lumber camps, road-building and construction. During the 'bad years' an immigrant could move from Canada to the United States and seek better chances there. And such economic crises were of relatively short duration and frequently localized. Performing the most menial and hardest jobs, Polish immigrants did not feel especially exploited or discriminated against. The wages earned appeared princely to people who could never hope to earn such amounts in Poland. Problems of isolation were not acute for the non-agricultural workers. There were other Poles or Slavs in nearly all work gangs and other projects. The separation from their families and communities was temporary. Prospects of eventual reunification provided further incentives to extra effort and frugality.

Economic conditions changed after World War I. The renewal of large scale immigration and the returning Canadian soldiers created a large pool of labour which the peace-time Canadian economy could not always absorb. Polish immigration to Canada resumed in 1920, but soon even those directed to specific locations and to seemingly vacant positions or jobs found on arrival that their services were no longer needed. Without further advice, without trades or training, with no English, and with little or no money, they were left to depend on the often unreliable advice of friends or casual acquaintances.

The memoirs[45] suggest that many who secured jobs, in some cases of a permanent nature, soon followed the advice of casual acquaintances, and began to 'chase after the rainbow' or travel in search of better paying work. Overwhelmingly, the information proved to be inaccurate or false; there were no better paying jobs or no jobs at all. During 1928-35 Polish immigrants traversed the country from one coast to another in search of elusive 'better jobs' or conditions.

While most worked during the harvest, extremely few jobs lasted more than a few months and those only during summers. During winters layoffs savings were exhausted and prospects of steady work grew dimmer after 1928. New arrivals coming with high expectations of regular work in Canada were deeply disappointed and wished to go back home, but had no funds for the return fare. Many, frustrated by their inability to provide properly for their familes brought over or left behind in Poland, became despondent or embittered.

One report notes that on December 13, 1928, about 60 people, mostly

Polish immigrants who came during the previous October and November, demonstrated at the CPR offices in Winnipeg. They arrived when seasonal unemployment was at its height and demanded work or support. Achieving nothing, they returned the next day in larger numbers (about 300), again demanding work or aid. The railway police were unable to cope with such large numbers and the city police were called in. The ensuing confrontation led to violence, damage to the CPR hall and the arrest of four protesters. There were still no jobs available.[46] For the immigrants of the 1918-1939 phase economic adjustment became the most problematic issue. Many were unable to establish themselves firmly and the economic crisis of 1929 effectively precluded chances of improvement.

THE LAND OF FREEDOM AND OPPORTUNITY

The post-World War II Polish immigrants no longer faced the problems their predecesors had known. Concentrations of Polish people and their descendants were now established in various Canadian communities. There was a viable and extensive Polish-Canadian organizational structure with numerous parishes, organizations, and services. Communications were well developed and frequent contact could be maintained with relatives and friends in Canada and in other parts of the world. Employment of some sort was always available and growing social services provided for those in need.

Again, some newcomers had specific problems of adjustment. The Polish veterans, many of whom were not in fact agriculturalists, were bound by a two-year agreement to work on Canadian farms. Recruited as single men and allowed appropriate accommodation, they were forced to remain separated from their families for the duration of the contract. Isolated in rural areas, working long hours, frequently exploited,[47] separated from companions, friends, and relatives, this period was one of great trials and tribulations for many. Over 80% of these individuals moved away from the farms once their contract was completed.

Polish refugees who came under group schemes had to agree to remain in the contracted employment for one year, after which they were given a document or certificate of satisfactory fulfilment of obligations. Despite unsuitable living and working conditions and regimentation or exploitation by some unscrupulous employers, the refugees remained in their assigned places, since the document was considered indispensable in acquiring other work and useful in applying for Canadian citizenship.[48] These very real problems of adjustment were of short duration and the affected individuals adjusted quickly to their new and more favourable conditions.

At this time other problems of adjustment emerged which have had deep and lasting effects for even the most recent Polish immigrants. These resulted from a severe status dislocation.[49] At least 20% of the post-war

Polish immigrants came with higher education, professions or other specialized qualifications. These individuals could enter into their profession or occupation only in rare instances. For some the problems were eventually solved with the acquisition of one of the official languages, or through a practical exposure in their specialized fields.

The Polish nation has never subscribed to the ethos that no work is demeaning and that all occupations are respectable. Pre-war Poland was characterized by strong and sharp class distinctions and a hierarchy of occupations. The post-war immigrants were products of this society. For those affected by severe and permanent status dislocation, problems of adjustment were great, requiring modification not only of lifestyle and attitudes towards others, but also of self-identity.[50]

CONCLUSION

After 1900, Canada's image for the vast majority of Polish immigrants was of a land of unlimited opportunities, with plentiful and well-paid work available for all; a land of refuge and democracy; and land of equal treatment and unequalled possibilities. The shock of reality, created not only by less than ideal economic conditions, by exploitation and prejudice, but also by the many different Canadian cultural and social norms and values, was bewildering. The struggles and hardships on the land and the coldness, indifference, and discrimination in the cities and work places, contributed to feelings of loneliness and isolation. All that was familiar was far way. Deep crises and broken dreams were made unbearable by the high expectations with which the immigrants arrived in Canada. But to fail was even harder than to succeed under difficult conditions, for back in the old community derision, scorn or jeering awaited those who were unsuccessful. For those coming after World War II, return was impossible.

The determination to succeed hardened. Insults from Canadians could be borne as long as one had work. What was lacking in education could be made up in extra physical effort and endurance. And there was always hope for the future. The husbands worked and saved, planning to bring their wives and children over. The families all pitched in, the women often working as hard as the men, the children contributing their share. With few material resources or savings, the despised traits of long-practised frugality, self-sufficiency, and tenacity stood them in good stead. And they have succeeded. The problems were surmounted, difficulties conquered and relatively few disgruntled or dissatisfied individuals found Canada inhospitable.[51]

NOTES

1. No further discussion will be undertaken of the first phase of Polish immigration ending in 1895 for lack of sufficient data.
2. Józef Okołowicz, *Kanada: Garstka Wiadomości dla Wychodźców* (Kraków, 1913), notes that Winnipeg had an Austrian consulate, and that the consul was a Mr. Jurystowski, a Pole. As Austrian citizens, immigrants from Galicia could undoubtedly rely on this office, but at present no details are available on the activities of this consulate.
3. It should be noted that memoirs are unanimous in their favourable opinion of Canadian immigration officials and other civil servants. What was startling to most was that they, landless peasants or farm workers, were treated on equal terms with all others, totally unlike the treatment they received from the petty bureaucrats and uniformed officials in their old country.
4. Henry Seywerd, "Integration in Canada," *Migration News* 7 (1), 1958, 1-5, suggests that this basically was the extent to which the Slavic immigrants were aware of the native institutions and social structure in their initial period of adjustment.
5. Seywerd also suggests that many Canadians believed that "one immigrant is very interesting, five are a bore, ten are a menace."
6. The Ukrainians who came in large numbers at this time were exposed to a similar reaction from the host society. See Michael H. Marunchak, *The Ukrainian Canadians: A History* (Winnipeg, 1970) and Ol'ha Woyecenko, *The Ukrainians in Canada* (Winnipeg, 1968).
7. One opinion, among the least vitriolic, was expressed by A.R.M. Lower, who commented that Sifton "seemed to be indifferent to problems of assimilation, social, political, religious, that he was entailing on posterity." Quoted in Michael Barkway, "Turning Point for Immigration," *Canadian Institute for International Affairs*, XVII (4), 1957, 14.
8. Woodsworth, *Strangers Within Our Gate.*
9. *Ibid.*
10. Robert England, *The Central European Immigrant in Canada* (Toronto, 1929).
11. Woodsworth, p. 139.
12. *Ibid.*, p. 305.
13. Anderson, p. 37.
14. Rev. Wellington Bridgeman, *Breaking Prairie Sod* (Toronto, 1920), p. 172.
15. Bridgeman, *op. cit.*; W. Burton Hurd, "The Case for a Quota," *Queen's Quarterly*, XXXVI (1929), pp. 145-59. Similar views and opinions may be found in: Ralph Connor, *The Foreigner* (New York, 1909); H.A. Kennedy, *The Book of the West* (Toronto, 1925); C.A. Magrath, *Canada's Growth* (Ottawa, 1910).
16. See Emerson, for example, who noted that the Slavs were not the only

poor nor the only bad farmers. Masses of English paupers, whom England had "kindly" sent to Canada, were no more desirable immigrants than the Slavs. This opinion is also shared by J. Woodsworth, *Strangers Within Our Gates.*

17. Anderson, *op. cit.*
18. According to Smith, *A Study*, p. 214, "[of] two battalions recruited in North Alberta for overseas, one contained 80 per cent and the other 60 per cent of Ruthenians whose ancestral home was Galicia." Undoubtedly, there were many Poles among these "Ruthenians." There are references by W. Kirkconnell, *A Slice of Canada* (Toronto, 1967), to the "Scottish" regiment in Winnipeg made up primarily of Poles, Ukrainians, and others.
19. A recruitment centre was established at Niagara-on-the Lake in Ontario where over 200 (and 22,000 Polish Americans) volunteers joined the Polish army, which later fought alongside French forces in Europe.
20. Pamiętniki Emigrantów.
21. *Ibid.*
22. The most hysterical advocate of this solution was W. Bridgeman, *op. cit.*, who, in poorly disguised terms, talked about benefits for Canadian society through the deportation of "Austrians" and "Huns," meaning primarily "the Galicians."
23. See John Porter, *The Vertical Mosaic* (Toronto, 1965), for his definition of the term and a further elaboration of this concept.
24. The Canadian farmers generally favoured Polish and other Slavic peoples for their willingness to work hard and without complaint.
25. Lubicz, pp. 85-7.
26. This was at various times competing with a strong self-complacency on the part of the hosts. There was nothing to learn from the newcomers since their culture and values were useless and worthless.
27. The main advocate of such policy was Hurd.
28. It must be remembered that these two years saw the greatest post-war influx of Polish immigrants to Canada. See page 31.
29. The ratio of males to females among the Polish groups at the period was 1.5:1.
30. Pamiętniki Emigrantów.
31. *Ibid.*
32. It is interesting to note that these opinions are once again popular among some Canadians. The liberalized immigration regulations of 1967 allowed visitors to claim 'landed' status from within Canada and saw thousands of unskilled workers coming from various parts of the world. High unemployment figures in Canada resulted in public outcry against this policy, contributing to the resignation of the minister responsible and a change in the regulation in November, 1972. Statistics suggest that only a miniscule proportion of these unskilled workers ever resorted to welfare or unemployment insurance. Further, employers decry the changes in the regulations, claiming that they cannot fill existing vacancies from among

the Canadian labour force (The Toronto *Sun*, The *Globe and Mail*, January/February, 1973).

33. Already in 1926, Foster urged greater understanding of the "strangers" among the Canadians. A similar position was taken by England, in *The Central European Immigrant*, who stressed the need for a civilized and rational approach to cope with the problems of adjustment of the Eastern Europeans. Perhaps the most popular was the work of Gibbon, portraying various Canadian minorities in a positive light. W. Kirkconnell, *The European Heritage* (Toronto, 1930), paved the way with brief historical sketches of the famous individuals in Poland and elsewhere. His work, *Canadians All* (Ottawa, 1941), re-emphasized the positive characteristics of the Slavs and other groups. See also L. Hamilton, "Foreigners in the Canadian West," *The Dalhousie Review*, XVII (1938), 448-60, who expatiated on the rich potentialities of minority cultures.

34. Canadian authorities took legal steps to ban both the Communist and Fascist parties in 1940. Included was the Polish People's Association. This organization was declared illegal and the publication of their newspaper was suspended. The newspaper began to publish again in 1941, under a different name, and a new name was adopted by the organization, which was active throughout the rest of the war years. See V. Turek, *The Polish Language Press in Canada* (Toronto, 1962).

35. B. Heydenkorn wrote for the *Dziennik Polski/Dziennik Żołnierza* for a number of years.

36. As one example, a Sorbonne-trained scientist with a Ph.D took the only available work – washing dishes in a restaurant. In time a more suitable position was secured, but this individual found that while professional adaptation in science was comparatively easy, social life posed many barriers to understanding and sharing common experiences. See George Sobolewski, "Reflections on my Experience as an Immigrant To Canada," *Migration News* 9 (5), 1960. For the experiences of a Polish army veteran contracted for farm work in 1946, see Józef Broda, *W Cieniu Kanadyjskiego Klonu* (Ottawa, 1966).

37. Vernant, p. 358.

38. See, for example, the position of Ellen Fairclough, "What Immigration Means to Canada," *Migration News*, 8 (2), 1959, 19-20. It can be added that occasional hostile views were expressed even at this time, as noted by F.G. Vallee, M. Schwartz, and F. Darknell, "Ethnic Assimilation and Differentiation in Canada," *The Canadian Journal of Economics and Political Science*, XXIII (1957), 540-49: "In 1956 the Orange Lodge requested the government to restrict Central European immigration and to prevent teaching of foreign languages in universities, publication of foreign newspapers, and ownership of hotels by foreigners."

39. See Rev. Boniface, OFM, *Pioneering in the West* (Vancouver, 1957); Bridgeman, *op. cit.*; Emerson, *op. cit.*; Rev. A. Gocki, *op. cit.*; and especially Douglas Hill, *The Opening of the Canadian West* (London, 1967), who deals with this subject at length and very perceptively. See also

Turek, *Poles in Manitoba*, and M. Wańkowicz, *Tworzywo*, for an in-depth portrayal of a few individuals and families. Wańkowicz's novel is based on extensive historical research and interviews held with original settlers and/or their descendants.

40. Mutual aid and co-operation was one of the common characteristics of that period and according to Hill gave rise to what is now known as "Western hospitality."

41. As an example, few were aware of or took advantage of bank loans to purchase equipment or build necessary farm structures. The Polish immigrants waited until the money was saved before buying these things.

42. The Prussian part of Poland was an exception, but relatively small numbers of Poles from this area settled in Canada.

43. Dawson and Murchie, *op. cit.*

44. M. Learner, "People and Place," in Peter I. Rose, ed., *Nation of Nations* New York, 1972).

45. *Pamiętniki Emigrantów.*

46. *Czas*, 1928.

47. The Minister of Labour, on hearing of exploitation and mistreatment that many of the individuals were subjected to, changed the duration of the agreement to one year from two and emphasized that workers could change their employers if conditions were unsuitable. Not many of the veterans were aware of these provisions.

48. See Vernant, pp. 543-69, for further details on both of these groups.

49. For an elaboration of this concept see A.H. Richmond, *Post-War Immigrants.*

50. This problem has been a neglected area for those writing on issues of Polish immigration to Canada or elsewhere.

51. See Zbigniew Abdank, "Jednak Wracam z Kanady," *Kultura*, 57/58 (Paris, 1952), 85-92, who decried the cultural poverty and pursuit of economic gains by all Canadians, returning to Europe where other values were important.

FOUR

Organizations

Man, a rational creature, in certain circumstances weighs the
advantages and disadvantages of joining a certain group or participating in a collective enterprise and, on the basis of the outcome of this deliberation joins the group.

A. Rose

The melting pot[2] orientation, prevalent at times in the United States, has
never been the official policy of the Canadian government nor has the
dominant group demanded total assimilation or Anglo-conformity[2] of
first generation immigrants. They were expected to learn English or
French, and adopt certain Canadian customs and values, especially those
related to the education of their children. Groups and individuals[3] concerned with the influx of 'strange' immigrants from Central and Eastern
Europe were convinced that the children of the immigrants would become
fully Canadianized through an effective public school system. Even where
pressures and discrimination against strangers prevailed, all immigrant
groups were able, if they so wished, to maintain a certain group identity
and cohesiveness. Further, illiteracy, different customs, lack of skills and
familiarity with Canadian culture and conditions had the effect of creating a wide social gap between the immigrants and the dominant segments
of the receiving society. Through choice or necessity the immigrants of the
1896-1914 phase became isolated from the Canadian mainstream.

The immigrants from Poland were prevented by differences in language, customs and attitudes from resorting to existing organizations,
even if they had wished to do so. Gradually the need for services and for
the re-establishment of contacts with their own people led to the emergence and creation of Polish organizations reflecting some aspects of their
old traditions and religion. This took place to a large extent in towns and
cities where concentrations of Polish immigrants could be found in the
early 1900s.

60

The Polish immigrants who settled on homesteads most often became a minority within a minority. Dispersed in small groups or single families among the predominantly Ukrainian settlers, they found it difficult both to establish a basis for co-operation with others from Poland and to create their own organizational structure. While some depended on the organizations which were being rapidly established by the Ukrainian communities, others lived for many years in isolation.[4] Deeply religious, with religiosity of a specific Polish character, their first concern was to establish a parish and have their own church where once again they could have understandable relationships with God, priest, and other Polish people. Other organizations were needed for companionship and protection in times of need. Mutual aid societies, social, political, sports, and cultural clubs sprang up in various locations, some to disappear quickly, others to continue to the present time.

A general pattern may be traced in the development of Polish associations in Canada. The years to 1920 saw the emergence of numerous local, multi-purpose organizations, usually associated with the parish, largely in the urban communities. The years 1920-1940 witnessed many mergers of local organizations, and the introduction of plans for mergers of others. The concurrent immigration from Poland resulted in the establishment of many new secular organizations of which only a few managed to last independently for any length of time. There was also the establishment and growth of parishes and parish associations. Numerous local, provincial and national conferences took place with hopes and plans for creating federated bodies. The hopes and plans were largely realized in the years 1930-1940 and the newly created bodies began recruitment drives for the established and independent but uncommitted associations as well as sponsorship and establishment of new branches. This period can be characterized by organizational struggles for power, conflict, withdrawals, alliances and other related problems. The period 1940-1950 saw the establishment of a new central body with further elaboration of organizational rules, processes, goals, and functions. The post-war phase of new immigration resulted in the rapid growth or rejuvenation of the existing associations and the establishment of many new ones. The last phase, encompassing the years 1951 onward, is a period of further recruitment and consolidation by the central body with continual redefinition of its goals and adaptation of new functions and aims. The most recent developments threaten the position of the central body and the leadership has expressed concern about its survival.

BROAD CHARACTERISTICS

The Polish organizations in Canada can be divided into three broad categories, all emerging during the earlier phases of immigration and retaining levels of distinctiveness even to the present day. Firstly, there are the

61

Catholic Church-oriented organizations, under the guidance and leadership of the clergy, generally having a character of faithful congregations, acknowledging the leadership of the clergy or clergy-sponsored individuals, adhering to the same faith, and wishing to associate with their fellow communicants. The structures of these associations have been, and are, most often rudimentary, staffed by the priests and a few lay people or pious individuals with no special expertise. Exceptions have been some parish (part-time) schools run by trained teaching nuns. Lately, the parish credit unions constitute another exception.

Secondly, there is a numerically large body of lay organizations, socially more encompassing, serving a great variety of special needs of Polish immigrants, generally stressing the culture and identity for the various phases and generations of the immigrants. This category includes fraternal associations, professional and business organizations, mutual aid societies, social, cultural, sports and hobby clubs and their numerous auxiliaries.

The third category involves the political organizations. Before 1940, this included various patriotic and Polish political clubs as well as Polish socialists and left-wing radicals. Today there are only a few organizations which can be termed explicitly political. The Polish Democratic Association falls into this category, and there are a few branches of an organization whose chief concern is the territories lost by Poland to the Soviet Union by the Yalta Agreement in 1945 (Związek Ziem Wschodnich). There are a few other groups concerned with the Polish territories recovered from Germany in 1945 (Związek Ziem Zachodnich), and a few branches of the London, England, Polish organization whose goals and activities concentrate on providing support and finances for the Polish government in exile in London, England (Skarb Narodowy).

A common characteristic of all Polish associations until 1920 was the small membership and lack of people able or willing to assume the extra effort connected with organizational activity. The associations in Canada were under some influence from the Polish-American associations, which were established earlier and displayed tremendous growth even before 1900,[5] and many of the founders and first leaders of Polish associations in Canada were Polish immigrants from the United States.

A curious feature of Polish associational activity is that although a large percentage of the immigrants settled on farms[6] there is no evidence of any farmers' organizations or co-operative activity among the Polish group. One writer[7] believes that this could be accounted for by the extreme dispersion of Polish settlers and the strength or availability of Ukrainian organizations which the Polish people utilized. Little is known about the numbers and structure of organizations which existed for the specific purpose of arranging passage from Poland to Canada for relatives and friends or providing loans for this purpose or about organizations which were formed in order to transmit monies to relatives in Poland.[8]

The fragmentary figures concerning the membership in various Polish associations strongly suggest that the membership was always small in proportion to the size of the larger group. This can be ascribed to three main factors: the absence of a planning and supervisory body for the Polish immigrants in Canada; the lack of experience in organizational life; and the poor communications, resulting from the great dispersion of the Polish group, especially in the western provinces. Other less important factors affecting participation in voluntary associations were economic considerations. There were always people too poor to pay membership fees or to join in building a church or community hall. A great many others, strongly isolationist, were suspicious of or uninterested in organizational activity outside of the church.

The initial periods of foundation were followed by waning zeal among some members; other withdrew because of lack of specific issues or because of conflicts of organizational aims with their own goals. The growing number of Canadian-born descendants of Polish immigrants, in frequent contact with the native society in schools and on the job and through the mass media, were less involved or interested in the Polish organizational structure outside of church membership and utilized Canadian associations.

The voluntary structure of the Polish community in Canada was able to function largely because of the reinforcement that it received through the arrival of new Polish immigrants. The recruitment of the native-born has been and remains one of the greatest problems facing the leaders and organizers of this structure. The resolution of this problem will determine the future of the Polish group in Canada as a distinct cultural entity.

RELIGIOUS AND PARISH ASSOCIATIONS

The early immigrants from Galicia and other parts of Poland to the western provinces found many Catholic churches in towns and other larger communities, but the clergy did not speak the language of the immigrants or understand the special relationship that the Polish peasant had with the church, and the service did not follow familiar rituals which were highly valued.

Some of the earliest, still informal organizations that arose almost spontaneously among the larger congregations of Polish immigrants were the *ad hoc* 'Polish Church-Building Committees.' The organizers hoped that Polish priests could be persuaded to come from Poland or the United States to serve the congregations. By 1900 a few priests did arrive from Poland. Others came from the United States and a number of Polish parishes were established. Many smaller groups of Polish settlers were unable to build their own churches, and chapels were constructed where a Polish priest visited periodically. By 1920 there were about twenty Polish parishes in Manitoba, fourteen in Alberta, seven in Saskatchewan, five in Ontario and six in other provinces.

The demands of the Polish immigrants for their own churches and

63

parishes were a reflection of their desire to recreate the community life they had left behind. The new parish was expected to become both a religious and community centre. The priests, seen as teachers, confessors and social directors as well as religious leaders, were expected not only to continue in these roles but also to provide guidance on various matters and undertake the propagation of the traditional culture and language as well. Few of the Polish parishes were able to provide these services for any period of time, and only in the larger urban centres.

Before 1920, there was an acute shortage of qualified priests able to cope with the pioneering conditions, and the parishioners were scattered over great distances, lacking communication channels and frequently consensus as well. The larger concentrations of Polish immigrants in some cities allowed for the establishment of associations with cultural or socio-economic aims or functions. The earliest such organization was established in Berlin (now Kitchener), Ontario.[9] In the Prairie provinces the first Polish organization was the "Holy Ghost Fraternal Aid Society" founded by the Winnipeg Polish parish priest in 1902. It drew its members exclusively from the congregation of the Holy Ghost parish which was established in 1898.

In some larger urban centres such as Montreal, Toronto and Hamilton, where there were concentrations of Polish immigrants, the churches were built within a few years of the first arrival and parish organizations followed soon after. Outside of the mutual aid societies, the main activities of these organizations were aimed at identifying, stressing, and preserving Roman Catholicism in the Canadian context, since the clergy felt that the scattered and disoriented immigrants were susceptible to the missionaries and other influences of the Canadian Protestant denominations. The membership was generally limited to those living close to the church who had the opportunity to attend the affairs of the church and parish outside the regular Sunday mass attendance.

Parish educational activities were generally minimal. The children of the parishioners were usually taught the Catechism in Polish once a week before or after the Sunday Mass, prior to their first communion. Usually this was the total extent of their education in the Polish language, history, and culture. In later years a number of parish part-time schools emerged with evening or Saturday morning classes taught by the clergy, nuns, or lay teachers; such schools provided an overview of Polish history, rudiments of grammar and language as well as religious instruction. On the whole these schools were characterized by a small enrolment, a limited curriculum, and a short life span.

The outstanding exception to this pattern was the parish school of the Holy Ghost Church in Winnipeg. This was a full-time elementary school, and later high school, with a full Polish curriculum in history, geography, religion and language, taught by trained nuns brought specifically for that purpose from the United States by the parish clergy. But by the 1920s Polish subjects were taught only at the request of the parents and the school ceased to be Polish in any sense. Another exception was an eight-grade school, first established in 1949 with enrolment of over 500, and run by the St. Casimir Church in Toronto.[10]

In the earlier period of development the parish organizational activities were unco-ordinated and weak. As early as 1912 an attempt was made at a convention in Regina to federate the various existing parish associations, but without success. The main obstacles were the difficulty in maintaining contact among the scattered parishes and settlers, and the problem of engendering among them a feeling of belonging to one cultural group rather than to a locality.

Individual Polish priests organized various religious bodies among their parishioners. Like the Holy Ghost parish many parishes introduced mutual aid or insurance plans; this was the most common activity of parish associations. Other activities included an involvement with chari-table activity and care of the needy, and safeguarding or maintenance of the Catholic moral ethic among the parishioners. Most Polish parishes had choirs, as have the majority of Polish parishes today.

Around 1925 a number of parish associations became dissatisfied with their limited and narrow goals and functions and defected to the secular side of the Polish organizational structure. Alarmed by this development, the clergy began to broaden the range of activities of the associations in order to retain the allegiance of those that remained. As a further step in this direction, the Association of Poles in Manitoba, a central body of parish organizations, was founded by the Polish clergy in 1933. The feder-ation was basically a reaction against the attempts by the Toronto-based secular organization to federate various independent (and willing) associ-ations in Ontario and elsewhere. Through competition for members and influence the Catholic federation entered into an intense and lasting feud with the various larger secular organizations which were also planning to federate. The rivalry and latent hostility prevail to some extent to the present.

Today, the Catholic federation represents the interests of Polish parish societies, is run by the Polish clergy, and derives its support mainly from the local branches situated in the Prairie provinces, where the influence of the clergy is still considerable. For a number of years (1908-1952) it maintained its own newspaper, the *Gazeta Katolicka*, but this organ has now ceased to publish. It is generally accepted that the scope or intensity of the activities of the Catholic federation were and are limited in compari-son with the activities of the secular federations.

One further type of association should be noted which is at least nomi-nally associated with the parish. This is the parish credit union which primarily plays an economic role, accepting deposits, making loans for various purposes and providing a type of life insurance for its members. While some of these organizations are extremely large,[11] they play only a peripheral role and are generally uninvolved in the cultural activities of the Polish community.

SECULAR ASSOCIATIONS

Immigrants found themselves, during the first few decades of this century, without the support of relatives or community and without social legislation providing for welfare or insurance against accidents, sickness or disability. They therefore established associations, generally in the form of mutual aid or insurance societies, giving members, in return for a small contribution, modest benefits in cases of misfortune. Most commonly the benefits were related to the burial of the dead and help for widows and orphans of the deceased members. Other benefits included help to the sick and injured. Besides protection, these associations often provided a place for meeting and learning about others with similar backgrounds, and afforded an opportunity to make social or economic contacts. In a short time they also became social clubs and community centres after working hours.

Even in the early stages of their development, most mutual aid societies and insurance organizations did not limit themselves to economic functions alone. The broadening of activities was often desired by the members, or by the associational officers, who wished to broaden their base of support, or was introduced as a counter-measure to other organizations which began to add insurance or other benefits to their main functions and activities.[12]

Even when fully diversified in their activities and interests, the mutual aid societies were more concerned with the economic needs of the membership than with political and cultural matters. A number of other organizations – cultural, social, or political – emerged, generally providing some forms of benefits for their membership, and attracted greater support than the more specialized mutual aid societies.

The post-World War II Polish immigrants were better able to cope with various problems individually since their economic opportunities were greater. There were now also public welfare measures eliminating the need for private bodies. After 1940, the mutual aid and insurance associations began to decline. However, the diversification of functions and activities allowed some to survive and at present there are two such organizations in Winnipeg, a number in Ontario,[13] and nine in the province of Quebec. This type of association no longer stresses its original economic goals, but serves the functions of brotherhood, with greatly diversified activities in cultural and social fields.

Almost simultaneous with the creation of informal Polish church-building committees, there emerged in some larger centres informal committees for determining ways and means of financing and building Polish Houses, designed to serve the cultural and traditional needs of the immigrants. Although such plans do not seem to have succeeded, the committees served another function, that of providing a basis for Polish secular associations in Canada. The first Polish secular association, the Sons of Poland,[14] was established in Montreal in 1902. The primary goal was to maintain and support Polish culture and identity, and Christian morals and ethics; the secondary aim was to aid members in time of sickness or accidents, and help widows and orphans. A number of organizations with similar aims began to form soon after. Some had a narrow base of support (especially the political clubs), and functioned only for a short time. Others encompassed almost all needs and interests of the urban Polish immigrant. There were mutual aid friendly societies, political-nationalistic clubs, cultural and sports associations, amateur theatrical groups, and others. No figures are available for the number of Polish organizations in Canada as a whole for any specific period of time but according to one source[15] there were 80 Polish organizations formed between 1904 and 1953 in Manitoba alone, not including parish associations, auxiliaries or sports and cultural clubs. Of this number about thirty had ceased to function by 1953.

DEVELOPMENTS AND ACTIVITIES

One consequence of the structure and role of the Catholic Church in Poland, which emerged almost unchanged in Canada, is that the clergy tended to be so bound by their office that it became almost impossible for them to see non-religious problems separately or with detachment.[16] They did not fully appreciate the new conditions facing Polish immigrants in a strange environment, and either ignored or could not fulfil the host of new needs; yet they often met individual or group initiative by concerned laymen with suspicion, distrust or outright opposition. The clergy did not wish to lose its influence over the Polish people in the new setting.[17]

The majority of the secular associations were formed as an expression of dissatisfaction with the limited functions of parish organizations, which were restricted most often to religious matters, and with the attempts by the clergy to control and dictate all associational activities. The Polish parish associations utilized church facilities for their organizational activities, but because of the issues involved the various secular associations depended for many years on the facilities of Canadian organizations, private halls, or their own homes.

These organizations embarked on various activities. The Polish press in Canada reported on social evenings, handicraft shows, libraries and part-time schools for children, amateur theatre performances, poetry readings, national or regional dance performances, and celebrations of historic and patriotic anniversaries. Each organization, once established, had the ambition to have its own choir or orchestra. In the first instance they were usually successful but the organization of orchestras was often deterred by lack of funds for instruments and a dearth of qualified music teachers.

A number of independent local associations began to co-operate on some projects around 1910, and the co-operation was intensified during World War I. From about 1915 to 1918 previous rivalries and animosities subsided, and there was a general organizational activity, focused largely

67

on Poland's struggles for independence. Polish associations in the western provinces campaigned for volunteers to serve in the Canadian forces as well and were successful in that there was a distinct Polish-Canadian battalion (250) formed in Winnipeg. Other Polish associations occupied themselves with defending the 'good name' of Poland and Poles, sending parcels to Polish troops fighting in France, and, after 1918, collecting and dispatching monies, food, and medicine to war-torn Poland. Before 1920, Polish associations did not have ladies' auxiliaries or youth branches, but two independent women's clubs were formed in Winnipeg in 1917.

Polish immigrants who began to arrive in Canada after 1918 found many Polish churches and parish halls and a variety of secular and parish associations with established structures and specific functions. The contributions of this group were directed towards the improvement and expansion of the existing organizational life of the Polish community in Canada. The next ten years (1920-1930) saw the establishment of professional and trade associations; ladies' auxiliaries focusing on charitable activity, arts and crafts; many new cultural clubs primarily concerned with the education of Polish children and the establishment of libraries; Polish-Canadian societies which were to provide a forum for concerned or interested Canadians; and Canada-Poland societies established for the maintenance of ties with the mother country. There also emerged at this time various patriotic, quasi-political and radical organizations, including the Polish Social Radicals, referred to by others as the Polish Communist Party.[18] The established associations solidified their position, recruited new members and occasionally merged for the achievement of specific goals. The leadership was now more experienced and financially able to undertake new and broader projects and activities.

The Polish government began in the early 1920s to take an active interest in the Poles living outside the state and to participate in some aspects of organizational life, providing advice, literature, and some funds to selected associations.[19] The Polish consulate in Winnipeg set up a number of political associations that were the counterparts of those in Poland in the late 1920s and 1930s. It met with a negative reaction from some of the older and larger associations, both parish and secular, especially in Ontario and ceased to support them. Many of these newly created organizations thereupon dissolved or were absorbed by others.

Unlike the governments of some other nations[20] the Polish government was not prepared to give any organization substantial financial aid, since Poland was economically poor and there were other more pressing priorities. While the Polish government attempted to influence if not control all immigrants through an organization known as the World Federation of Poles Abroad (Swiatowy Związek Polaków z Zagranicy), its influence in Canada was minimal, concerned largely with the maintenance of support for its domestic policies and leadership and with maintenance of allegiance to Poland.

Among the strategies employed by the Polish government representatives in Canada were attempts at control of the appointment of editors for the Polish-language press, especially *Czas* (*Time*), and *Polonia*.[21] It was hoped that certain individuals would stress a more favourable attitude towards the government in Poland and its policies, provide an alternative position to the Polish-American press (popular among large numbers of immigrants in Canada), and oppose the 'destructive' activity of the *Workers Voice* (*Głos Pracy*), a radical weekly devoted to sharp attacks on the Polish government, and the 'unfriendly' attitude of the new publication *Związkowiec*.

Information and advice for new immigrants was now provided by many of the established parish and secular associations, but between 1922 and 1930 a new type of organization emerged in Ontario and in the western provinces to aid new Polish immigrants. Few such organizations survived more than two or three years and the membership was always small, ranging from five to twenty concerned individuals. They were considered ineffective by other Polish associations which also performed these functions.

THE RADICALS OF THE LEFT

Another type of organization which emerged in the early 1900s were the political associations and clubs. Never numerous, they generally followed the socialist ideologies of Poland up to the year of independence in 1918. Among such organizations were the Stefan Okrzeja Society of Montreal, the Potęga of Toronto, and Sokołs of Winnipeg and Brandon. Following the Bolshevik Revolution of 1917, some members of these organizations, adhering to the more radical ideology stressed by the Soviet Communists, broke away from the socialist bodies to form separate associations.

Before 1929, the radicals could claim only a handful of followers or supporters, but after that year their numbers grew impressively. The radicals received support from various organizations, but in 1931 one organization emerged, the Polish Workers' and Farmers' Association (Polskie Towarzystwo Robotniczo – Farmerskie). Its aims and activities attracted a large following among the Polish immigrants and the Association boasted of 15 branches in Ontario, four in Montreal, one in Nova Scotia and twenty in the western provinces.[22] This organization or its successor has never publicized details of its strength.[23] The estimates are that at the peak of its popularity between 1930-1937, between 3,000 and 4,000 Polish immigrants were members of its various branches. If such estimates are correct, it was probably the largest single Polish organization in Canada at that time.

The growth of this organization is not surprising. Canada suffered from large scale unemployment which left many Polish immigrants not only without work but also without social security of any kind. They were also open to prejudice and discrimination from the competing Canadian workers and employers. Poland also was under the clouds of large-scale unemployment and its government was considered totalitarian. Individuals were attracted by the slogans which the Association stressed: social justice, racial equality, progress, democracy, peace and brotherhood of all men.

Another factor which has a great bearing on the recruitment and support by individuals and organizations is the self-definition of this Association. The leaders and spokesmen for the Polish churches, lay organizations, and editors of the Polish press in Canada have always defined this Association as Communist and considered its leaders as tools of the Communist regimes of the Soviet Union and since 1944 of the Polish governments.[24] But in order not to discourage potential members by open Communist propaganda or names, the leaders avoided disclosing its party affiliation and "used as front various small organizations formed ostensibly for educational and cultural purposes."[25]

According to another source[26] the growth and position of this Association was derived partially from the Canadian Communist Party and from the Canadian Ukrainian Communists, who not only joined its ranks but offered advice and financial aid. But the present leader[27] of the Polish Democratic Association, the successor to the Polish People's Association, asserts that the organizations were never communist. The spokesman stressed[28] that the organizations were established to satisfy a number of needs of Polish immigrants in Canada and were concerned largely with improving and bettering their economic conditions. The organizations were not specifically political but "progressive and independent." The membership was composed of peasants and workers of many political orientations, and while a proportion of both the membership and leadership were probably Communists, others were totally apolitical. The spokesman does not define himself as a Communist[29] and claims that the Polish Democratic Association in Canada has a similar political position to the New Democratic Party.

The organization maintained its own press organ which began publishing in 1932 as a weekly[30] and was suspended by the Canadian government in 1940. The organization and its branches were also dissolved in June of 1940 but re-emerged in 1941 with a different name[31] and became active in the general war effort against Germany. It joined with other Polish organizations in 1945 in a united effort to give aid to Poland, but the last vestiges of co-operation disappeared by 1948. Thereafter, the organization was totally isolated from the Polish community in Canada and weakened rapidly.

A number of factors were influential in this development. The improving economic and social conditions in Canada in the post-war years, combined with the growing unpopularity of Communist or radical ideologies in North America, resulted in the withdrawal of many members from this organization. Under the urging of the *Weekly Chronicle* and some influential people a number of committed individuals returned to Poland to help reconstruct the nation under a new ideology. The post-war immigrants provided few recruits if any. Thus the Polish Democratic Association is faced with a rapidly diminishing and aged membership, with little hope of replacing members from the Canadian-born Poles.[32]

A major part of this organization's difficulty lies in its narrow aims and functions, stressing primarily the overall betterment of the lower classes and putting little emphasis on Polish culture, traditions and social activities. In addition the leaders and press organs of other Polish organizations and institutions strongly condemned its policies, attitudes, and activities with relation to the Soviet Union and the post-war Polish government.[33] The masses of churchgoing and traditional Polish Canadians reject the organization and its ideology as well.

Until recently both sides have resorted to frequent recriminations, accusations and attacks on each other in the Polish-language press in Canada, at meetings, special celebrations, and elsewhere. This has now largely abated and the two sides remain in largely unvoiced indifference if not hostility. Although both the leaders and members of the Polish Democratic Association identify themselves as belonging to the Polish group in Canada and they desire closer and harmonious relationships with other Polish organizations, this is unlikely in the near future, for the majority of Canadians of Polish descent retain a strong dislike for social radicalism and Communism generally.

FURTHER DEVELOPMENTS

One Toronto-based Polish association, the Alliance Friendly Society, first established under a different name in 1907, was somewhat of a maverick among Polish associations. It was democratically or socialistically oriented, but held that it could have progressive aims without being an agency of a foreign power,[34] and condemned the parish associations as well for their narrow focus and for their ineffectiveness in providing social and cultural services for the Polish immigrants.[35] It was also strongly critical of the Polish government and the activities of its representative in Canada, frequently pointing out their shortcomings through its press organ *The Alliancer* (*Związkowiec*).

Around 1927, the Alliance Friendly Society began a campaign for the federation of the numerous existing Polish organizations, especially in Ontario. Many secular and parish bodies were sympathetic to this plan. However, both the Catholic Church and the Polish government reacted by establishing their own federations of associations. The next few years saw continuous struggles, conflicts and rivalries among the various factions, each attempting to attract the largest possible number of associations and the greatest number of members. By 1933 there were four large organizations, each with a number of affiliates or auxiliary association and clubs:

1. Stowarzyszenie Polaków w Kanadzie (Association of Poles in Canada) was established in 1933 in Winnipeg, Manitoba. This

71

federation was exclusively parish-based, directed by the clergy and a few individuals chosen by them, deriving its strength exclusively from the western provinces, with headquarters in Winnipeg.

2. Związek Polaków w Kanadzie[36] (The Polish Friendly Alliance in Canada) drew its members only from Ontario. This secular organization, established in 1907, included by 1933 parish organizations of the Polish National Catholic Church[37] and a few of the Roman Catholic parish associations. The headquarters of this organization was in Toronto.

3. Zjednoczenie Zrzeszeń Polskich w Kanadzie (Federation of Polish Societies in Canada), a numerically large federation under the guidance and influence of the Polish government, was established in 1931. It soon encompassed various secular and religious associations in all parts of Canada. The headquarters of this organization was in Winnipeg, Manitoba.[38]

4. Polskie Towarzystwo Robotniczo-Farmerskie (The Polish Workers' and Farmers' Association) emerged in 1931, following a consolidation of various types of radical organizations across Canada, with headquarters in Toronto.[39]

The first three bodies were hostile towards the Polish Workers' and Farmers' Association but they also continued rivalry among themselves in recruitment up to the outbreak of World War II, while at the same time increasingly broadening and intensifying their aims and activities. These included a stress on education for the Canadian-born descendants of immigrants in the language and culture of their fathers, greater involvement and participation in the life of Canada by all immigrants, and concern with the improvement of their own organizational structures and facilities.

During the war years each organization undertook various projects aimed at helping the war effort of Poland and of Canada. In the later parts of the war the federations even co-operated with the radicals on a project aimed at helping Poland.[40] The rivalries, suspicions and conflicts were submerged in the overall effort. Only in crisis situations, especially wars, have Polish organizations in Canada co-operated closely and in unity.

THE CANADIAN POLISH CONGRESS

The year 1944 saw yet another unification of Polish associations. The organizations of the Polish Friendly Alliance, the Federation of Polish Societies, all independent secular organizations such as the Polish Boy Scouts and the Association of Polish Engineers in Canada, all parishes of the Polish National Catholic church, and a number of Roman Catholic parish associations from Ontario and Quebec joined in a single federation with a co-ordinating central committee and a new name: the Canadian Polish Congress (Kongres Polonii-Kanadyjskiej).

The urban Roman Catholic associations in Eastern Canada and all parish associations in the western provinces remain within the organization of the Association of Poles in Canada, which is directed by the clergy and sponsored by the Roman Catholic Church. The initial mottoes of the Congress were 'For the good of Canada, for the good of Poles in Canada, for the good of Poland.' The new orientation followed the final crystallization of the ambiguous aims of various Polish associations on the question of how the Polish immigrants were to perceive themselves. The position adopted by the Congress, with the general agreement of the member bodies, was that the Poles in Canada were to consider themselves as CANADIANS of Polish extraction and not as POLES in Canada. But this position was soon put to a severe test by yet another phase of Polish immigration to Canada.

The characteristics of the post-war phase have already been described.[41] Because of their background and wartime experiences, the veterans, displaced persons, and political refugees were highly conscious of their Polish identity and had a strong interest in various aspects of Polish culture and political life. They were also ready and qualified to undertake the preservation of the values and beliefs that they considered important. The old immigrants had never held the same values and perceptions as strongly, and those that they possessed were being slowly eroded in proportion to their length of residence in Canada.

The post-war immigrants began to enter into the existing organizations and take part in their activities, infusing new ideas, providing fresh impetus, and declaring their readiness to participate in all levels of the organizational structure, especially in the higher echelons of the Congress and its local branches. It was inevitable that a significant proportion of the newcomers were strongly oriented towards Poland, preoccupied with the question of ideology, political matters in Europe, and with the exiled Polish government in London, England. Many considered themselves only temporary residents in Canada, hoping that the Cold War would result in political changes which would allow them to return home. Their position was reflected in their views on Polish associations in Canada and on the role that they should play.

For the old immigrants and their leaders this was unacceptable, and the demands for changes in the organizational policies or aims were generally rejected by the leaders and members of the Congress-affiliated organizations. The Association of Poles in Canada, although sympathetic to the views of the newcomers, was unwilling to adopt the aims and functions proposed by the post-war immigrants. The newcomers therefore established their own associations. Primarily, these took the form of veterans' clubs, ex-political prisoners' associations, combatant organizations and clubs with the focus on cities or territories lost to Poland by the Yalta agreement in 1945. Within a few years the majority of the post-war immigrants reconciled themselves to permanent residence in Canada, and while maintaining support for their own associations began increasingly to co-operate with the Congress and other Polish organizations.[42]

The organizational structure of the Polish group in Canada is extremely well-developed, especially in the provinces of Ontario and Quebec. The Polish communities in the western provinces, on the other hand, have experienced weakening in their organizational activities since World War II, and, except for a few larger urban centres, the parishes provide the only platforms on which cultural contacts between Polish immigrants are possible. After 1940, the majority of their best and most energetic leaders moved to other provinces or to the United States. Even in Winnipeg, the centre of Polish organizational activity well into 1940, by 1949 only 2,000 out of the 8,000 residents of Polish background were influenced by Polish organizational life.[43]

The Polish organizational structure at present consists of the following:

1. The Canadian Polish Congress, a co-ordinating body with head-quarters in Toronto, Ontario, and with twelve regional offices representing districts in various provinces. The Congress represents about 140 member organizations, all of whom maintain their own structures and aims. At present, the Congress is made up of the four branches of the Association of Polish Engineers in Canada, the eight branches of the Federation of Polish Women in Canada, the four branches of the Polish ex-Political Prisoners Association, the Polish National Union in Canada with 16 branches, the Central Committee of Education with about 20 part-time schools, 27 Veteran Associations, six branches of the Polish Mutual Aid Society in Quebec, Polish university students clubs, and a number of smaller organizations in various parts of Canada. The ladies' auxiliaries, youth groups and other auxiliaries of the member organizations are also automatically included in the membership of the Congress.

2. The Polish Alliance of Canada with 30 branches in Ontario, the Educational Commission with nine schools, ladies' affiliates and youth organizations. The headquarters are in Toronto, Ontario.[44]

3. The Polish Boy Scouts and Girl Guides Association in Canada which is made up of four separate branches: the Scouts, Girl Guides, Senior Scouts and Friends of Scouts. The headquarters are in Toronto but the association has close ties with the Polish Scout movement in London, England. The Association has six districts, one each in British Columbia, Alberta, Manitoba and Quebec, and two in Ontario. It runs five recreational and summer centres, and its membership is around 2,250, of which 1,500 are Girl Guides, 1,300 are Scouts, 700 Senior Scouts and the rest Friends of Scouts.

4. The Association of Poles in Canada, which encompasses all parish associations which do not have an affiliation with the Congress, and with headquarters in Winnipeg, Manitoba. No details of the member organizations or their numerical strength are known to the writers.
5. The Federated Polish Combatant Associations in Canada, with 19 branches in Canada and with headquarters in London, England. This Federation has five ladies' auxiliaries and sponsors two Polish-language schools as well.
6. The Polish Democratic Association, made up of a branch of a trade union, the Polish Canadian Friendship Societies and the Democratic Association. The headquarters are in Toronto, Ontario.

The details of the structure, composition or other aspects of these organizations are extremely hard to obtain and what is now available is sketchy, fragmentary and suspect.[45] Generally, the organizations are a part of international, national, regional or district associations and the central committees of each such body provide organizational links with the member associations. Within the main associations contacts are maintained through conventions, literature, visits of the head office representatives, and a two-way exchange of resources – material, ideological and human. Polish associations in Canada still devote some effort and money to Poland, but the areas of 'aid' or concern are now chosen by the associations themselves, and are purely non-political: funds for school building or restoration of historical monuments or memorials in commemoration of some great historical figure.[46]

This broad portrayal of the Polish organizational structure in Canada cannot possibly enumerate the development of the whole range of individual associations or institutions, nor their varied and numerous activities. The establishment of a Polish research institute, cultural foundations, scholarship funds, institute of arts and sciences, and the growth of numerous dance, song and theatre groups all constitute an important part of the overall structure and activities of this ethnic group in Canada. A more detailed portrayal of some of the organization's activities and development can be found in numerous anniversary or commemorative publications.[47]

FUNCTIONS

The associations and organizations have performed a variety of functions[48] for the Polish immigrants in Canada. They have also served to create a number of problems.
Power Distribution: The organizational structure, especially as represented by large unified bodies, was generally able to receive recognition from the Canadian political institutions. Enjoying a broad support from the members of the Polish group, speakers or representatives could influence the

decisions or policies affecting this group in Canada. The most effective body in this respect was the Canadian Polish Congress, which at various times used its position as a spokesman for the majority of Polish Canadians in relations with the various levels of the Canadian government. The leaders of the Congress and of other large independent associations have been recognized as having influence both within their own ethnic community and with the Canadian government, a position which allows them to wage battles and campaigns against restrictive immigration policies for preservation of the group's status, and upon other such issues.

This has not always been so. The participation and representation of the Polish immigrants in the political life of Canadian society was retarded initially by their identification with Poland and its political developments. It was further slowed by the fact that the vast majority of the earlier immigrants from Poland had little knowledge and practice of democratic political processes.

The organizational structure can be seen as a training ground for people who were largely uninvolved in the political system in their old country and generally ignorant of the structure, functions and processes of a democratic political system. For those people, membership in associations provided the first awareness and experience of the political power that they could exercise in the new democratic society. Organizational participation served to train leaders not only for the Polish group but for the Canadian society at large. A number of individuals involved in various aspects of organizational life of the Polish community run for political offices at various levels of Canadian government. One, the Hon. Stanley Haidasz, achieved the rank of Minister of State for Multiculturalism in the Trudeau government.

Orientation: For an immigrant coming from a society differing strongly in language, traditions and customs from the receiving society, the associations of his group are usually at first the only sources of information on social, political, and economic processes in the new context. Through membership an individual gains greater knowledge of the immediate local environment and of the broader society. The functions of membership are both adaptive to the new environment, and integrative into a new set of interactions. The most significant role in this respect was played by the press, which provided not only advice for a healthier adjustment but also offered information, in an understandable language, on the various aspects of the host society.

In the earlier stages of development the Polish associations in Canada served another purpose. Before 1935, Polish organizations stressed the identification of their members with Poland. The role of the Polish government and its representatives in the years 1920-1940 added to this orientation. Members of organizations were generally asked or urged to consider themselves as Poles in Canada. Few organizations emphasized the permanency of residence in Canada for their members, and advocated a greater focus on and allegiance to the new country. Generally, the Polish associations provided a source of affirmation of attachment to Poland. The Polish Roman Catholic churches purposely or unwittingly tended to serve a non-integrative function since they were identified with, and represented for their congregations, Polish culture and traditions. The role of the Polish churches in cultural maintenance has been and remains significant, to the extent that the parishes maintain the use of the Polish language for the services and offer other means of cultural maintenance, such as part-time schools, choirs and youth clubs.

More recently the aims and policies of the majority of Polish organizations have stressed the adjustment of Polish immigrants and their descendants in the Canadian society without the total loss of their ethnic identity. They have attempted to relate individuals to the Canadian society, urging them to consider Canada as a permanent home. They have also discouraged total assimilation by stressing the preservation and maintenance of what is considered the best of the Polish culture and traditions, and retention of some ties with the mother country. The new motto is: "An immigrant adopts a loyal stance towards his new country but retains ties and identity with his old homeland."[49]

Social Change: One of the most important functions of the organizational structure of the Poles (or of other ethnic groups in this society) is the presentation of a distinct ethnic community and culture as an important contributing factor to the 'mosaic' of the Canadian society. Various techniques are utilized in this process. The most popular is the publication of accounts of the cultural, economic and other contributions from the ethnic community, or some of its members, to the development of the Canadian nation. Various Polish organizations have encouraged and supported the publication of the histories and achievements of some of the early immigrants,[50] the contributions of the pioneer settlers in the Prairie provinces, the numbers of intellectuals and professionals and their role in the overall development of Canada, and other related information.

Polish organizations have submitted briefs and other representations to the federal and provincial governments on issues related to immigration policies and the role and place of ethno-cultural minorities in Canada. The results of such activities are perhaps best exemplified in the recommendations of the Royal Commission on Bilingualism and Biculturalism, contained in Book IV of its report.[51] The involvement and activities of the Polish and other ethnic organizations have resulted in the long run in significant changes in the immigration policies as well as policies reflecting on the very conception of Canadian identity. As was officially stated by the Prime Minister, P.E. Trudeau, on October 8, 1971, Canada henceforth would be bilingual, but multicultural rather than bicultural.

Various organizations of the Polish and other ethnic groups have been active in seminars, conferences, and meetings designed to plan strategies for meaningful involvement in Canadian society and to inform or re-educate the general Canadian public about their presence and role in

Canada. Numerous undertakings supported or organized by ethnic bodies such as Toronto's yearly festival "Caravan" and cultural exhibitions, further illustrate and explain to other Canadians the ethnic group or groups involved. It may now be claimed that as a result the Canadians are less xenophobic, less likely to be prejudiced or to stereotype the numerous ethnic groups residing in Canada. If not fully accepted, the immigrants now find greater tolerance and understanding of their cultural or biological differences.

While the ethnic organizations are largely responsible for advocating changes within the receiving society, they also serve to implement social change of the immigrants themselves. By necessity, the members had to abandon many traditional beliefs and values and adopt a new set just to be able to function effectively in the new society. Participation in organizational activities unavoidably affects members' behaviour, attitudes and lifestyles, and for the Polish immigrants this served the function of breaking many traditional isolationist barriers that long characterized them.

Social Cohesion: Ethnic organizations minimize for the members the shock of a new and strange environment, and cushion the period of transition while helping to prevent personal disorganization. For the Polish immigrants to Canada, the associations served to provide some familar aspects of the old community where human fellowship and companionship were highly valued. It is likely that many achieved family-like satisfaction from the participation in small associations. Probably this was an important motive for joining Polish associations and may still be one of the strongest motives for joining and participating in organizational activities.

Personal Identification: Polish organizations also served an important role of clarifying and maintaining the immigrants' perception of their identity as Poles or Canadians of Polish descent. Immigrants from Poland in the second phase (1896-1914) did not form a self-conscious, unified group. The consciousness and the bond of identity grew later, and only through the efforts of a few dedicated leaders of organizations and their activities. In many cases the immigrants learned that they were Poles only after immigrating to a new society, and this consciousness arose through a common language and religion in the context of the Polish parish and other secular organizations.[52]

World War I provided a unique opportunity for Polish organizations to reach isolated groups and individuals, and, with patriotic slogans or demands for concern over the struggle for independence in Poland, claim their allegiance, if not for their own organizations, at least for their country of origin. The publicity campaign carried out by various Polish associations during the war years led many previously uncommitted or uninterested individuals and groups to reaffirm their nationality.

While prior to World War II various Polish organizations were to a degree responsible for large segments of Polish people in Canada considering themselves as Poles first, resident in Canada but not necessarily citizens, recently the aims and policies of the Polish organizations focus on preventing the total assimilation of the Polish group into the Canadian society. There is little concern in this respect for the mature immigrant, but efforts are made to provide some aspects of Polish identity for the Canadian-born descendants of Polish immigrants.

Socio-Economic Advancement: For a mass of unskilled peasants and workers, membership or office in an organization often provided the only social distinction that they could achieve in the new society within their lifetime, a release from a restrictive environment characterized by the absence of upward socio-economic mobility. Such membership, or especially office, represented status recognition, unavailable except in this particular context.

Organizational membership or office served a special role for those suffering from a severe status dislocation in the socio-economic spheres of the Canadian society.[53] For those individuals a part of their previous position, influence and prestige could be maintained through playing a significant role within the Polish organizational structure, where their old symbols of social status could be recognized by the other members.

There were also economic benefits to be derived from membership in some associations. For example, the St. John Cantius Society of Winnipeg paid out in the course of the years 1918-1952 the sum of $119,000 in sickness benefits, $43,000 in death benefits, and $17,000 in aid to the needy. On the other hand, the economic benefits to the organizations themselves were also considerable, allowing them to build or purchase their own edifices and generally retain large sums of monies under their control. Finally, those with common business or professional interests, by uniting in organizations or associations, were able to strengthen their position in relation to their own ethnic community as well as the host society.

Problems: The Polish organizational structure in Canada, comprising numerous institutions, organizations, associations and other formal groups, was frequently influenced by the religion, occupation, political orientations, and military backgrounds of the members, their time of arrival in Canada, and place of birth. It was thus inevitable that few bodies had similar standards, values, or goals. Some organizations reflected narrow or limited sets of orientations, attitudes or positions on such matters as relationships with Poland or attitudes towards the youth; others took a neutral or opposing stance on the same issues. The members themselves did not necessarily support all the positions of their own leaders.

The absence of consensus led on many occasions to confrontations among the organizations, or else fragmentation of the membership of a particular body. The discord, suspicion and hostility precluded co-operation and joint efforts, endangering group cohesiveness. The struggles and acrimony, combined with the selfishness or obstinacy of some organizational leaders, led to non-involvement of many potential members and withdrawal of others from participation, and created an atmosphere of indifference, apathy, and even dislike for Polish organizations among the younger generations and those born in Canada.

The continual factionalism resulted in unnecessary duplication of services and facilities, and a waste of efforts and funds. Those are the less positive aspects of the Polish organizational structure in Canada. They must be judged and weighed against the fact that for some decades the institutions and organizations provided the only sources of information for the Polish immigrants on social, political, and economic processes in Canada, allowing for greater factual knowledge of the immediate environment and of the broader society.

The organizational structure served to maintain memories of communities left behind, of wartime comradeship and of newly developed ties of friendship. As well as providing cultural and social facilities for their members, organizations offered financial and even legal assistance to those in need. The organizations have always been a reservoir of potential leaders who not only knew their own people but also various aspects of Canadian life, which allowed them to serve as interpreters of two cultures and bridge-builders between two groups. Finally, the organizational structure of the Polish community has probably been the main factor responsible for the maintenance of the group's distinct culture, yet its numerous components have been concerned with the immigrant's adjustment in the new setting, preparing the newcomers for entry into and participation in the life outside of the ethnic community.

Canadians of Polish descent and Polish immigrants in the eastern provinces[54] possess an extensive and seemingly viable organizational life which satisfies the needs of enough people to keep the organizations functioning for some time to come. But the present membership is overwhelmingly composed of immigrants who have been already partially or fully socialized in Poland and thus are more likely to want to maintain and preserve some of these values in the Canadian context.

Within the last few years, the number of new Polish immigrants has dropped to about 1,000 yearly, and the existing organizations cannot depend on such small numbers to replace the retired or deceased membership. The children of immigrants are a potentially unending source of support and continuity, but spokesmen and leaders of the Polish community do not foresee that enough of them will want to maintain ties with their own ethnic community through membership in organizations to allow the organizational structure to continue. The questions of replacement and continuity have preoccupied the thoughts of the Polish community and organizational leaders for some time now. Organizations that are to remain relevant must adapt to new conditions, solve problems, and learn from experience, thus moving to greater organizational maturity.[55] To a degree, this has been realized and acted on.

As the largest and most influential Polish organization in Canada in the last few decades, the Canadian Polish Congress gradually undertook the reformulation of aims and ideologies which would explain the need for continuation of a distinct community and culture as represented by a viable and broad organizational life. In a large measure, this was facilitated by the position of the federal and provincial governments, with their policies of cultural pluralism. More importantly, the Canadian Polish Congress modified its aims and range of activities to appeal to the interests not only of the first generation immigrants but also of their children, and thus prevent large scale defection from the Polish community through assimilation. To facilitate this process, the ideological basis has shifted from the "mother country" orientations, and the policy of the Canadian Polish Congress is that the continual existence and active functioning of Polish organizations are necessary, not for Poland, but for Canadians of Polish descent, striving to preserve what is best of the culture, values and traditions, enriching the lives of individuals and of Canadian society as a whole.

The modified organizational aims resulted in much intensified activity on two fronts, one directed towards the Polish group, the other involving interaction with the Canadian society, including other ethnic aggregates. In the first instance, there were intensified efforts to instil a positive and clear self-image, pride and awareness of cultural background and heritage, especially among the old immigrants and their children. The campaign was carried out through the available mass media, and included elaborate celebrations of historical and religious anniversaries, symbolic and cultural activities, publicizing of prominent Polish Canadians and their contributions in the past, stress on the contemporary contributions to Canadian society made by the Polish group as a whole, and presentation of Polish culture as important on the world scene. The second and later generations were constantly reminded in such terms as 'we should be proud of being Canadians of Polish descent – look at the rich history, at the world famous Polish writers, musicians, artists, and fighters for freedom.' At the same time, Polish organizations were concerned with maintaining or improving the 'image' of the Polish group in Canada, by guarding against prejudice and discrimination, by making representations (in co-operation with other ethnic organizations) to the government for the improvement of their status, and, on special occasions, requesting the presence of governmental representatives to lend prestige to their activities.

The outcome of such activities cannot be predicted with certainty. Since 1971 there has been renewed interest among Polish-Canadian youth in their cultural background, demonstrated by the formation of numerous youth groups – theatre troupes, choirs, folk dance ensembles, university students clubs, and a publication directed at this generation.[56] All such activities are carried out with the support or under the auspices of the established organizations.

It is premature to conclude that these activities will in time broaden, and that the youth will enter into and participate in other aspects of the organizational life of the Polish community. The leadership is divided on this question, but all agree that a great number of the present organizations will cease to exist when the membership dies or retires. This would especially affect the combatant and veterans associations. But it is envisaged that a number of parish and other associations and organizations will continue to function, drawing their members from the small numbers of new arrivals, and from the Canadian-born individuals who wish to maintain or re-establish their distinct identity in the Canadian 'mosaic.'

NOTES

1. The discussion of the Polish voluntary structure in Canada is based largely on H. Radecki, "Ethnic Organizational Dynamics: A Study of the Polish Group in Canada," unpublished Ph.D dissertation, (Toronto, 1975)

2. For a fuller elaboration of those terms see M.M. Gordon, *Assimilation in American Life* (New York, 1964).

3. For example, see Anderson, *op. cit.*; R. England, *The Central European Immigrant*; and Woodsworth, *Strangers Within Our Gates.*

4. Turek, "Jeszcze o Polonii Kanadyjskiej; Polacy w Manitobie: Liczba i Rozmieszczenie," *Promlemy Polonii Zagranicznej*, Tom III (Warsaw, 1964); *Poles in Manitoba* pays special attention to the settlement of Poles among the numerically superior settlements of the Ukrainians in the Prairie provinces.

5. Wytrwal, *op. cit.*

6. Until 1941 over 50% of Polish newcomers engaged in agriculture, according to census data.

7. Turek, *Poles in Manitoba.*

8. J.W. Jenks and W.J. Lauck, *The Immigration Problem* (New York, 1912); *Pierwszy Polski Kalendarz Dla Kanady Na Rok 1915* (Montreal, 1915).

9. Refer to page 23 of this study.

10. Part-time schools are discussed further in the section devoted to language and culture maintenance.

11. As an example, the St. Stanislaus and St. Casimir Credit Union in Toronto claims 11,583 members and assets of $22,000,000, and publishes its own monthly, *Nasza Credit Union*, for its members.

12. The fraternal and mutual benefit societies were made redundant by the introduction of various social services by the Canadian government.

13. The Polish Alliance in Canada with its 30 branches in Ontario maintains a protection insurance and funeral benefits for its older members.

14. The full name of this organization was "Towarzystwo Synów Polski pod Opieką Matki Boskiej Częstochowskiej, Królowej Korony Polskiej."
15. Turek, *Poles in Manitoba.*
16. According to T. O'Dea, *American Catholic Dilemma* (New York, 1959), p. 87, "in the power structure of the Catholic Church the appointed priest must exercise a supervisory functional relationship with all parochial activities."
17. For similar points of view see Turek, *Poles in Manitoba*, and Arthur Evans Wood, *Hamtramck: A Sociological Study of a Polish-American Community* (New Haven, 1955).
18. For further discussion of this organization, see pages 69-71.
19. It is likely that the funds were provided to a small number of organizations concerned exclusively with aiding new arrivals from Poland. They were established for that purpose and generally ceased to function after a year or two of activity. There is no evidence that any other organization received financial aid from the Polish government at any time.
20. Germany and Italy are examples.
21. This is based on a copy of a pre-war governmental document – a correspondence to the Polish Foreign Ministry, concerned with the selection of the "most suitable" editors for the highly esteemed and popular Polish newspapers in Canada in the 1920s and 1930s. Documents are in the possession of the editor of *Związkowiec*, Mr. Heydenkorn.
22. According to Mr. W. Dutkiewicz, who is the First Secretary of the Polish Democratic Association and also the editor of the *Weekly Chronicle*, its press organ.
23. This information was requested but not received.
24. According to Vincent C. Chrypinski, "Unity and Conflict Among Canadian Slavs: Two Examples of Alien Infiltration," *Slavs in Canada*, Vol. I (Edmonton, 1966), p. 130, the Polish Democratic Association was long considered "auxiliary cadres of the Communist Party."
25. Turek, *The Polish Language Press*, p. 117.
26. B. Heydenkorn, *'Związkowiec' – Monografia Pisma Polonijnego* (Toronto, 1963), and "Problemy Polonii Kanadyjskiej," B. Heydenkorn, ed., *Sympozjum 50* (Toronto, 1972).
27. Mr. W. Dutkiewicz.
28. In an interview with H. Radecki, December 20, 1972.
29. Turek, *The Polish Language Press*, p. 119, sees him as "one of the best known Polish Communists in Canada."
30. And semi-weekly in 1939.
31. Relief Society for Poland and Allies.
32. The information was requested about the number of branches and the approximate membership of this organization but this has not been provided in any detail. Mr. Dutkiewicz claims that at present the Association consists of about 1,000 members in 10-12 localities with the following organizations: The Polish Democratic Association, branches of trade

unions, Canadian-Polish Friendship clubs. Accuracy of this information cannot be ascertained.

33. The organization was generally disapproving of the Polish government prior to 1939 and has been uniformly approving of the Polish rulers since 1944.

34. With reference to the Polish radicals whom it considered a tool of the Soviet Union.

35. This Association was in part instrumental in forcing the clergy to expand the limited and church-focused orientations of the parish associations, earning in the process the lasting enmity of the church.

36. For an in-depth discussion of the Association see B. Heydenkorn, *Pionierska Droga Związku Polaków w Kanadzie* (Toronto, 1973).

37. For further discussion of this religious organization see pages 157-159.

38. By 1938 this Federation had 74 member organizations from Quebec to British Columbia.

39. This organization changed its name to Polskie Towarzystwo Ludowe (Polish People's Association) in 1935. From Turek, *The Polish Language Press*, p. 119.

40. The organizations involved insist that they were pressed by the Canadian authorities to co-operate with those whom they considered Communists, for the sake of greater war effort.

41. See pages 32-34.

42. There are no relations between this or other organizations and the Polish Democratic Association.

43. *Czas*, March 14, 1949.

44. The Polish Alliance in Canada was one of the founders and a member of the Congress until December, 1972, when it withdrew claiming that the original purpose of the Congress had been subverted in recent years.

45. For a number of reasons the officers of various organizations exaggerate the size of the membership of their organizations, others provide inaccurate information, and still others are unwilling to part with any information.

46. As examples, the Polish organizations in the community at large were concerned with funds for the rebuilding of the destroyed Royal Castle in Warsaw and sums of money were collected for this purpose in 1972 and 1973. The year 1973, the anniversary of Copernicus' birth, witnessed another spurt of activity among Polish organizations in Canada.

47. For a more detailed portrayal of the Polish organizational structure see Radecki, *op. cit.*

48. The discussion follows the typology of Arnold M. Rose, *Sociology* (New York, 1965).

49. Garczyński, "Od Atlantyku."

50. For the Polish community in Canada, Sir Casimir Gzowski provided the main source of references in this context. See page 19 of this monograph.

51. *Report of the Royal Commission, op. cit.*

52. Handlin, *op. cit.*; Turek, *Poles in Manitoba*; Wytrwal, *op. cit.*

53. Refer to p. 49 of this study for illustrations of this point.
54. Where about 65% of them reside.
55. This issue was raised in some detail by H. Radecki, "The Polish Voluntary Organizational Structure: Issues and Questions," in B. Heydenkorn, ed., *Past and Present* (Toronto, 1974).
56. The bi-monthly *Echo*, published in English and Polish with contents largely of interest to the younger generations.

FIVE

Language Maintenance

Learning the language means learning social conventions
through which individuals form images of what others expect,
and decide upon their own reactions as determinants of the reaction of others.

H. Landau

THE BACKGROUND[1]

Before Confederation, French-speaking and English-speaking communities established and supported schools, teaching in their own language. Many of those schools were under the auspices of churches and the religious schools received some state support. The British North America Act of 1867, Section 93, confirmed control of education by the provinces, "protecting denominational rights as they existed by law at the time of Confederation."[2]

The educational section of the British North America Act assured the rights of minority groups (Protestants in the Province of Quebec and Catholics in other provinces) to separate education. The act did not stipulate a uniform approach to the standards of education or curriculum; the language of instruction was left to the discretion of local authorities or school trustees. The language of instruction became a controversial issue since the British North America Act assured rights for minorities (British or French) based on religious differences rather than on language. Minority language rights were not clearly defined. As one researcher noted, provincial legislatures in all but the three Prairie provinces "were inconclusive or silent on the language rights of the official minority."[3] The interpretation of the educational section of the British North America Act led to conflicts and controversies which are only now being resolved, following the recommendations of the Royal Commission on Bilingualism and Biculturalism.[4]

Since the overwhelming majority of Polish immigrants in the years

86

1895-1914 were destined for the newly opened Prairie provinces, the issues of education in these areas are of special interest. Until 1870 the population in Manitoba was predominantly French-speaking but on entering Confederation in 1870 a denominational educational system was established, assuring the British settlers of schools satisfying their needs. The opening of the West saw many Ontario-born pioneers settle who came with memories of bilingual school conflicts and controversies. In the late 1880s, the English-speaking settlers were in the majority in the Manitoba legislature and the denominational school system was abolished. "Church schools were allowed to continue but they received no support from public funds."[5]

The French-speaking population of Manitoba protested vigorously, taking their case to court and to the Dominion government, but to no avail. The Manitoba school question became an issue in federal politics, contributing to the defeat of the party in power at the time. The new administration negotiated with the Manitoba government, which agreed to amend the Public School Act in 1897. The new Act, in Section 258, Clause 10, accorded special privileges to schools where ten or more children in any school spoke languages other than English. While maintaining the regular curriculum in English "a portion of the school day was set aside for religious exercises, and the use of the French language and all other languages were authorized in the public schools."[6]

By 1911 there were 126 French bilingual schools in Manitoba with 234 teachers, 61 German schools with 73 teachers, and 111 Ruthenian[7] and Polish bilingual schools with 114 teachers and 6,513 students. By 1914 the number of the Ruthenian and Polish schools rose to 132.[8] A special 1916 report on bilingual schools in Manitoba established that Ruthenian was the predominant second language in 87 schools, both Ruthenian and Polish were used in five schools and Polish was the second language in only two schools.[9]

The early developments in education in the present provinces of Saskatchewan and Alberta were similar to those in Manitoba but special concessions were made to the French-speaking settlers which provided for a system of separate schools. In Saskatchewan and Alberta local schools boards were allowed to teach languages other than English on the bilingual basis, but such courses of instruction could neither supersede nor in any way interfere with the English-language instruction given by the teacher in charge of the schools, and could take place only after the regular classes were finished. Further, instruction in languages other than English was to be provided by employing one or more 'competent' individuals, whose expenses were to be paid by special rates imposed on the parents who wished such instruction.

The educational departments insisted on qualified 'other language' teachers and at that time there were not many who could qualify. The special tax was rarely imposed, perhaps because the new settlers were unable to afford it in their first years on the homesteads, and the results were that

of one hundred schools in foreign settlements where the language concessions might be taken advantage of, during the past few years only five or six of those districts had anything but English taught in their schools."[10]

Theoretically, school attendance in Manitoba was compulsory, but in many districts the enforcement of this law was lax. It was said that "the children from homes where education was most needed are most likely to be irregular in attendance,"[11] and that parents kept children at home, arguing that there was much to be done on their new homesteads. It is also possible that parental reluctance to send their children to school was influenced by the fact that most schools were "scandalously overcrowded," not only in the cities but in rural districts as well.[12] There were, of course, exceptions, and some Polish parents took every advantage of the opportunities to educate their children at great cost to themselves.[13]

In Alberta and Saskatchewan until 1916, the enforcement of compulsory attendance in rural districts had been left to the discretion of local school boards and they generally had done little or nothing about it among the children of new arrivals. The majority of the new immigrants were not really concerned with maintaining their language through education in public schools but rather wanted their children to learn English. In a few districts where Polish settlers were concentrated, some individuals insisted that the Polish language be taught, but such requests were hampered by the scarcity of qualified teachers. Polish immigrants of the 1896-1914 phase found conditions in the educational systems of the three Prairie provinces which could facilitate the maintenance of Polish language among those born or raised in Canada, but few took advantage of this situation with the result that their children received the bulk of their learning in Polish at home.

Manitoba in 1916 and Saskatchewan in 1919[14] abolished the bilingual system. No languages other than English were to be used for teaching in public schools with the exception of the French language in certain districts. Ontario maintained the bilingual system until 1927 when it was no longer practised, although it remained theoretically available for some school districts after this date.[15]

In the Province of Quebec, especially in Montreal, Polish-language teaching has been made possible by the establishment of special language classes by the Catholic School Commission "in those French language schools where the number of pupils of Polish extraction have been sufficient."[16] In Montreal, Polish language, history, and geography classes began in 1915, following petitions to the Catholic School Commission by a Polish priest and members of a Polish organization.[17] The Catholic School Commission responded favourably to the requests, providing free facilities and nominal teachers' fees for this instruction.[18] The arrangement with the Catholic School Commission lasted until the early 1950s when a number of independent schools were established and sponsored by the Polish organizations in Montreal.[19] The Quebec government has continued to provide provincial grants towards the educational expenses of these schools.

Generally, other provinces with substantial minorities have until recently designated English as the only language to be used for teaching in public schools. Thus, it is not only the Polish and other ethnic minorities in Canada that have been denied financial support for education in their ancestral languages, but "the French-speaking minorities have also been deprived of their right to an education in their mother tongue."[20] This is not to say that education in other than the English language was prohibited. Any group wishing to avail itself of private schools, meeting public school criteria, could do so, but the costs of education, school buildings or facilities, equipment, resources and aids and teachers salaries, were to be borne exclusively by those desiring such schools.[21]

In the history of the Poles in Canada there has never been a strong desire for totally separate or private educational institutions, so prevalent and firmly established among the Polish communities in the United States.[22] Generally the Polish immigrants have availed themselves of the educational facilities of the Canadian society, sending their children to the separate Roman Catholic schools where they were available. Perhaps they believed that the family and the church would continue to serve the role of language and culture preservers.

While the organizational structure of an ethnic community plays a vital role in the preservation and maintenance of a distinct frame of reference for ethnic identity not only for the active members, but for the whole ethnic aggregate,[23] the position that the part-time schools occupy in this complex is of crucial importance. Only by establishing and supporting such institutions can an ethnic community maintain a significant degree of cultural distinctiveness among the native-born members, in effect preventing total assimilation to the host culture, and assuring a distinct cultural continuity among the descendants of immigrants. Part-time schools are limited in time and resources,

> but at the same time attempt to pass on the students the total cultural heritage of their parents and to do so in such detail as is possible in a society where everyday life is conducted in another language.[24]

In this educational process language is the crucial factor, as was stated by the Royal Commissioners: "the language is the most typical expression of culture . . . the natural vehicle for a host of other elements of culture,"[25] and, "it is said that those who care about their cultural heritage also care about their ancestral language."[26] " . . . it is through language that the individual fulfils his capacity for expression. It is through language that a man not only communicates but achieves communion with others. It is language which, by its structure, shapes the very way in which men order their thoughts coherently. It is language which makes possible social organization. Thus a common language is the expression of a community of interest among a group of people." [27]

THE EARLIER PROBLEMS AND EFFORTS

Poles have a long history of culture and language maintenance under adverse conditions, and for over a hundred years the partitioning powers were not able either to Germanize or Russify the Polish population under their control. In the Prussian and the Russian parts of partitioned Poland, education in Polish was eventually forbidden. Clandestine schools continued to exist but there were no textbooks and only the most patriotic and dedicated teachers risked imprisonment to propagate Polish language and history. Conditions were more relaxed in the Austrian part of Poland, where after 1867 freedom in education was granted, and Polish was established as the official language. Here, other factors precluded the development of viable educational institutions well into the twentieth century. Yet Polish identity and culture have survived 125 years of foreign rule and the Polish language, maintained within the family and reinforced by the Roman Catholic Church, was the crucial factor in the preservation of 'Polishness' among successive generations.

In Canada, English-French dualism and the absence of strong pressures for rapid assimilation allowed those ethnic groups to flourish who desired and were able to preserve and perpetuate their culture, including language. Those Polish immigrants who came to the western provinces before 1915 found the official attitudes towards education insofar permissive, that the establishment of schools, teaching a regular curriculum but also lessons in Polish and about Poland, were subject to comparatively few conditions, and as was already noted a small number of bilingual schools, English and Polish, were in existence at that time. After 1919, all western provinces adapted a unilingual system of education but here, as elsewhere in Canada, immigrants could continue to teach their children and grandchildren aspects of the culture of the Old Country in private schools, or through other means.

Some individuals or groups from all phases of Polish immigration to Canada have been concerned with the problems of cultural maintenance among the younger Canadian-born generation. They maintained that if the children were to have a meaningful exposure to the Polish culture and enjoy its expressions, they would first of all need to know the Polish language. The concern was shown by some members of the Polish clergy as well as by leaders of lay organizations. For some time the efforts at culture maintenance focused on values and traditions brought over from Poland and were generally within the context of religion. Polish language maintenance was taken for granted as the responsibility of each individual family.

The first Polish-language lesson, in the form of Catechism, was probably given by the parish priest of Wilno, Ontario, around 1875. There is little information on this subject from this and other parishes but it is likely that at one time or another every Polish priest provided some instruction, at least in language, to children of Polish immigrants. The established parishes, with a resident priest, were able to assure a modicum of language training for children preparing for their First Communion. The outlying and isolated settlements and homesteads in the West were visited by Polish priests once a month or less; they attempted to teach Catechism in Polish, but their visits were brief, and it is unlikely that they taught non-religious subjects. Often the situation was complicated by the fact that many children were learning English at school or from neighbours, and many adults were becoming assimilated by Ukrainian groups and were transmitting the Ukrainian language to their children.[28] In larger towns and centres, especially Winnipeg, Toronto and Montreal, residential concentration and the presence of Polish parishes and other organizations allowed for a time more favourable conditions for culture maintenance, and Polish families were able to continue to function as teachers and perpetuators of traditions and language.

The acute shortage of qualified teachers retarded or precluded the establishment of private or part-time schools and the concern of the Roman Catholic clergy led to the establishment of a training school for bilingual teachers in 1905 in Winnipeg. The training school was established through the efforts of the Oblates and this had its effect on the Catholic character of its curriculum and on the forms of education provided by its graduates in later years. The school trained both Poles and Ruthenians until 1907 when it was moved to Brandon as an exclusively Ruthenian school. The Polish section reopened in Winnipeg in 1909 and was finally closed in 1916. Little is known concerning this school, neither the number of trainees, their levels of achievement, nor their effect on language maintenance among the Polish immigrants and their descendants.[29]

Most Polish parishes conducted, at some time, Polish-language classes. Usually the parish priest himself served as teacher; a few parishes recruited teaching nuns from the United States for this purpose. The courses focused heavily on the Catholic doctrine with some rudiments of grammar, geography and history. The classes were usually held on Saturdays or in the evenings in the church halls or basements. The teachers possessed few teaching aids, especially suitable textbooks. They were often not fully prepared or qualified to teach, attendance was never compulsory or regular, and few parishes maintained regular education on a part-time basis.

The school of the Holy Ghost parish in Winnipeg was the sole exception to this generalization. The school was established in 1901 and until 1903 was taught in the church basement. Until that time there were two female teachers, who taught two hours daily in Polish and provided the regular Manitoba curriculum in the mornings. The Dominican nuns took over teaching duties in 1903 when the first school building was erected. It has been noted[30] that these teaching nuns were not adequately trained in the teaching profession and some spoke Polish with difficulty. In time the professional qualifications of the teaching staff improved, but the Holy Ghost school began to compete with other private schools for students and Polish-language courses became optional subjects "taught only on the special request of the parents."[31] The Polish community in Winnipeg ceased to regard this school as an exclusively Polish institution in the 1920s. As a separate Roman Catholic School the curriculum was expanded and Grades 9 and 10 were introduced in 1934. In 1935 Grade 11 and in 1936 Grade 12 were provided as well. The expansion referred to the required curriculum of the Province of Manitoba. A number of problems emerged and after a few years the school once again became an eight-grade elementary school.

Concern with education was also shown by some lay organizations established in the first decade of this century. They made great efforts in the promotion of cultural and educational programmes for the Polish communities, collecting money for the purchase of textbooks, recruiting suitable teachers, providing facilities and moral encouragement, organizing libraries and initiating various cultural activities, and urging the Polish immigrants to support these efforts. The first Polish part-time school in the Prairie provinces was established in Winnipeg by the Polish organization Sokol in 1904; another school was sponsored by the Polish-Canadian Club Oświata, but lasted only two years. Other schools were organized in Winnipeg, Montreal, Toronto, and larger urban centres where Polish people settled more or less permanently. Despite the activity and the concern of some organizations and individuals, the number of part-time schools was never more than a dozen in all of Canada before the end of World War I.

With few exceptions these part-time schools were of short duration, mainly providing some education for children for a year or two. Most were characterized by the absence of clearly defined aims and organization and there was little co-operation between schools and teachers, even in the same community. Limitations on curriculum and laxity in attendance further complicated matters. Often, on the day scheduled for the classes, the children gathered but the teacher or the priest was absent because of other duties; the following week many of the students were unable or unwilling to attend.[32]

A number of individuals from the second phase of Polish immigration to Canada, concerned about culture and language maintenance among the immigrant children, advocated the establishment and maintenance of more permanent schools where the children could learn not only reading, writing, and Catechism, but also the history, geography and literature of Poland. As was suggested above, the plans and hopes of the concerned activists were far removed from reality, and it must be admitted that the Poles initially showed little inclination to organize and maintain schools in Canada.

RENEWED ACTIVITY

The influx of Polish immigrants to Canada began once again in 1920. While the majority in this phase were still economically motivated individuals and families, there were among them a few intellectuals, educators, organizers and professionals who affected the development of the part-time schools in later years.

Poland regained her independence in 1918 and in 1920 following the Russian-Polish war a period of reconstruction began. As in other societies, some intellectuals, such as teachers and professionals, were unwilling or unable to come to terms with the new Polish regime and followed the economically motivated migrants to the New World. In the 1920s the Poles in Canada acquired, for the first time, a number of professionally trained and qualified teachers and educators who could give leadership in the language and culture maintenance efforts of their group.

The American Polish community had developed an extensive and comprehensive network of organizations by this time, both secular and religious, including a whole structure of parochial educational institutions, with a full range of texts and other educational aids suitable to the needs of immigrant children. These resources were now to be relied on by the Polish immigrants in Canada. Parochial part-time schools especially drew on personnel and textbooks from the United States.[33] The Polish government, through its consular representatives in Winnipeg, Montreal, and Ottawa, also participated to some extent in the development of the Polish organizational structure, including part-time schools. The consular offices donated a number of textbooks to Polish schools and provided advice and expertise on matters of education.

Most importantly, Polish organizations in Canada began to take greater interest in the education of children and the period 1930-1940 witnessed greatly increased activity in this field. An important event was the foundation of the Federation of Polish Societies in Canada (Zrzeszenie Stowarzyszeń Polskich) in 1931. One of its main concerns was education and it imported great numbers of primers and textbooks in the Polish language, organized travelling lending libraries, set up and supported a few schools in larger urban centres and generally encouraged and promoted the Polish community to greater effort in this field. "Even then its work was hindered by the differences among its members of diverse ideological orientation and by the Great Depression."[34]

Another organization, the Alliance Friendly Society, created an educational council in 1932 with powers to establish and manage Polish language schools in Ontario, with special funds set aside for this purpose. In 1937 the council was replaced by a Board of Education consisting of five elected members. They in turn engaged teachers and published a number of textbooks. In 1933 the Polish Academicians Club was formed at the University of Winnipeg which, for the next five years, provided a forum

93

for debate on the shortcomings and problems facing Polish-language schools.

At present, information is far from complete on the Polish part-time schools in Canada. As far as is known, only the teaching orders of nuns kept regular records of their educational and other activities prior to 1960.[35] The records of the Felician Order of Nuns, reaching back to the first years of their teaching in 1937, contain information as to the number of children attending Polish-language schools taught by them. There were six such schools in Ontario, all of which are still functioning. The six are attached to the following parishes: St. Stanislaus, St. Casimir, and St. Mary's, all in Toronto, St. Stanislaus in Hamilton, St. Hedwig's in Oshawa, and St. Mary's in St. Catharines.

The archives also provide data on the sex of students (but not their ages), schedules of classes, and the number of teachers in each school. The Felician Sisters also taught Catechism and religion in both Polish and English as a separate subject on weekends and during the summer; other than this there are no references to the subjects taught in various schools. There are few or no references to the facilities, aids, or methodology used nor to the numbers of graduates, grades taught, and the drop-out rates.

It is likely that the number of Saturday or evening part-time Polish schools, including those run by parishes, varied between twenty and thirty.[36] By 1946 there were eleven evening schools with about 700 students under the supervision of the Board of Education of the Alliance Friendly Society. It is difficult to judge the effectiveness of these institutions in language and culture maintenance, but it is evident that despite the effort and time expended by some organizations and groups of individuals a considerable percentage of second-generation immigrants did not speak any Polish, and the number of those who could command the literary language and read Polish literature was extremely small. The Canadian census shows that the ratio between those claiming Polish as their mother tongue and those claiming Polish as their ethnic origin has constantly decreased since 1931.

A more significant fact found by a recent study is that only 23.3% of those of Polish origin under the age of 15, and 31.2% in the 15-24 age group, still claim Polish as their mother tongue. Even those who do so are generally characterized by a poverty of vocabulary, carelessness of accent and frequent use of slang expressions or of Polonized English words.[37]

So far as could be determined, part-time education with objectives of language and culture maintenance among the children of Polish immigrants in Canada up to 1946 was only partially developed and did not seemingly produce the desired results. The numbers of children utilizing Polish as their everyday language even at home diminished with every year. Whatever was learned in schools was soon forgotten and increasingly larger percentages of the younger generations used only English even in conversations with their parents.

TABLE 6

POLISH ETHNIC GROUP IN CANADA – MOTHER TONGUE POLISH

Year	Polish Ethnic Origin	Polish Mother Tongue	
1931	145,503	118,559	(81.4%)
1941	167,485	128,711	(76.8%)
1951	219,845	129,238	(55.8%)
1961	325,517	161,720	(50.0%)
1971	316,430	134,680	(42.6%)

Source: DBS, Statistics Canada.

This development was decried and condemned by organizational leaders and others in the Polish press, in public meetings and in private. The major responsibility was placed on the parents for their lack of interest in the maintenance of the Polish language among the children. It was pointed out that the parents were lax in insisting on the use of Polish at home and apathetic towards part-time schools, unwilling to support them financially or through involvement.[38]

Polish organizations were also criticized for 'inadequate' performance, lack of co-ordination and co-operation on this issue and insufficient support, financial and moral, for part-time schools. The peculiar form of Polish parish education, with emphasis on religious subjects, was considered by some as useless, even harmful to the maintenance of language and culture.

ANALYSIS

There are a number of reasons why the Polish group in Canada was not able or willing to establish and maintain a more extensive network of part-time schools before 1946. Among the more important factors are the background and the composition of immigrants who came to Canada in the years 1896 to 1939. Well into the present century, the Polish society was composed primarily of two classes: the first were the landowners, who were the lesser nobility or 'szlachta,' the greater nobility composed of the old families, members of the royal blood, and great latifundists, some of whom were the *nouveaux riches*. The other class were the peasants who comprised over 70% of the society. There was no Polish middle class to speak of; the commerce and financial matters as well as most professions were in the hands of minorities, Germans and Jews, or members of one of the occupying powers, from Austria, Russia, or Prussia. The masses of peasants lived in ignorance and extreme poverty, without an opportunity for social or economic mobility, and without power or influence in even those important decisions that affected them directly. Rural communities in Galicia[39] were especially isolated, both from modernizing currents and social reforms and developments.

The rate of illiteracy was high at the turn of the century. Some sources[40] place it at over 50% for males over the age of ten and much higher for females, who were considered not to need formal education since they were to be wives and mothers anyway. Education was considered superfluous to the needs of the farmers, neither valued greatly nor appreciated.[41] Gradually it was accepted that being able to read a newspaper and write letters gave a person a special position in the community. Village schools in Galicia began to be established only in the late 1880s, and attendance, though officially compulsory, was seldom enforced. The children who attended rarely managed to go beyond the basics of reading, writing and religion. The concerned activists and Polish educators who attempted to explain the benefit of education to the peasants were most often met with disbelief. Children always learned from the parents, imitating their performances and roles.

The family performed the main educational function for the Polish peasants well into the 1900s, but this did not include reading or writing. The parish priest served an important auxiliary role in this process, by teaching the children Catechism and prayers and reminding the adults of the religious values in weekly sermons. Travelling storytellers or beggars brought news of the outside world, recounted important happenings in other parts of the country and served as agents of informal education for a few interested and bright children by teaching them to read and write.[42]

It was beyond the comprehension of the average peasant that education was necessary in order to maintain his language, culture, and traditions, or that education could serve important functions, allowing, for example, for upward social mobility. The only possibility that existed was for a lucky or bright boy to be picked out by the parish priest and sent through the schools in larger towns and cities, to prepare for the priesthood. To peasants, this was an honour, and it was encouraged if their son was so chosen. Other types of education were not seen as useful for the future of the children.[43]

Canada attracted the poorest Polish immigrants, the landless day-labourers and small landholders. The adults who made up the bulk of immigration in the 1896-1914 period had derived little benefit from schools. "These were peasants without a developed feeling of nationality and without a class of educated men to lead and guide them in the new environment,"[44] and "it was unreasonable to expect them to become enthusiasts for education all at once."[45] In addition, the general poverty and the financial struggles of the first years did not allow time or money which could pay for the education of children in the Polish language and culture in the bilingual schools even when they were still a reality. Education for children was rarely on the priority list of the Polish peasant and far behind the acquisition of livestock, farm implements, or a house in the city.

The children, exposed to the public education in Canadian schools and in frequent contact with non-Polish peers, acquired the new language and culture quickly. Most parents did not object, but were alarmed that in the process of acquiring a new language and cultural identity their children quickly forgot the Polish language, values and customs. This is not surprising. In public schools they learned nothing of their culture or background. In the context of the family they were exposed to an oversimplified version of their heritage: folk dances, songs, and special food. Prayers were said in church and Catechism was learned in Polish. There were few incentives for the retention of the Polish language and many opportunities to lose it.

Thus, it was only after they immigrated that language preservation and cultural maintenance became a prominent issue in the minds of many.[46] But as a result of their lack of education they may well have been too inarticulate to explain to their children who they were and how important this background was. As one writer put it, in most cases "the parents themselves were too illiterate to teach their children at home."[47] Deprived now of the supporting role of the Polish church and the community, they were unable to transmit the values important to them to their children who at best thought of themselves in partially ethnic terms only.

The new arrivals found themselves in a strange culture where exploitation and discrimination was common towards the strange immigrants unable to communicate in English. Concerned and aware of their shortcomings, they made attempts to learn, and most mastered the English language to some degree.[48] Faced with the necessity of possessing a means of communication in order to find work or to improve their economic and social position, more emphasis was placed on acquiring the new language than on preserving or maintaining the old. The parents were happy that at least their children, exposed to Canadian education, had chances to enter and participate fully in the new society. Part-time schools were luxuries which many relegated to the background in the struggle to establish themselves in Canada.

But it was also felt that the family would continue to be able to socialize its new generations in the traditions, attitudes, beliefs and language as it had always done. The families settled in rural areas, in contact with other Poles and isolated from the disruptive influences of the urban environment, were able to maintain this pattern of socialization to a large measure in the absence of influential native peer groups and with the continuation of the extended family system. The role of grandparents was significant in the past and probably remains important at present. The grandparents, permeated with the culture and traditions of the Old Country, too old to adopt new values, often 'forced' their grandchildren to speak to them in the old language, exposing them to or teaching them different customs and traditions. The pattern of socialization was further facilitated by the absence of television and lack of exposure to other mass media.[49] The results were that the Canadian-born descendants of the earlier Polish immigrants remaining in rural areas learned to speak Polish and maintained other aspects of culture and traditions well into the 1950s.

The urban Polish families were less successful in transmitting their language and culture. Exposed to the full impact of Canadian public schools, mass media and peers, the immigrant children were quickly absorbed into the mainstream of Canadian life. To counteract assimilation the families could rely only on a few Polish organizations and institutions. The children, who were generally coerced into attending part-time Polish schools where they existed, had to do so after regular school hours or on weekends, when other children were free or at play. Not many understood the necessary sacrifices. Polish grammar is extremely difficult to master, and this subject provided an additional burden for the young students. It is also likely that children resisted identification with the negative image Poles had in Canada before 1940.

In addition, many urban Polish families were mobile, in search of work or better prospects, and thus could not always remain close to Polish institutions and other Polish people. In such cases the family was seldom sufficiently strong to socialize the children into the Polish culture. Also, many mothers went out to work, and with both parents working there was little time or strength left for language and culture maintenance within the family.

Before World War II, Polish immigrants came with few intellectual or professional leaders and without a broad experience of participation in organizational or civic affairs at home. Most were unaware of the importance or functions of educational institutions. Without speaking or understanding English, they were ignorant of the laws and services affecting them in Canada. Before 1916, some demanded that the provincial governments in the Prairie provinces provide their children with complete facilities for their own language and culture maintenance; more often they were not aware of or unable to take advantage of the facilities which existed already.

The majority settled either in isolated rural areas or were scattered in all urban centres where work was available. Polish parishes, other organizations and eventually part-time schools were established only after the intitial periods of adjustment to the new conditions were over, and religious and economic needs took precedence over education or culture maintenance. A few concerned activists proposed co-operation and mutual aid within the whole organizational structure in order to solve the problems related to Polish part-time schools, but the proposals were not acted upon.[50] Some immigrants were unable to participate and support such efforts, others were apathetic, and there was little unity or consensus among the organizations.

Most damaging in the development of the educational institutions was the absence of co-operation and understanding, which on many occasions turned into outright hostility between the clergy and the lay leaders. The parish-affiliated schools were accused of stressing religious instruction to the detriment of history, geography and related subjects.[51] On the other hand non-parish schools were seen by the clergy as godless institutions, downgrading the most important aspect of the Polish culture which was provided by Roman Catholicism. Other agencies were able to alleviate the lack of Polish schools to some extent.

Since the establishment of the first Polish parish in Canada the religious institution served as an important agency of culture preservation. The sermons or lectures given in the Polish language, the singing of traditional hymns and national songs, participation in the choir, and the celebration of the many specifically Polish anniversaries or holy days all provided some reinforcement to the language and culture maintenance efforts of parents and of part-time schools.

An important role was also performed by the Polish-language press. A number of Polish-American journals were available to the immigrants by the 1890s and by 1904 they could read Polish-language newspapers published in Canada.[52] The Polish press could claim that it preserved and maintained a relatively pure style of Polish while at the same time battling against encroaching dialect, or development of "pidgin English." It was even claimed that the Polish-language newspapers contributed more than any other single factor to the general improvement in the educational and cultural standards of the Polish immigrants.[53] Similar roles could be ascribed to various libraries and reading rooms that were established in larger cities in the first or second decade of this century. Folk art and music may also have been resposible to a lesser degree for language maintenance although it is likely that traditions rather than language were really affected.

MORE RECENT DEVELOPMENTS

Despite all these factors the Polish community in Canada was losing the battle for the allegiance of its Canadian-born descendants. Neither the Polish family nor the organizational structure was able to counteract the attractiveness or pressures emanating from the Canadian society. A new development took place following the influx of the post-World War II immigrants. The number of part-time schools, especially in Ontario and Quebec, rose significantly, and parents showed strong interest in these institutions. There was also a growth of specialized bodies concerned with language and culture maintenance, while many of the established organizations displayed renewed interest in part-time schools, offering encouragement or support to plans for educational activities. This concern remains to the present day, and new ideas and strategies are constantly being sought in an effort to maintain and expand the opportunities for Canadian-born youth of Polish descent to acquire aspects of the culture of their forefathers.

The Polish immigrants of the fourth phase, arriving in Canada between the years 1945 and 1956, differed strongly from all previous immigrants to this country. The numerically large group of people contained for the first time a substantial number of intellectuals and professionals, representing scholars and doctors, lawyers and engineers, army officers, educators, and other white collar workers.[54] As political refugees or exiles these immigrants are strongly conscious of their nationality, their history and their traditional background. There were few illiterates among them; most had been exposed to formal education in Poland, which was broadened further by circumstances of war, immigration and resettlement. The unsettled political situation in Europe and the Cold War between the Soviet Union and the Western nations up to the early 1960s deluded many into believing that world conflict was bound to ensue at any time and the Western Powers would be victorious in such a conflict and would liberate Poland from Soviet domination, allowing them to return to their rightful places. This provided an important spur and incentive for language and culture maintenance among the younger generations.

The arrival in Canada of a large number of professionals and intellectuals after World War II, many of whom harboured strong political and nationalistic views, could not fail to have a powerful effect on the development of organized life, including educational institutions. Numerous individuals, leaders and influentials from among this group quickly became aware that the existing Polish part-time educational institutions were too few to serve the needs of the new arrivals and, furthermore, that the curriculum was unsuitable. Helped by the experiences of the immigrants who had come to Canada earlier and by the methods of Polish education developed in the United States and Great Britain, in addition to their own resources in experience and expertise, the new arrivals made concentrated efforts to provide education for their children in the language, history, geography and traditions of Poland. As a result, since 1945 over forty new part-time schools have been established in various parts of Canada.[55][56]

THE NATIONAL SURVEY

In 1965 a survey was initiated by the Canadian Polish Congress in order to provide data for the Royal Commission on Bilingualism and Biculturalism.[57] The first and only survey conducted in the Polish community on a national scale was designed to determine the overall situation of Polish-language maintenance efforts, and was carried out in the years 1965-1968. While a number of Polish schools known to exist in various parts of Canada failed to respond to the survey, a majority of the institutions returned the questionnaires and the results provided, for the first time, a broad and fairly accurate portrayal of Polish part-time schools in Canada.[58]

In 1965 there were about 5,000 children attending 57 Polish part-time schools in Canada, which were sponsored by the Canadian Polish Congress, parishes and various lay organizations. There were in Ontario 38 schools with 2,285 students, 12 of them in Toronto, 5 in Hamilton, 2 in Brantford, 2 in Thunder Bay, and others in various smaller urban communities; in Quebec 10 schools with 760 students, all of them in Montreal; 5 schools in Manitoba with 265 students; 2 schools in Alberta with 100 students; and 2 schools in British Columbia with 152 students. On the basis of the survey the following data emerged:

The majority of the part-time Polish schools taught Polish language (grammar, reading and writing), history and geography. The parish schools emphasized also normative or religious instruction. Some schools included lessons in traditional dancing, singing and crafts.

There were three types of schools: parochial schools, Congress schools and those sponsored by other organizations. Polish schools were characterized by a lack of uniformity or co-operation even among schools located in the same city, and this was reflected in different curricula and standards of education. Lack of central organization and direction entailed extra costs for all the schools involved, and lack of central planning resulted in a "hodge podge" of textbooks, methods of teachings, aims and goals. The sum allocated by the Polish group towards the costs of part-time schools in 1965 was $73,300.

Only 41 out of 57 Polish schools replied to the survey, and the data provided below are based on this number. The statistics show that 73.2% of the schools were sponsored by organizations while 26.8% were parochial schools. Of the schools, 80.5% held no more than two or three hours of instruction per week; 65.9% held instruction on Saturdays while the other 34.1% held weekly evening classes.

The number of grades varied considerably; 2 grades – 7.3%, 3 grades – 17%, 4 grades – 17%, 5 grades – 22%, 6 grades – 9.8%, 7 grades – 22%, 8 grades or more – 4.9%.

The average number of children per school was 57. The language of instruction was exclusively Polish in 80.5% of the schools; some English and/or French was used in others. School libraries were to be found in only 14 schools (34.1%). Of the children attending, 48.5% spoke the Polish language well, 41.5% spoke Polish poorly and 10% did not speak it at all. The majority, 53.7% of Polish schools, used the facilities of the Canadian separate schools while only 14.0% had their own rooms or facilities, mostly parish schools.

The school budget was divided in the following way:

Teachers' salaries 73%
Fees for rental of space...12%
Texts and books 7%
Other 8%

The school budget was derived from the following sources:

101

TABLE 7

SCHOOL ATTENDANCE BY CHILDREN OF POLISH DESCENT - 1966

	Children 5 - 14		Number attend- ing School		% of Total
Metropolitan Centres	36,574	(53.4%)	3,067	(86.1%)	8.4
Cities	5,042	(7.4%)	382	(10.7%)	7.6
Town and Villages	26,807	(39.2%)	113	(3.3%)	0.4

TABLE 8

YOUTH OF POLISH BACKGROUND BY PROVINCES
AND POLISH SCHOOL ATTENDANCE

Province	Age 5-14*	No. attending Polish School	%
Newfoundland	30	–	–
Prince Edward Island	26	–	–
Nova Scotia	705	–	–
New Brunswick	161	–	–
Quebec	6,269	760	12.1
Ontario	32,802	2,285	7.0
Manitoba	8,506	265	3.9
Saskatchewan	6,157	–	–
Alberta	8,685	100	0.3
British Columbia	5,018	152	3.0
Yukon and N.W.T.	55	–	–
TOTAL	68,414	3,562	5.2[59]

* Data of age based on the 1961 Canadian census.

Contributions of organizations
or parishes and individuals..35.4%
School fees paid by parents...48.8%
Special collections, etc..8.6%
Provincial grants (in Quebec)..7.6%

There were 142 teachers, of whom 25 were male and 117 female. The educators were a mixed group. The largest percentage, estimated at about 75%, were qualified teachers, having been trained in teachers' colleges in the United States (as most of the Felician Sisters and other orders of teaching nuns are), or either in Poland or in Canada, and some were regularly teaching in Canadian separate schools. The pay usually did not exceed $200 yearly.

The survey found a great variety but a general shortage of textbooks. Some of the texts were outdated, many were too complex, others unsuitable for the special condition of immigration. The teachers complained that there were never enough books available to provide a meaningful reading programme for the children. They advocated a suitable text for grammar for all Polish schools which would facilititate the learning of the subject and eliminate the negative factors associated with the change of teachers or change of school for a child.

A further finding was that there were no training or upgrading facilities for the teachers. As was noted, a large number of them were qualified, yet the special circumstances did not allow the application of techniques and teaching methods employed in public schools in the part-time schools.[60] Often, too much was expected of a child or too much was assumed.[61] Since attendance was voluntary, too many demands tended to discourage the children.

There was lack of interest among the parents and various organizations in the financial needs of the schools, and this was evident in the shortage of books and other teaching aids. There were many comments and complaints by teachers and the Polish-language press that the education in the majority of the part-time schools was limited to bare classroom instruction, often without maps or blackboards, with insufficient books, pens, and other aids.

The absence of co-ordination in the programmes and textbooks among the various schools produced far from uniform results. Because it is hard to master, Polish grammar was an unpopular subject among the children, while history, dance and songs enjoyed greater popularity. Just to keep the children attending regularly, many teachers glossed over the more difficult subjects and concentrated on singing, recital and history, a strategy of doubtful value in regard to the child's level of knowledge of the Polish language, especially if the child had to change schools for one reason or another.

The findings of the survey established that one of the main obstacles preventing or retarding the establishment and growth of part-time schools in areas where facilities were available and the number of children would warrant a new school was that the Polish-language schools were not seen as filling a vital role for future generations. Not only the parents but many of the leaders of communities as well did not view them as important.

There was no concrete action that the Canadian Polish Congress, the sponsor of the survey, could take to deal with the various problems, although it represented more than 180 organizations in Canada at the time. It had no funds to allocate to individual schools and was in no position to levy taxes for education among its members and other Polish immigrants, and its authority was insufficient to dictate and implement a uniform programme of education and introduce a uniformity in textbooks. Its only recourse was to appeal to the Canadian Polish community and encourage it to take greater interest in the support of these schools. One encouraging note in the survey was that the majority of the schools in the past were organized independently by groups of parents who expressed a need for language maintenance among their children, and this spontaneous desire for schools could be rekindled, given a few dedicated individuals and a little extra financial outlay.

THE LATEST DEVELOPMENTS

Since the time of the survey, information is more easily available and the latest information is provided by the Polish Teachers Association in Canada (Związek Nauczycielstwa Polskiego w Kanadzie).[62] According to this source, the number of children attending Polish part-time schools in the 1972-1973 academic year was over 3,600. This is a substantial drop since 1965, when the national survey estimated that over 5,000 children attended Polish-language schools. At the same time the number of schools increased from 57 to 72 in all of Canada and the number of teachers rose from 142 to 167. The Polish Teachers Association further notes that there are a number of privately conducted lessons in Polish for smaller groups of children.

The numerical decrease in the numbers of children attending Polish part-time schools in understandable. The dynamic period of post-war educational activity resulted largely from the peculiar characteristics of this phase of immigration. As refugees or political exiles, the parents were deeply concerned with Poland and Polish culture and these feelings were translated, in part, into a concern for language and culture maintenance among their children. In time, the post-war immigrants have reconciled themselves to the permanency of their stay in Canada, many losing in the process their concern for maintaining language and culture among the youth. By 1970 their children have largely grown up, many have married and moved away from the areas where there are Polish organizations. The continuation of Polish part-time schools depends to a large degree on whether they in turn will send their children to Polish part-time schools, for as the Report of the Royal Commission points out, "the fate of language depends on the persistence of its use by the native-born. While immigrants provide immediate support to the language, it is the native born who determine its retention in the long run."[63] The number of immigrants to Canada from Poland has for some years been small. There will probably be a further reduction in the number of schools and teachers and decline of enrolment. Their survival is in doubt unless native-born children of Polish descent enrol in greater numbers than at present.

The attitudes and beliefs of the Polish aggregate have changed considerably in the last decade, including views concerning language maintenance among the children. A number of pragmatic leaders within the Polish community advocate abandoning the slogan, "As a good Pole it's your *duty* to see that your children speak Polish," and stressing instead the concrete benefits of knowing the additional language, and of being aware of and having pride in one's origin. To this end they say that the schools must be made more attractive to the children and "wide publicity and effort should be devoted to invoke the good will and interest of the parents."[64]

Within the last few years significant developments have taken place which may strongly influence the future development of the Polish educational institutions in Canada. In 1958 the Mickiewicz Foundation was established to provide scholarships to outstanding Polish students, grants for publication, aids to Canadian Polish artists, and awards for Polish-language competitions among the students attending Polish part-time schools. Another such body, the W. Reymont Foundation, was established in 1969 to support Polish studies at the university level in the areas of language, history and sociology.[65] This Foundation also provides some financial aid to Polish schools and teachers, organizes competitions with prizes for students, and sponsors various cultural events. More recently, the Foundation, in co-operation with a number of Polish universities, has organized summer courses in the Polish language, literature, and history. Courses are also available in methodology for Polish-language teachers from Canada and elsewhere, and in 1972 there were 170 students who took advantage of this offer.[66]

The Polish Teachers Association, founded around 1950, in the last few years has held regular conventions and discussion meetings. The Association has published a journal[67] since 1963 aimed at co-ordination, exchange of views and sharing of problems. The journal offers advice to teachers on methods and other problems related to Polish part-time schools. The Association is planning to write and publish a Canadian-Polish textbook that could be used by all Polish part-time schools in Canada.

Since 1971, local school boards in Ontario have had the power to set up credit courses in languages not normally taught in secondary schools if the boards decide there is sufficient demand for such courses, and Polish language and literature credit courses are now offered in Grades 12 and 13 in two high schools in Thunder Bay and one in Toronto. A separate school in Vancouver provides a daily lesson in Polish. George Brown College in Toronto offers a credit course in Polish language and history, and the Board of Education in Brantford, Ontario, offers evening courses in the Polish language.[68]

A number of Canadian universities offer courses in Polish language and literature. Participation in those courses in the past was not high. For example, there were two students taking Polish courses in the Department of Slavic Studies at the University of Manitoba in 1949-50, three in 1950-51, three in 1951-52, and one in 1952-53. In the evening classes arranged by this department there were six students in 1950 and seven in 1952-53. Recently there are signs of renewed interest shown in Polish language and literature courses offered by the Canadian universities. To cite one example, the University of Toronto, offering elementary and advanced Polish-language courses and a course on Polish literature, had an enrollment of about 50 students for language courses in the 1972-73 academic year. Other universities offering such courses note increasing interest and rising enrollment.[69] The young people are themselves becoming more concerned and involved, as suggested by the issues raised at a convention held at York University in October, 1969. One of the main resolutions was that since

> a knowledge of Polish is important for a fuller appreciation of Polish culture and traditions, and the Polish school is one of the main agents of culture and language dissemination. Polish should be therefore taught and spoken as well as possible by all members of our community.[70]

The propensity of future generations to identify with their own ethnic group may not in the final analysis depend so much on the knowledge and the use of Polish language as on the knowledge of the culture and history of the Polish nation. One writer feels that "the members of the third and fourth generations find that the longer the lineage they can claim, the greater the social respectability,"[71] but that the knowledge of language is not necessary for such claims.

NOTES

1. The discussions in this chapter are based largely on the unpublished monograph by H. Radecki, "Culture and Language Maintenance Efforts of the Polish Ethnic Groups in Canada," York University, 1971.
2. Dawson and Younge, p. 67.
3. *Ibid.*, p. 68.
4. *Report of the Royal Commission on Bilingualism and Biculturalism*, Book

II, "Education" (Ottawa, 1968). This source portrays the historical development of schools and education in Canada, focusing on British and French groups.

5. Dawson and Younge, p. 166.

6. Anderson, p. 120.

7. The term "Ruthenian" was generally used to denote the Ukrainians in Canada prior to World War I.

8. Cornelius J. Jaenen, "Ruthenian Schools in Western Canada, 1897-1919," *Paedagogica Historica*, 10 (3), 1970, 517-41.

9. This is a largely unexplored area so far and is open to re-examination and correction of statements given here.

10. Anderson, p. 105. For further elaboration on developments in education in Western Canada see Dawson and Younge, Chapter IX.

11. H. Kennedy, *op. cit.*, p. 287, referred specifically to the Slavs as most guilty of breaking this law. See also Anderson, *op. cit.*

12. See especially S.D. Clark, *The Social Development of Canada* (Toronto, 1942), p. 441 *et passim*.

13. One such example is given by Anderson who talks about an individual, Niemczyk, attending university and generally achieving a very acceptable level of education.

14. Alberta never stipulated bilingual education in public schools but in 1914 it was officially stipulated that they would not introduce bilingual education. See Jaenen, p. 539. British Columbia has never introduced a bilingual educational system.

15. For further discussion of these issues see Book II of the *Report of the Royal Commission*. The bilingual issue never included the Slavic groups.

16. V.J. Kaye, "People of Polish Origin," *Encyclopedia Canadiana*, Vol. 8, 1965, p. 226-30. Instruction in French was, of course, a precondition for receiving a subsidy for teaching in Polish.

17. Reverend F. Pyznar. The organization was the Towarzystwo Synów Polski, established in 1902.

18. According to B. Makowski, "Historia Towarzystwa Białego Orła," *Złoty Jubileusz Towarzystwa Białego Orła w Montrealu* (Toronto, 1952), the teachers were volunteers from among the Polish immigrants in Montreal, and were without qualifications or teaching experience.

19. Five Polish schools were established in the 1950s and another five since then (*Związek Nauczycielstwa Polskiego*, 1972/73).

20. *Report of the Royal Commission on Bilingualism and Biculturalism*, Book I, "The Official Languages," p. 121.

21. It is likely that for the Polish immigrants the greatest problem was finding qualified or suitable teachers.

22. See K. Wachtl, *Historia Polonii w Ameryce* (Philadelphia, 1944), for further details.

23. For further discussion on this topic see R. Breton, "Institutional Completeness of Ethnic Communities and the Personal Relations of Immigrants," *The American Journal of Sociology*, LXX (1964), 193-205.

24. *Report of the Royal Commission*, Book IV, p. 149.
25. *Ibid.* Book I, p. xxxiv.
26. *Ibid.*, Book IV, p. 13.
27. *Ibid.*, Book I, p. xxix.
28. For a further discussion on this process see Turek, "Jeszcze o Polonii," p. 89, and Hunchak, p. 26-30.
29. Jaenen, *op. cit.*, discusses some of its developments but focuses largely on the Ruthenian section, while Dawson and Younge, p. 171, quote a study of those schools, carried out in 1915, which showed that the "teachers trained in them were deficient both in English and in general knowledge."
30. Turek, *Poles in Manitoba.*
31. *Ibid.*, p. 225. Turek does not provide the exact date when this transformation took place.
32. From a private account by Father Puchniak, OMI, in March, 1971. Father Puchniak, a graduate of the Holy Ghost Polish parish school in Winnipeg, has served in a number of Polish parishes in Canada, and was involved with problems of education throughout his service.
33. In 1902 Father Kulawy invited a Polish-American order of nuns, the Benedictine Sisters, to Winnipeg where they took over teaching duties in the Holy Ghost parish school. The aforementioned Father Puchniak requested the help of teacher-nuns from the Polish-American order, the Felician Sisters, in 1937.
34. G. Grodecki, "Polish Language Schools in Canada," in Cornelius J. Jaenen, ed., *Slavs in Canada*, Vol. III (Toronto, 1971).
35. Archives of the Mother House, The Order of the Felician Sisters, Mississauga, Ontario.
36. Some of the commemorative sources consulted mention 'plans' for the establishment of schools, others refer broadly to children being 'taught' the Polish language, but few concrete details are avilable.
37. Kogler, p. 35.
38. H. Radecki, "How Relevant are the Polish Part-Time Schools," in B. Heydenkorn, ed., *Past and Present* (Toronto, 1974), discusses these questions further.
39. This area provided the majority of immigrants to Canada in the period 1896-1914.
40. See for example Balch, *op. cit.*; Estreicher, *op. cit.*; Turek, *Poles in Manitoba.*
41. Especially for the girls.
42. See an illustration of such an individual in Władysław S. Reymont, *Chłopi* (Warsaw, 1970).
43. For further elaboration on Polish attitudes towards education see Rose, "Russian Poland."
44. Estreicher, *op. cit..*
45. Gibbon, p. 301.
46. It may well be that a great many did not wish to preserve or maintain

cultural distinctiveness from their first years in Canada and others, isolated or separated from other Polish immigrants, reconciled themselves to the fact that their children would acquire and maintain only a minimum of the culture of their fathers.

47. Anderson, p. 57.
48. Even the Polish immigrants in Montreal generally accultured to the English group, sending their children to the English separate schools. Of those of Polish origin in the 1961 Canadian census, 24.5% had English as their mother tongue and only 6.3% French.
49. The ubiquitous transistor sets are a recent innovation.
50. For example, attempts were made in 1909 by one organization in Winnipeg, the Sokols, to provide a more extensive summer course, which would allow those children unable to attend weekend or evening classes a chance to immerse themselves in the language, history and traditions, but those plans, like many others, met little response on the part of the Polish community in Manitoba.
51. This issue was further complicated in that even among themselves non-parish school advocates did not share the same goals or attitudes towards the purpose and functions of these institutions.
52. Turek, *The Polish Language Press.*
53. *Ibid..*, p. 28.
54. B. Heydenkorn, "Emigracja Polska w Kanadzie," "Polonia Kanadyjska," *Kultura*, 144 (Paris, 1959), 85-107; "The Social Structure of Canadian Polonia," in T.W. Krychowski, ed., *Polish Canadians: Profile and Image* (Toronto, 1969), estimated that at least 20% of this phase were of professional or highly qualified occupational categories.
55. *Związek Nauczycielstwa Polskiego w Kanadzie.*
56. The portrayal of the past history of the development of the educational institutions of the Polish group in Canada was, by necessity, broad and generally unsubstantiated by statistics or other data. We have based this portrayal on the various available sources, academic works, commemorative brochures issued by various organizations, and other references, and believe it to be largely correct but admit that some errors or biases may be present. The reason for the absence of school records may be that teachers of the Polish language did not necessarily possess administrative or accounting skills necessary for keeping full records. On the other hand, some information may be available in the archives of various organizations, in parish records, even in provincial archives, but gathering and collecting such data is beyond the resources of the authors at present.
57. Some of the findings of this survey were published. See *The Report of the Royal Commission*, Book IV, pp. 149-65.
58. The data were compiled by R. Kogler, *"Ankieta Szkolna"* (Toronto, 1965). Additional analysis was provided by B. Bieniasz, J. Gładuń, B. and F. Głogowski, and H. Pierzchalska.
59. The number of students was estimated at about 5,000 on the basis of enrollment in all known Polish part-time schools. There were 16 schools

that did not answer the survey but the number of students enrolled in those schools was approximately 1,400 in 1965. On the basis of the total estimated figures, 7.4% of all eligible children attended Polish schools in Canada in 1965.

60. The Polish Teachers Association, established in 1950, has taken steps to rectify this problem and there are annual methodology seminars organized by this Association.

61. For example, that he or she was familiar with the language to a much greater extent than was actually the case.

62. *Związek Nauczycielstwa.*

63. *The Report of the Royal Commission*, Book IV, p. 119.

64. Grodecki, *op. cit.*

65. This Foundation was established by the Polish Alliance in Canada.

66. The participants pay a certain sum ($300-$400), which includes all the costs involved. The Foundation covers additional costs and expenses. No financial aid is solicited or accepted from the Polish government.

67. *Biuletyn Związku Nauczycielstwa Polskiego w Kanadzie.*

68. *Związek Nauczycielstwa.*

69. Private correspondence, H. Radecki with Professor D. Bieńkowska, May, 1974.

70. Resolution of the Convention reported in *Jak Tam Idzie?*, Toronto, October, 1969.

71. Jerzy A. Wojciechowski, "The Future of Canada's Polish Speaking Community – Polonia's Problems and Possibilities," in T.W. Krychowski, ed., *Polish Canadians: Profile and Image* (Toronto, 1969).

SIX

The Press

Access to . . . information in their own languages is of greatest importance to immigrants, particularly those who have not acquired skill in either English or French.

Report of the Royal Commission on Bilingualism and Biculturalism, Book IV (1970)

Polish immigrants in Canada have at all times displayed a deep interest in publications in their own language. Between 1904, when the first Polish language newspaper was founded in Winnipeg, and 1963, there were over 125 different publications available to the Polish immigrants at one time or another.[1] These publications represented a whole spectrum of interests, from those deeply religious or concerned primarily with Polish churches and parishes to those stressing traditions, culture, humour, or socio-political issues. The Polish-language publications enjoyed complete freedom of the press in Canada[2] and the main problems encountered were the lack of support from their potential public, or inefficient management.

A GLIMPSE INTO THE PAST

The Polish press in Canada grew not out of commercial enterprise but out of the needs of the community. With few exceptions this is still true. The publishers clearly realized that their efforts would not meet with commercial success, and to keep the whole venture going would be up to the concerned reader and the Polish group itself. Each publisher in the past – and these were not individuals but organizations – had to rely on donations in the first stages of publication. Lack of capital and insufficient subscriptions within a short period of time made the publication of an independent weekly newspaper impossible.

The need for a sponsoring organization is demonstrated in the case of the *Polish-Canadian Courier*. This fully independent newspaper is facing an uncertain future after only two years of existence. In June, 1974, the *Courier* issued an appeal for support in its endeavours, word-of-mouth publicity from its present subscribers, public recruitment of new readers, and advertisements from merchants and others. It also established a press fund and asked for financial support.

With the exception of the *Gazeta Katolicka*, the Polish weekly published by the Oblate Fathers in Winnipeg, all of the other weeklies were sponsored by secular organizations. This does not of course apply to the strictly religious publications such as bulletins of individual parish churches, local newsletters and the like.

The first Polish-language newspaper, the *Głos Kanadyjski*,[3] was published in Winnipeg in 1904 by the Oblate Fathers who came early to the conclusion that the written word would be a valuable aid in their work. It would facilitate contact with the faithful beyond the reach of the pulpit, and would make it possible to contact those faithful who were prevented from attending Mass in a Polish church by distance or isolation. The Catholic newspaper was also meant to deepen understanding and consolidate the community by venturing beyond strictly religious themes. Each number, besides containing the appropriate text from the scriptures for that particular Sunday, carried articles dealing with faith and morals which served as a sort of surrogate priest. The rest of the contents examined such questions as what attitude to adopt towards the native land and towards Canada. The religious publications preserved Polish culture and traditions in the broadest sense and helped to consolidate the Polish community by giving it a feeling of closeness regardless of geographical, financial, and other differences; above all, they united the Polish people spiritually. In addition, the Polish Roman Catholic clergy was anxious that utmost care in every possible way be given to the Catholic immigrants in order to shield them from the proselytizing efforts of Protestant missionaries and from the strong influence of the Ukrainian Greek Orthodox churches.

The religious weekly, the *Gazeta Katolicka*, was first published in 1908, and though it changed its name on two occasions, it retained its character until 1951, when it merged with the *Głos Polski*, a weekly published in Toronto since 1950. Since 1951 the publication bears the name *Głos Polski-Gazeta Polska*. Until the end of its independent existence, the *Gazeta Katolicka* was under the auspices of the Oblates, but neither the bishops nor religious authorities of the Oblate Order in any way hindered the work of its spiritual and secular editors as far as their views pertaining to Poland or to the Polish-Canadian aggregate were concerned.

The *Gazeta Katolicka*, a religiously-oriented weekly, enjoyed a near monopoly of the Polish-language publications in Canada for some years. At the same time, the ideology stressed by this weekly was not acceptable to some Polish immigrants who relied on the secular Polish newspapers published in the United States. Realizing that an opportunity was present for another Polish-language newspaper in Canada, an enterprising individual began a weekly publication named *Czas*, in 1914.[4] This weekly had a clearly anti-clerical character since the publisher hoped to draw all the dissatisfied readers from the *Gazeta Katolicka.*

While the secular weekly *Czas* was started through private initiative it received some support from the local Polish organizations in Winnipeg and others from Manitoba. The weekly remained independent until 1931, owing its longevity to the publisher, Mr. F. Dojacek, who was the printer and publisher of a number of other publications in different languages.

In 1931, as a result of basic political differences and especially of harsh criticism of Poland's policy toward minorities which appeared in this paper, the Polish organizations bought the weekly from its Czechoslovak-Ukrainian combine. The financial situation of the publication was shaky, so that in 1934 an effort was made to procure funds from the Polish government. This was successful, and the publishers received the sum of $580, nominally from the World Federation of Poles Abroad, but in reality from the Ministry of External Affairs in Warsaw, in the form of a purchase of 50 shares in the stock of the company. The Polish consultate was not only deeply interested in the Polish ethnic press in Canada but attempted to exert a definite influence, if not outright control, over it. The effort to influence or control the Polish press in Canada is illustrated by a secret report which was issued by the Consular Department for Poles Abroad of the Ministry of External Affairs entitled, "A Survey of the Polish Press Abroad," No. E. II. 303/1-140 January 1st, 1935.[5]

1. *Czas*/425½ Selkirk Ave., Winnipeg, Manitoba. Weekly Pub. Polish Press Ltd./the Polish Press Society Ltd./the organ of the Federation of Polish Organizations in Canada. Loyal to all official policies of the Republic of Poland. Sympathizes with the labour movement, especially with the Progressive party in Manitoba. Distr. Canada. Circulation 4,000 copies. Exec. Ed: J. Sikora/secretary of the Fed. of Polish Organ. in Canada.

2. *Gazeta Katolicka*/619 McDermont Ave., Winnipeg, Manitoba. /Weekly. Publ. by Canadian Publishers Ltd./a Catholic limited company subsidized by Archbishop Sinnot of Winnipeg/also publishes newspapers in French and English./Admin. exclusively Catholic and religious. Sympathetic to the Polish National Democratic Party. Opposes the official policy of the Republic of Poland./Distr. – Canada, esp. western Canada. Circ. 2,500. Exec. Ed.: J. Pazdor/a former teacher.

3. *Głos Pracy*/Winnipeg, Manitoba./ Bimonthly. Publ. by Polish Union of Farm Labourers./a Communist organization/its Communist administration attacks the government and Polish organizations in Canada./ Distri.-Canada. Circ. 4,000 copies. Exec. Ed.: M. Dutkiewicz/a gifted agitator and public speaker.

4. *Słowo Polskie*/ 1723 St. Denis St., Montreal, Quebec/ Weekly.

Publ. by J.M. Kreutz. Inimical to the official policies of the Republic of Poland. Sympathizes with the Polish National Democratic Party./a radical who exploits weaknesses of the unemployed and unhappy element among the Polish immigrants./ Dist. Canada. Circ. 1,000 copies. Exec. Ed.: J. Kreutz/without character or any moral conviction/Was criminally charged with the robbery of a train terminal in Ostaszewo (Poland).

5. *Związkowiec*/62 Claremont St., Toronto, Ontario./Monthly. Published as the official organ of the Polish Alliance of Canada. Loyal to the official policies of the Republic of Poland.[6]/Distr.- Southern Ontario. Circ. 600 copies, Run by Editorial Committee/A. Piekarz, a tailor by trade and a radical/S.F. Konopka, president of the Executive Council of the Polish Alliance/K.J. Mazurkiewicz, president of the Head Executive Board of the Polish Alliance – the editorial committee is aided by the office of the Consul General of the Polish Republic in Montreal.

This document is not merely a description and brief analysis of the Polish-language newspapers, but also an evaluation of the editors, especially their political views and background.[7] Among documents at present in the Archives of the Ministry for External Affairs in Warsaw, one can find a later evaluation and analysis of the Polish press in Canada and consular correspondence between Winnipeg, Montreal and Warsaw, dealing with various issues of the Polish press. These documents portray Polish consular activities in Canada in matters of Polish-language publications, illustrating clearly attempts to influence or control by providing support for some, and clearly recognizing and evaluating "unfriendly" publishers, editors and their newspapers.

The Polish consular activities in Canada regarding the Polish-language press are further illustrated by the following document. An internal policy statement, the document was undated, but from the text it can be established that it was written in 1934, at the time of the financial difficulties experienced by the weekly *Czas*.

Canada at present has a population of 145,000 Polish immigrants. This territory should be treated as a promising field for the future, since it has great possibilities and the right sort of environment. The Ministry for External Affairs is somewhat cognizant of this state of affairs. Up until this time this territory was not properly cultivated as far as organizations, education, and so forth is concerned. At the moment, the efforts of our agents are beginining to give promising results, especially in the field of developing solidarity and proper attitudes among the immigrants.

This policy should be energetically implemented particularly at this stage when the immigration is young and unformed. The future character of this community depends upon whether it is properly moulded. The field of action is hindered by a lack of funds. The

Ministry for External Affairs has not allocated the smallest sum to Canada. Specifically, it is desirable to strengthen and support co-operative publication, one of which is *Czas* (as an aside comment, the editor, Mr. Sikora, is closely involved in organizational work, acting in close relationship with the Directors of our agencies, who always refer to him with the utmost respect). The possession of such an outlet is necessary:

1. In order to promulgate a positive policy through our agencies.
2. For the purpose of overcoming the destructive activities of *Głos Pracy*, editor/Kreutz, and of the ultraclerical faction.
3. In order to furnish the immigrants with a healthy press outlet and weaken the not always satisfactory influence of the Polish press from the United States which has a wide readership in Canada.

Until this time *Czas* was financially solvent. But with the current Depression it is seriously threatened. Consul Pawlica suggests that a loan of $800 or around 5,000 złoty's be extended for its upkeep. This motion also has the support of the Consul General Adamkiewicz. Basically, it would be advisable to extend a nonprofit loan, repayable on terms, and to advise Consul Pawlica to work out the details.

A few lines below, written in a different type, are added to the following sentences:

Section E I thoroughly agrees with the above stated position of Section E II. Considering the nature of the publication, which is thoroughly grounded upon a Polish national foundation and its trend toward communal solidarity the granting of a loan for its upkeep is essential.

A copy of this publication is enclosed. (Please note the high calibre of its contents.[8])

For the Head of the Department Dr. Jan Rozwadowski.

Under the signature of Dr. Rozwadowski there appear the following notations by hand:

Słowo Polskie – $30 per month., *Czas* – $50 – $960-5,000 zloty's yearly. After a year a reduction of the outlay should be expected due to advertisements, which will be increased after a trade agreement has been reached/the opinion of the Trade Consul/

Then *Słowo* – nothing, *Czas* – $35-$40 monthly. This is undersigned by an indecipherable signature. Lower in the right hand corner " – p it is agreed," and then another unintelligible signature over a stamp reading "Dr. Witold La . . . . ."

It can be assumed that the present Polish government representatives in Canada have at least as lively an interest in the Polish ethnic press today. This is the result of the changed political, economic and social conditions in Poland, the notable increase of Polish immigrants to Canada, and the natural growth of the community. The present regime in Poland is increasingly more concerned in overcoming enmity towards the Communist system and the regime itself, and is seeking, if not acceptance, then at least a friendly neutrality. However, one of the tenets of Communist ideology distinctly calls for a constant war of propaganda. This in itself casts suspicion on the regime of the Peoples' Republic of Poland in relationship to the ethnic press of this country.

At one time, the Polish consulate in Ottawa published a news bulletin which appeared sporadically in Polish as well as in English. More important is the reading matter supplied by press agencies specifically designed for the use of Poles abroad, and distributed free of charge. For example, the Polish-Canadian press receives two bulletins especially geared for use of the Polish press abroad, containing a wide range of information, articles on a variety of subjects, correspondence and so forth. Other materials distributed to Poles abroad are various magazines, some of which contain sections written in a foreign language such as English. The material is carefully selected to avoid flagrant propaganda, so that some of it finds its way into all of the Polish-Canadian papers.

In the previously quoted report of the Ministry for External Affairs (dated January 1st, 1935), in reference to *Związkowiec*, which started its existence as a stencilled monthly, there occurs the phrase: "The Consulate General of the Republic of Poland in Montreal is helping the editorial work." This fact did not apply only to *Związkowiec*. The editors of the Polish-Canadian press were recruited by the organizations as essentially more sophisticated individuals than average, or those possessing a sense of mission. In most cases they lacked journalistic training and had no previous experience for the job. They were amateurs with a sense of mission and social responsibility. Naturally, over the years they acquired experience, and in some cases a high level of competence, by broadening their knowledge, their scope, the techniques of the trade, and so on. These were dedicated people, such as Jan Pazdor, Jan Sikora, Julian Nowacki, A.F. Chudzicki, and Alfons J. Staniewski. On the far left of the political spectrum, W. Dutkiewicz became outstanding in the field of journalism; he was a thoroughly gifted and professional editor.

The position of a Polish-language newspaper editor was never a well-paying one. As was noted by Stanisław Zybała, a professional post-war editor, the earlier editors and their helpers devoted much time and effort in the service of their newspapers and the Polish community, but their financial rewards were frequently less than the pay received by the printing shop workers, who received union wages.[9] The publishers of the Polish newspapers in Canada always relied on the fact that sooner or later a poverty-stricken intellectual, willing to take over the editorial seat, would show up and there was little need to reward him by a high salary.

The post-war period witnessed fundamental changes in the existing Polish publications and the emergence of a number of new ones. The arrival of the new Polish immigrants created new and broad demands on

116

Clifford Sifton's ideal Polish Family at immigration sheds in Quebec City, Quebec, 1911.

Winnipeg – the main staging point for the new arrivals, c. 1908.

Good neighbour policy. Helping to clear land for a new settler, Prince Albert, Saskatchewan, 1928.

The important first potato crop, especially with another mouth to feed.
Manitoba, 1928.

As fortunes improved, sod huts were replaced with more solid structures. Alberta.

Contacts with other Polish settlers were established slowly and visits were a joyful occasion.

Some traditional farming techniques were brought from the Old Country. Home-made apparatus for grinding wheat into flour. Alberta.

*Wedding of a Polish coal miner and his newly arrived bride,
Coleman, Alta., 1923. With parents and families still in Poland
friends share this happy occasion.*

*Honouring Polish Constitution Day, May 3rd, with authentic Polish
military uniforms and traditional costumes. Fraternal Aid Society,
Coleman, Alta., 1933.*

Polish volunteers for the Canadian Army. A farewell party, Calgary, 1940.

One of the part-time schools under the auspices of the Polish Alliance in Canada. Toronto, 1946.

Many Polish pilots were trained in Canada during World War II.
These two are entertained by a Polish dance group from McLeod,
Alta., 1943.

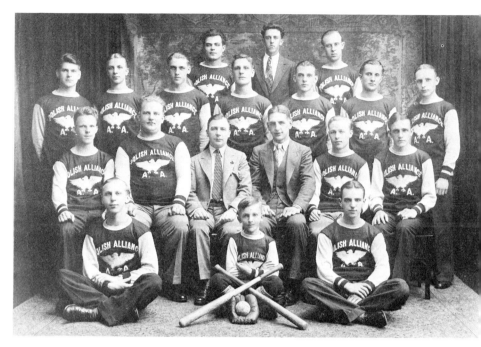

Sports activities were not neglected. Athletic association, Polish Alliance in Canada, Toronto, 1946.

Post-World War II settlers. Barrie, Ontario, 1957.

Poles, once again to work the land on a two-year contract. Veterans recruited for farm labour, 1946.

Concern with their language and culture is demonstrated by the popularity of libraries and bookstores. Toronto, c. 1950.

Girl and Boy Scouts – among the most popular organizations for the young. Kashuby-Barry's Bay, Ontario, 1959.

Poles participate in various civic and national Canadian holidays. Polish float at the Calgary Stampede, 1950.

Blessing and installation of the "Black Madonna" of Czestochowa in the newly erected Polish church in Oshawa, 1955.

One of the many demonstrations of religiosity. Polish clergy, followed by lay organizations at the Martyr's Shrine, Midland, Ontario, 1956.

Expo, 1967. Unveiling of the monument to Mikotaj Kopernik (Nicolas Copernicus), founded by the Polish community in Montreal.

The White Eagle – Polish national symbol. Art and handicrafts at the Canadian National Exhibition, Toronto, 1955.

One of many lively and colourful Polish traditional dances.

Ready to entertain. Young Polish song and dance group, Toronto,
c. 1950.

the Polish-language press, while at the same time providing numerous individuals capable of participating in the publication of the Polish newspapers. The changes began during the war when the *Związkowiec* found itself in the editorial hands of people who were mature politically and competent profesionally. In the post-war years, only the *Kronika Tygodniowa* retained the same editor throughout; all the other Polish-language newspapers were guided by a succession of individuals, characterized by editorial skills, journalistic know-how, and dedication to their tasks and duties.

In the post-war period two important issues came to the forefront: what position the Polish community was to take towards the new political and social order in Poland, and what its relationship to Canada was to be. Bound up with the first issue was another problem: what was to be the attitude towards the existing Polish government in exile located in London, England. All these burning themes were intensified by the appearance of a new publication. The weekly *Głos Polski*, making its appearance in July, 1950, as the official organ of the Polish National Union of Canada, took a pro-London line, in defence of the legality of the Polish government abroad, and proposed that funds for its support be sent to Britain. Without contradicting the need of adaptation to this country, it simultaneously urged the Polish immigrants to think of themselves as political exiles and not as permanent settlers.

Związkowiec took the opposite position, and declared that it was time to "unpack one's luggage" and stop treating Canada as a transit terminal, but consider it as a country of settlement, with the responsibility of accepting Canadian citizenship and joining fully in the life of its society. While remaining firmly anti-Communist and stongly critical of the new regime in Poland, *Związkowiec* insisted that as a Canadian one owes allegiance to only one government – the one in Ottawa. Political exiles were free to act on their own responsibility, but neither the paper nor the Polish Alliance of Canada meant to condone any kind of political commitment to outside influences, whether they came from London or Warsaw.

Czas took a similar stand but less affirmatively. It granted that there was enough room for everyone, with the exception of Communists, but editorially it never formulated a concrete policy. However, since most local organizations in Western Canada were solidly pro-Canadian, and since relatively few post-war immigrants settled in the western provinces, the issue for this publication was not of paramount importance.

Kronika Tygodniowa took a diametrically opposed standpoint to all other Polish newspapers. If in the pre-war period *Czas* approved all the official policies of the Republic of Poland[10] then in the changed post-war era, *Kronika Tygodniowa* formally took over this position. It was, and remains to this day, the spokesman and promulgator of the Warsaw regime. It could not have been otherwise, since the paper began its existence as an organ of a group which glorified Communist ideology, so that when

117

it became implemented in Poland, the *Kronika Tygodniowa* welcomed the changes with open arms.

The diverging positions taken by the various press organs led to sharp polemics in the editorials, articles and letters to the editors. *Kronika Tygodniowa* was condemned for its pro-Communist stance by all the other Polish-language newspapers but the fights and recriminations were not limited to this paper alone; the editors of the *Głos Polski* and *Związkowiec* also resorted to mutual accusations and epithets, labelling each other "pro-leftist" or "reactionary," or as "tools" of one or another political faction.[11] The enmity was strongest between these two newspapers in the post-1956 period, following the change of rulers in Poland, but has now abated and the various Polish-language newspapers maintain positions of mutual tolerance and respect.

With the passage of time, many of the basic differences in the Polish community concerning Canadian status disappeared, all finally agreeing that the first loyalty should be given to Canada. A faction remains which stresses that the loyalty to Canada should not prevent a continuing effort towards freeing Poland from the rule and influence of the Soviet Union, but the attitude towards Poland has witnessed many changes and this is reflected in the Polish-language press in Canada. The three largest circulation newspapers, *Związkowiec, Głos Polski* and *Czas*, remain anti-Communist, but each of them evaluates certain events in its own fashion, not necessarily or consistently in a positive or negative way. The attitude towards the Polish government in exile has changed in time as well. While *Głos Polski* continues to print certain pronouncements of this government and its 'president-in-exile,' and *Czas* does it less often and more subtly, none of the editors fully believes in the effectiveness or the rationale for the continual existence of this body.

POLISH-LANGUAGE NEWSPAPERS TODAY

The Polish-language press is a viable institution exhibiting at present few signs of problems which would lead to its eventual demise.[12] The individual press organs are not wealthy and the editors are among the lowest paid professionals in the Polish community, but they are dedicated and concerned individuals, and the modest deficits have been on occasion made up by the sponsoring Polish organizations, by financial aid of the readership, or by payments for advertising from various government departments and private businesses.

The number of Canadian publications available to readers in the Polish language in Canada today may well reach 50. This includes newspapers, church bulletins, journals and magazines published more or less regularly. Various Polish organizations issue a number of publications in Polish, focusing on special anniversaries or other occasions, and some of these contain a wealth of information for their readers. There are at present five major publications of general interest, four of which publish weekly, and one semi-weekly:[13]

Głos Polski-Gazeta Polska (Polish Voice) is the organ of the Polish National Union of Canada and of the Associated Poles in Canada. It is published weekly in Toronto with a circulation of about 5,500 copies. The *Polish Voice* is concerned with the activities of the two sponsoring federations and some other Polish associations, prints news of general interest from Poland, Canada and the world and includes literary and other articles of special interest to people of Polish descent. This newspaper began as *Gazeta Katolicka (Catholic Weekly)* in 1908 in Winnipeg. Following changes in name and ownership the editorial offices and the printing press have been in Toronto since 1951.

Czas (Polish Times), established in 1914, is the only newspaper now published in Winnipeg and serves primarily the western provinces. In the past this newspaper was sponsored by, or represented, various Polish federations or organizations in Canada but presently it defines itself an independent and non-partisan weekly. The *Polish Times* prints information of general interest from Canada, Poland and other parts of the world and every issue contains announcements or news of Polish organizational activities, in Winnipeg and further west. The present weekly circulation of this newspaper is estimated at about 4,000.

Związkowiec (The Alliancer) is the organ of the Polish Alliance of Canada and publishes news from Canada and the world and the editorial comments focus on Canadian issues. Selected news from Poland, based either on Polish press releases or on first-hand observation and information, are a regular feature on its pages. Its reviews and political, literary, and social commentaries are acknowledged to be of high quality. Since its beginnings in 1933 this newspaper has grown to the largest publication in the Polish language in Canada with a circulation of about 8,500. All three of the above newspapers publish, as a regular feature, serialized Polish novels.

Kronika Tygodniowa (The Weekly Chronicle) is the successor to *Głos Pracy (Voice of Labour)*, established in 1932, and is published in Toronto with a circulation of about 2,000 copies. *The Weekly Chronicle* is the voice of the Polish Democratic Association. The contents are of general interest with special emphasis on events and developments taking place in Poland which are portrayed uncritically. There is at present very little emphasis placed on the concerns and activities of the Polish aggregate in Canada or on the maintenance of its cultural distinctiveness.

Kurier Polsko-Kanadyjski (Polish-Canadian Courier) was established only in 1972 and its present circulation is estimated to be about 1,000 copies weekly. This fully independent newspaper, began as a business venture, is published in Toronto. The contents encompass news of general interest from Canada and other parts of the world, based on releases from press agencies and other publications. This is the only newspaper that publishes a number of articles in English, prints a large number of illustrations and attempts to provide a great variety of topics of general interest which are reprinted from various sources.

Kronika Tygodniowa provides the widest coverage of matters pertaining to Poland, and devotes the smallest space to Canadian affairs and those of the Polish aggregate. *Związkowiec*, on the other hand, prints mostly Canadian news and covers the activities of the Polish communities. *Głos Polski* and *Czas* take a position somewhere in between these two, and contain a great deal of information about Poles outside of Poland and Canada. *Kurier Polsko-Kanadyjski* is more in the nature of a monthly than a weekly paper. There are no editorials, and there is no discernible policy. Lavishly illustrated, it carries many items of information, reprints from the press in Poland and other Polish publications elsewhere, in a combined Polish-English format.

There are a number of monthly or bi-monthly publications, sponsored by one or other organization. There is the Polish teacher's bulletin, publications of Polish Scouts, engineers, veterans, the Polish National Catholic Church, Polish Federation of Women, Polish credit unions, and the Federation of Youth bulletin. Among the more noteworthy of those publications is the *Echo*,[14] a magazine devoted to the concerns and interests of the Polish youth. This independent magazine began in 1969 in Toronto, and there were about 20 issues published by the end of 1973. The *Echo* provides a forum for the varied talents of the young people of Polish descent in Canada. Past numbers of this magazine included articles on the history, geography, customs, traditions and culture of Poland; historical sketches of some Polish concentrations in Canada; poetry, literary endeavours and graphic art. The circulation of this magazine is presently estimated at about 600 copies, and the articles are published in either Polish or English.

ROLE AND FUNCTIONS

Unlike the 'regular' press of any society, which generally adopts and follows the policies of the editors or executive boards, the immigrant press has had to adapt to many special conditions and circumstances facing their readers in a new society. Having of necessity a limited public, the press had to take under consideration the needs and interests as well as the level of intellectual sophistication of this public. It had to provide information and content that would be of value and interest to readers who were in Canada for different reasons, who were from diverse areas of Poland, and who did not necessarily have similar religious or political orientations.

In coping with those problems, the Polish-language newspapers emerged to play an important role in helping the immigrants adjust to the new conditions in Canada. While the Polish group has now experienced varying degrees of acculturation, this role remains important for many of the first generation immigrants. In easing the immigrant's adjustment to

Canada, the press had several roles. Polish-language newspapers have always devoted space to events taking place in Poland, the extent of such information increasing greatly during periods of emergencies, wars, natural calamities or political upheavals. Frequently the press organized plans and strategies of material or financial aid to people in Poland, and provided leadership for others in participating in some significant event taking place there.[15] This involvement, and the information about events in the Old Country, provided a degree of continuity with Poland for the immigrants, allowing them to feel less estranged or homesick.

There were other, equally significant roles. The press, more than any other agency, was able to introduce the newcomers to their host society. All newspapers, at one time or another, published articles explaining the complexities of the Canadian political, legal, economic and educational systems, as well as history and geography. The press informed its readers of the behaviour and attitudes which were current in Canada. It provided information on, and often urged its readers to avail themselves of, Canadian citizenship status, elaborating on the related duties, obligations and privileges. One member of the press, the *Alliancer*, called on its readers to consider Canada their permanent home, to consider themselves not Poles in Canada but Canadians of Polish descent, urging them to become full members of their adopted country.[16] It may be accepted that the Polish-language press, more than any other Polish or Canadian agency, allowed easy and speedy acculturation of the various first generations of immigrants to Canadian social norms and values.

Another role that the Polish-language press played was related to the strengthening of Polish ethnic identity, culture, and traditions. Through its concern with the political developments in Europe in the years 1914-1918 and 1939-1945, the press rekindled the dormant ethnic group identity in many uncommitted or unconcerned individuals, retarding the process of assimilation and full identification with Canada. The rekindled feelings of Polish identity resulted in a greater awareness and interest in the events and developments taking place there, and in an awareness and appreciation of their cultural richness; in some cases it led to individuals returning to Poland. The press served an important role in maintaining the purity of the Polish language among immigrants who rapidly devised a 'patois,' an admixture of Polonized English terms and expressions in everyday speech.[17]

The press noted all traditional and patriotic anniversaries, frequently describing how and by whom they were celebrated in Canada. While stressing acceptance of Canada as a permanent home, the press generally insisted that Polish customs, traditions and language should be maintained not only among the immigrants themselves but also among the succeeding generations.[18] It may be that the Polish-language press served as the most important agency in the maintenance of cultural distinctiveness among the dispersed, confused, or unconcerned individuals who saw little value or advantage in preserving their own language, values and traditions.

A further role served by the press was that of a spokesman, a representative, not only for the sponsoring federations or organizations, but also for the whole Polish aggregate within the Canadian political, legal and other institutions. It fulfilled the same role in relationships with other ethnic groups in Canada, and with the government in Poland. It was generally on its pages that protests were voiced against economic and social discrimination experienced by numerous Polish immigrants. It was the Polish-language press that stood in defence of the Polish 'good name,' defending the integrity and worth of Polish people generally, and the decisions of the Polish government which affected indirectly other ethnic groups in Canada.[19]

A further role served by the press was that of a social agency for many readers. Letters or visits to the editors requested help in dealing with the immigration department or law enforcement agencies, and in finding missing persons, work, or even a marriage partner. The pages provided means of advertising social functions such as dances, picnics, anniversaries and other occasions. The editorial offices served as meeting places for discussions, concerned little with the publication itself. The Polish-language press provided information but also served as employment agencies, marriage brokers, missing persons bureau, offices of legal aid and social activities co-ordinators. The editors were expected to perform functions and duties ranging far beyond the immediate concerns of the newspapers themselves.

Another role that the press performed was in the area of education. The press repeatedly urged parents to send their children to the Polish part-time schools, and encouraged mature readers to upgrade their education by attending courses in the English language and to improve their Polish through reading literary classics which were available to readers in serialized form in the press. The press provided for many the only understandable reading matter, and attempted to improve the intellectual level of the readers by high standards of writing. For many years, it allowed the talented the only platform for expression of creative thought, and through constructive criticism improved the quality of poets, writers and educators. The press also stressed the desirability of improvement in social behaviour and ethics, serving to educate the readers as citizens, parents, people.

Lastly, the press has played another role which is being increasingly appreciated by many historians, sociologists and other writers. The files, archives and libraries of the Polish-language press contain a veritable gold mine of information. In the publications a researcher can discover detailed statements of the experiences of groups and individuals, their trials and difficulties, and their successes in Canada. The establishment and later development of organizations can be traced; all that was important to the Polish immigrants in Canada, all that concerned them deeply was reported by one or another of the newspapers. The Polish-language press serves as the most accurate and extensive record of the experiences, changes, and developments of the Polish people in Canada to be found, and undoubtedly historians and others will take advantage of this storehouse of information.

NOTES

1. Turek, *The Polish Language Press*, provides an exhaustive portrayal of the establishment and later developments of all publications in the Polish language from 1904 to 1960. Heydenkorn, *'Związkowiec,'* focuses on *Związkowiec*, which began its publication in 1933 and at present has the largest circulation of the semi-weeklies. Other sources that deal with the Polish-language press in Canada are Jacek Adolph, "The Polish Press in Canada," York University, Toronto, mimeograph (1970); S.J. Jaworsky, "Newspapers and Periodicals of Slavic Groups in Canada During the Period of 1965-1969," MA Thesis (mimeo), University of Ottawa, 1971; Stanisław Zybała, "Foreign in Language, Canadian in Spirit, Human in Every Other Respect," in J.M. Kirschbaum *et. al.*, eds., *Twenty Years of Ethnic Press Association in Ontario* (Toronto, 1971). For an overview of issues related to the ethnic press see Robert E. Park, *The Immigrant Press and Its Control* (New York, 1922).

2. With one exception, where the *Głos Pracy* was ordered to close down for its pro-Soviet and pro-German stand, in August, 1940. The publication resumed, under a changed name, in February, 1941.

3. The Oblates published the *Głos Kanadyjski* in the years 1904-1905, and the *Gazeta Katolicka* beginning in 1908. See V. Turek, *The Polish Language Press, op. cit.*

4. According to Turek, the publication of *Czas* began in April, 1915.

5. The facts relating to Canada are found on pages 19 and 20 of the report, and constitute Chapter X. Photostat copies of these and other documents related to the Polish press in Canada are in the possession of B. Heydenkorn.

6. This newspaper did not remain "loyal" to the official policies of the Polish government for long, criticizing strongly its attitudes towards the workers and peasants. The Polish government demonstrated its displeasure by taking away its rights of distribution in Poland in 1937.

7. Not always accurately. For example, the initial of the editor of the *Głos Pracy* is "W" not "M."

8. This sentence was added by hand, bearing the initials T N 28/V with the stamp of Tadeusz Narzyński in the margin.

9. Zybała, *op. cit.*

10. That is since 1931, when it was acquired by Polish interests.

11. S. Zybała, "Jak Tam Na Wojence Ładnie," *Związkowiec* No. 100, candidly admits that some accusations were unfounded but the resulting publicity "sold the newspapers."
12. The survival of the press is closely related to the arrival of new immigrants from Poland. The numbers of newcomers in the last decade or so does not bode well for the future of those publications.
13. The other weeklies are the church bulletins which focus on the announcements of the activities revolving around the parishes, religious holidays, and anniversaries.
14. Not to be confused with *Echo*, a bi-monthly publications of the Polish National Catholic Church.
15. More recently, the rebuilding of the Royal Castle in Warsaw and the Copernicus anniversary received much publicity in the Polish-language press in Canada.
16. The post-war immigrants especially were encouraged to unpack their 'kitbags' and reconcile themselves to accepting Canada as their permanent home. See Heydenkorn, *'Związkowiec'*, for further elaboration of these issues.
17. "Pajda," meaning pay day or wages, "kara" for an automobile, and similar expressions.
18. In this day were generally less sucessful.
19. Following the political developments in Poland in the 1920s, both the Ukrainian and Jewish groups in Canada made strong representations to the Canadian government to elicit condemnation of the policies of the Polish government towards the minorities in Poland. The Polish-language press defended these policies.

SEVEN

The Family

Among the several forms of association that constitutes the microstructure of a society, families are the most influential.

Jan Szczepański

THE FAMILY IN POLAND

Some of the earliest literature on the family in Polish history, dating to the early fifteenth century, suggests that stable patriarchal family relations were characteristic of Polish society. Three-generation families flourished and survived well into the present century despite various political, economic and ideological changes which have taken place in the last few hundred years.[1]

Until 1945, Polish society was basically traditional.[2] There were social class differences in family life. The peasant's was determined by the farmwork cycle; the family life of a small entrepreneur was closely linked with the functioning of his enterprise; among the upper and middle classes the family was an institution for the maintenance of status and power. But common to all classes were a strong patriarchal tradition, a strong influence of religion (and church) on family life, and strong ties of family solidarity.

According to one Polish sociologist, "almost all families were three-generation families and the influence of grandparents on the conduct of family affairs was strong even if the grandparents were not living with their married children,"[3] while another found that "traditional and past-oriented social relations were strongly evident among all social and economic groups."[4]

An ideal concept of the family was shared by all Poles. Popular values stressed the feeling of belonging to a family group, which could include all relatives by blood or marriage. The ideal advocated the integration of

125

activities of the family members to obtain common objectives, the utilization of family resources for relatives who were in need, and the maintenance of strong ties between the parental family and the new family units. In the event of the death of parents, even distant relatives were expected to help in raising the orphaned children. Another highly stressed value was that the grown children should care for their old parents or grandparents.

In the predominantly rural society the man regarded himself as his wife's superior or master. One widely known and applied proverb was that "a woman had to be constantly reminded that she was incapable of ever having any wise or important thoughts and opinions."[5] It was generally accepted that the duty of the wife, at home or outside, was to make clear that her husband was the head of the family, even if she shared in or exercised influence over family decisions. A high value was placed on the obedience of the children to the rules and wishes of the parents.

Among both the rural population and the urban working classes, the wife was regarded more as "the mother of children than as companion or a sex mate."[6] The choice of marriage partners was strongly influenced, if not dictated, by parental choice or approval. The approval hinged on the size of the dowry or possessions, social status, and family background. A wife who could do the washing two hours before giving birth, and feed the livestock two days after,[7] was valued by the peasants; age or personal appearance were of lesser importance. Love as such was not given much weight in the selection of marriage partners. The peasant marriages were most often arranged according to strict customs, and Polish wedding ceremonies are famous for their traditions[8] (which are usually appreciated by those who have attended such occasions in Canada).

In everyday relations with the children, affection or tenderness was seldom openly shown by the father for fear of spoiling the children or making them soft. Only the middle classes, especially the intelligentsia, deviated somewhat from this norm. For the peasants and the urban workers, the children were seen primarily as workers, as members of the economic structure, assigned specific tasks or duties around the farm, the house, or the workshop. They were "auxiliary staff,"[9] helping to run farms and family enterprises.

The family role structure adhered to the traditional division of labour into 'man's work' and 'woman's work' for the peasant and the working class families in towns and cities. While everyone within the family performed certain tasks, it was unacceptable for a married woman to perform work for pay outside her home since such activity would certainly lower the esteem and prestige of her husband in the eyes of relatives, friends and community. When the wife worked, doubts were cast on the adequacy of her husband as a provider, and thus as a man. The wife's or mother's place was at home, with her children.

Polish families were, as a rule, large. The size of the family depended on the woman's fecundity, infant survival, and later sickness or epidemics. The size of the family played an important role in the prestige of the father; he was considered a virile, manly person if he sired many children. The children were the most visible demonstration of his health, strength, and ability to provide. Many children, especially sons, represented security for the future, potential power in the community decision-making, and reserves of manpower as well as strength in times of trouble.

Traditionally, the husband and father was the head of the Polish family in all social classes. The pattern of authority encompassed the whole family – sisters were expected to obey or defer to brothers, the seniority of brothers was observed and emphasized. The mother had her own area of influence and authority but acknowledged and complied with the overall position of authority and power of the father and husband.[10] The authority of fathers, especially among the nobility and peasants, frequently bordered on despotism.[11] This authority generally included the final decision in purchasing or selling property and contracting marriages for the children.

While the husbands and fathers decided on the disposition of any savings, among the peasants it was the wife who was entrusted with their safekeeping. Since banks were either unavailable or mistrusted, each wife had her own special hiding place for cash of which even the husband was ignorant.

The traditional authority and position of the father was never questioned, but the balance of power was frequently open to negotiation and depended on the personality traits or resourcefulness of each individual. One writer illustrates a number of cases of peasant wives who over time did achieve significant power or influence with the family through withdrawal of favours, nagging or manipulation, and were the *de facto* heads of the households.[12] Another suggests that the mother and wife can become the full master of her household through subtlety, in effect becoming the "power behind the throne."[13]

In Poland, as elsewhere, there were wife-dominated families, but these were never seen as satisfactory, even by the wives themselves. The standards, norms, and values of society saw a good marriage as one in which the father was the head of the family and conducted himself accordingly. When the father was inadequate, allowing or forcing the mother to take over roles and functions normally performed by the husband, the results were frequently disorientation and unhappiness, accompanied by scorn, derision or pity by kin, friends and community.

Strict discipline was a part of a child's training for all social classes, since it was meant to toughen the child for the struggle of later life. "The discipline exerted by the father was strict and harsh, especially among the peasant and worker families."[14] The pattern, common to all social classes, was that of "a stern father and a mother who tries to defend the child and mediate between him and the father when the punishment becomes too severe."[15]

It was taken for granted that the sons of a farmer would follow their father's footsteps and remain on the land. The urban workers or craftsmen usually decided into what occupations or trades their sons should enter and when. The middle and upper class parents decided on the future occupations of their children, and only the most rebellious or independent youngsters could go against the father's wishes, usually on pain of disinheritance or banishment from the family.[16]

THE EFFECTS OF MIGRATION

The bulk of the mature Polish immigrants who came to Canada well into the 1950s arrived with these values and beliefs, unaware that different family relations were possible. However, the family, the bastion or foundation of Polish and other societies, has been almost totally neglected or ignored by writings dealing with the Polish group in Canada. Only one novel, based on research, deals extensively with Polish families in Canada.[17] Available statistics provide some data related to family size, death of one of the spouses, and rates of intermarriage between Polish and other ethnic groups and religions,[18] and there are a few vague references in works by Canadian authors to the incidence of juvenile delinquency and other family problems. This would seem to be the extent of the information available to discuss Polish families in Canada and little can be stated with any certainty about the changes that took place in this venerable institution.[19]

Few prospective migrants had sufficient resources to pay the passage for the whole family at once even if all possessions were sold and additional monies borrowed from relatives or money lenders. It is likely that the important decision to emigrate was not undertaken with finality, and wife and children as well as possessions were left behind as a form of security or insurance in case the 'promised land' was not all it was purported to be. The few organizations offering advice to the prospective emigrants in Galicia before 1914 strongly discouraged whole families leaving at once on a permanent basis. One especially[20] urged that the fathers alone go to Canada, work, earn and save their money and return to Poland. Many impoverished families sent sons to North America for the express purpose of helping them financially and the sons, realizing the better opportunities available in Canada, persuaded the rest of the family to join them. More often the father went first, to find work and accommodation, and when all debts were paid sent money or steamship tickets for his family to join him.

Before 1914, Polish immigrants were directed to the Prairie provinces, and families were encouraged to settle on the land and claim their homesteads.[21] The rural settlers, isolated from the dynamic and often disruptive influences of city life, were able to maintain their traditional lifestyles for many years. The transition from one society to another had little effect on the father's authority. The farm or homestead required the wife and children to pitch into the many tasks of farming under the father's leadership. The wife was a junior partner in these initial struggles and all children were unpaid workers who were assigned tasks or duties suitable to their age and sex. Separated from its old community, the family became "the basic unit of production and consumption, of socialization and recreation. In the absence of secondary groups it had to assume many functions that were performed by the community and institutions in their old country. The dependence of individuals intensified."[22] In the strange and often hostile environment, separated from their friends, relatives and peers, the children relied on moral and physical support provided by the immediate family and adhered to the traditional patterns of relationships with their parents.

The rural families changed only very slowly.[23] The reinforcement, which could be provided by other Polish families and institutions such as the church, was most often missing, but there were also few pressures for change. Other European immigrants, especially the Ukrainians among whom many Polish families settled, shared similar patterns of family relations and held similar values and attitudes. The youth were not exposed to 'modern' ideas from the mass media.[24] Family life, subject to the demands of compulsory public education and economic necessity, resisted changes and innovations.

The urban families were fully open to the influences of the receiving society but as long as the mother remained at home she served as a guardian of customs, traditions, and values, warding off pressure from the outside society. In this she was aided by the Polish churches, which continued to stress the traditional patriarchal ideal of family relations as the most desirable one. The custom of having grandparents living with the family was maintained, and they not only helped with a variety of tasks, but further reinforced the guardian role of the mother.

Yet it would be miraculous if the traditional family system remained unaffected by the process of migration and the situations within the new environment, and a number of factors began to affect the Polish family. The absence of the supporting extended family,[25] friends and immediate community, and the dearth of agencies reinforcing values and traditions, especially Polish churches and clergy and Polish schools, were especially influential.

Regarding the first factor, it has been noted that there were a number of Polish rural 'colonies' in the three Prairie provinces, especially in the first three or four decades of this century.[26] These rural concentrations were exceptions rather than the rule. The vast majority of Polish farmers in Canada were scattered among other ethnic groups, especially the Ukrainians. Even when there were concentrations of Polish immigrants, these were not made up of people from the same communities or even districts in Poland.

Faced with strange customs, struggling to establish themselves in the new society, without supervision and guidance, the Polish immigrants had to interpret and cope with their problems by themselves. Their values, customs and traditions served them well and there is little to suggest family disintegration, moral turpitude, juvenile delinquency and prostitution.[27] As an example, one study found that the rate of convictions for the Canadian-born in the 1951-1954 period was 86.56 per 10,000 males in the 15 to 49 age category. The corresponding figure for the Polish-born was 42.73.[28] The absence of supporting and reinforcing agencies to the traditional forms of family interaction left its members isolated at best, but more often open to the influences and pressures of the surrounding environment. While the adults were less open to such influences the effect on the youth was undoubtedly very great.

There were other conditions which added to changes which took place in the established Polish family system. Great need for funds to purchase the necessary farm implements and livestock, or to pay off debts, forced the husbands to seek any available work and often resulted in prolonged absences from their wives and children. During those periods, the mother had to assume many of her husband's roles: decision-maker, disciplinarian, head of the family. After the father's return the transition back to the traditional pattern was not always easy.

The older children, both male and female, were encouraged to seek remunerative employment. The young men were exposed to life in work gangs, lumber camps, or factories, new situations and experiences for individuals who had seldom left their villages. New ideas and values were learned or heard about: strange notions of economic independence, influence in decision-making and decisions about their own future. The older girls were engaging in domestic service where they could observe different lifestyles and patterns of family interaction.

The authority and power of the Polish father was now less secure, even threatened. While he remained the legal owner of his property he was not always certain of the Canadian laws affecting his status. There was no supporting environment to reinforce his supremacy. There were no relatives or neighbours to watch over and criticize any infractions of customs or traditions. In the new environment he no longer could exercise the many prerogatives available to him in Poland. In the early stages of mass migration (1896-1914) and settlement on homesteads, marriages were most often dictated by necessity. Since the families were scattered and strangers to each other, there were few opportunities for the young people to meet one another and unions were arranged by the parents with little consideration for the two people most concerned. There was also little consideration of the all-important details of the girl's dowry or the boy's position or wealth, and the marriages were not generally satisfactory to all concerned.[29]

Because of the great preponderance of males, Polish girls of marriageable age were in short supply. Young men resorted to travelling to Poland to choose a wife, or else sent for their sweethearts or girlfriends to join them in Canada. Others married girls from other ethnic groups, especially the Ukrainian.[30] The young people were increasingly exercising their wishes in the selection of marriage partners and the concept of romantic love as a prerequisite to marriage was beginning to be stressed. The parents could still influence, approve or disapprove of the selection, but were no longer the main instigators of new marital unions.

The father could no longer dictate to his children how they should be educated or what occupation they should pursue. The daughters, having fewer outside working opportunities, generally remained under the influence of parents in this respect,[31] but the sons, exposed to or aware of the potentials of earnings in other types of work and other locations, were no longer dependent on their fathers' possessions. Perhaps one of the sons was anxious or willing to take over the father's farm or business, but there were many opportunities available to the others. Land was plentiful and comparatively inexpensive. A young man determined to have his own farm could accumulate the necessary funds in a few years of work for another farmer or in a city. Independence was easily achieved. Other work in towns and cities, in mines or forests, on construction or railroads was generally available to the young, healthy and strong.

Education in Canada was compulsory, and while some fathers kept their children from attending school, especially during the season of intensified farm activities, all had to reconcile themselves to the new laws. Education in public schools has been and remains one of the most important factors of change in the traditional patriarchal Polish families. In public schools the children learned of new values and customs which were defined as the most civilized.[32] Their own cultures and histories were usually ignored or derided. In informal relationships with their peers they came to realize that other types of family relationships were practised, with a less severe authority structure and a more liberal or democratic set of relationships.

Most importantly, the children acquired in public schools the means of communication with the outside society, which their parents lacked or possessed only to a limited degree. On many occasions the fathers had to rely on the newly acquired skills of their children when faced with the necessity of translation, and such dependence was bound to undermine the father's authority and power.

Public school education created a communications gap and a lack of understanding between parents and children. Fragmentary or partial exposure to Polish values and traditions within the family, only partly reinforced by churches and part-time schools where they existed, did not produce the results the parents desired. For the youngsters the old customs and traditions became more and more incomprehensible and meaningless. Incomprehension was often replaced by dislike for the 'foreign' and 'bad' customs and traditions of their parents. The children wanted to avoid the negative stereotypes and labels attached to their parents by Canadian society and the quickest means of achieving this was by becoming "Canadian" like others, dissociating themselves from the customs and language, even changing their names in maturity.

131

The parents could not provide a meaningful alternative view to the one their children acquired in the 'outside' world. Many were incapable of coping with the new situation because of unconcern, ignorance or lack of time. Others encouraged their children to become 'Canadians' as quickly as possible. Some who wished to preserve and maintain the traditional lifestyle were too weak to oppose the impact of Canadian institutions and values.

Many traditional patterns of family interaction had to be modified; despotism was no longer possible since the children could leave home and seek other opportunities. Discipline had to be adjusted to meet Canadian standards. As a result, although the immigrant parents tried to maintain the traditional patterns of relations as practised in Poland, each succeeding generation born and raised in Canada adopted more and more the family lifestyles of the host society.

ISSUES OF SOCIALIZATION

The children of immigrants, especially those coming from traditional societies such as pre-war Poland, faced a host of problematic situations which until recently have received scant attention in Canada.[33] The child of an immigrant in the first few years of residence in the new society was under continuous pressure from two different and often conflicting sets of values, attitudes and perceptions. He was not yet completely permeated by the values, cultural patterns, literature, customs, and history of his own ethnic group. This made it easier to shift to the norms, values and roles of the receiving society which he had to adopt to be able to function in certain contexts, especially in school. The parents, on the other hand, attempted to socialize their child into the culture of his forefathers through encouragement, entreaties, directives and any other means available. But his allegiance would only be won if the family and the ethnic group as a whole provided a meaningful frame of reference or comparison for self-appraisal.

By the very fact that the immigrant children usually have a simultaneous membership in two groups, many of them developed incongruous self-images; they were not certain if they were Canadian first and also 'ethnic,' or if they were ethnic and also Canadian; some felt completely Canadian and a few defined themselves as exclusively 'ethnic.' The immigrant child was exposed to conditions which are seldom faced by his Canadian peers: two different reference groups impinging simultaneously with diverse sets of values on the unformed character of a child, which if about equal in strength, may have resulted in two sets of loyalties. Marginality followed if the immigrant child was unable to relate himself in a consistent way to either of his two available groups of reference.[34]

To what extent the children of Polish immigrants were faced with the issue of identity resolution and with what results cannot be stated with any certainty, but the various sources suggest that the vast majority opted for acceptance of the Canadian norms and values and identity with the Canadian reference group and abandonment of the Polish language, customs and traditions.

TORONTO AREA STUDY

Research[35] was conducted among Polish post-war immigrant families in the Toronto area in order to consider and examine the attitudes and values of these people towards familism, the authority structure within the family, and the religiosity of its members. The questionnaires were submitted to the fathers and interviews were held with other family members wherever possible.

The study found that the Polish families in Toronto were strikingly smaller than the norm in Poland only two or three decades back. Of those interviewed, over 60% came from families where there were five or more children, while only about 10% of the families studied in Toronto had five or more children. More importantly, the majority of the parents had consciously decided the number of children that they would like to have and their attitudes towards artificial birth control methods corresponded closely to those of other Canadian Roman Catholics. About 25% of those who considered themselves good Catholics stated that they approved of artificial birth control and over half approved of divorce 'under certain circumstances,' or else no longer believed that people, even if married in church, should 'stick together no matter what.'' A number of comments were made to the effect that smaller families are now desirable; among the reasons given for this were that parents can afford to provide better education if the family is smaller, housing conditions do not allow for large families, and it costs too much to raise a large family.

Orientations were focused primarily on the members of the nuclear family. The adults maintained contact with relatives in Poland through mail and even occasional visits but only small percentages of their children had even sporadic contact with their relatives in Poland. If cousins and other relatives were in Canada the children met them when families came together for special occasions but did not necessarily maintain friendships or contacts with them. Fewer than 10% of the children had friends from other Polish families and in some cases the fathers were unaware who their children's friends were.

The traditional familism was not very evident among the post-war immigrants. The great majority had meals together only on weekends or special holidays. Family activities in leisure hours were enjoyed only on special occasions. Polish teenagers tended to develop and pursue interests which did not necessarily include other family members. The majority of fathers noted that their children did not come to them for help or advice. Nearly half of the fathers considered their children disrespectful on many occasions and often rebellious, and about 35% had problems of communication and mutual understanding.

133

Asked about the Polish youth generally, the majority of fathers responded with negative opinions. The Polish youth were too ready to accuse them of being "old fashioned," too traditional or rigid, and not adaptable to the new environment. Children were accused of a lack of understanding for the vast differences between the Polish culture and that of an industrial modern society like Canada. The fathers could not understand the lack of interest in their attempts at retaining traditional values, which to them were as good or better than Canadian values. Many blamed this situation on the general "generation gap" and hoped that with maturity the views of their children would change.

Working Wives

Of the group studied, only 31.6% of the wives did not work at all while 32.2% had regular full-time jobs. The husbands of the working wives provided many explanations and justifications for this development. Many of them argued that it was the norm of Canadian society. Others pointed out that as immigrants they had come to Canada with few material possessions, and in order to secure the best possible chances for their children, both parents had to make an effort to build up the necessary savings. Others gave assurance that it was only temporary and as soon as possible their wives would be back in their rightful places, at home with the children. The majority of the fathers reaffirmed the belief that the mother's place was at home and blamed Canadian society or industry for encouraging married women with children to work.

The wives themselves did not necessarily concur with those views. Some were satisfied with their work, which offered them challenge and a change from housework. Others liked the partial independence with which the financial rewards now provided them. Some felt that they would continue to work to purchase the various extras or "luxuries" which could not be acquired on the husband's salary alone. Wives working occasionally or part-time in particular had specific purposes or goals: holiday trips, clothing for themselves and the children, or other extras. Only a few mothers considered that it was the duty of the father alone to provide for the family; even those who did not work would take jobs if the family needed financial support.

The study also found new family relationships and new structures of decision-making and authority. The authority of the father in pre-war Poland was seldom disputed, and ranged over all of the important issues and decisions. The study found that even of those fathers whose wives did not work, 72.2% shared final decision-making with their wives in matters concerning larger purchases, while 27.8% of the fathers shared such decisions with the whole family. None said that they decided alone. In changing jobs the fathers now consulted their wives. The family budget was controlled by the father alone in 18.3% of the cases, while others shared this responsibility with their wives.

Other Findings

The study suggests that the Polish fathers had little direct influence on the choice of marriage partners for their children. The one factor of seeming importance concerned religion. Over half of the Polish fathers stated that they would want their children to marry within their own religion, but many of the same individuals later modified their statements by holding that any marriage is happier if there are no differences or conflicts over religion, facilitating child upbringing, easing family relations and generally reducing misunderstandings which mixed religious couples are bound to encounter. Thus, in the final analysis, the happiness of the couple was brought to the fore even for many apparently religious individuals. The young people themselves stressed such values as compatibility, personality, kindness, and love as important in the selection of their marriage partners. Only rarely was ethnic background or religion considered as all-important.

The authority and decision-making, connected with the punishment of children as well as the type of punishment given, differed greatly from the pattern which existed in pre-war Poland, where the father of the family had the final word, and the punishment, especially in rural areas, was predominantly physical. In Toronto as many ex-villagers as former residents of cities and towns used scolding when their children deserved it. In 80% of the cases, the decision to punish children was taken by the parents together. The father no longer made decisions on the children's education and occupation alone; in more than half of the cases this was done by both parents, while in 35.0% of cases the children themselves had the final decision. In their attitude to parental authority most young people were quite satisfied with the present relationship in the family, although some thought the older people too conservative on the issues of sex, artificial birth control, and divorce.

The Aged

While the study did not inquire about the status of grandparents, a few developments are significant. The most important is the utilization by the Polish community in Canada of homes for the aged, senior citizens' residences and nursing homes. A cursory enquiry would suggest that the Polish community no longer considers it wrong to have people other than members of the family look after the aged. Further, there are at present four Polish homes for senior citizens and plans for the establishment of others.[36]

The grandparents' wishes are seldom considered since it is held that the Canadian residences are usually inadequate for the family as well as for the grandparents, or that since the wife is working there is no one to provide the necessary care and attention, or that the children cannot get along with the grandparents. It is also held that the grandparents will get the best care and attention in institutions and are lucky to be able to live in them. The grandparents seldom agree. Many of the elderly Polish do not have a perfect command of English, adhere to different customs and traditions, and have been raised to believe that the grandparents' place is with their children and grandchildren. The activities in the public institution, such as sing-alongs, have little meaning for the Polish oldsters. The next Polish generation may be better prepared to cope with the enforced retirement and institutions for elderly, but the present residents (many of whom refer to themselves as inmates) find the experience very stressful.

Conclusions

The whole traditional pattern of authority and parental prestige has disappeared or is greatly weakened among Polish immigrants in Toronto, and one may safely predict that it is weakened in other urban centres in Canada as well. There seem to be relatively few "holdouts" who retain the traditional division of labour.

The post-war Polish immigrant father has little in common with the traditional ideal of pre-war Poland, the stern and all-powerful figure. He allows his wife to work for wages. He no longer makes any important decision by himself, but most often asks his wife for advice and counsel. More significantly, the children are now allowed to add their voices regarding both the purchase of important items for the house and the family, and decisions about their own education and occupation.

As in other traditional European societies, housework, cleaning, cooking and washing the dishes, and child care were the exclusive responsibilities of the mother, and the father (or any male) would consider it degrading to help or do such chores. But there are cracks in this male redoubt and the fathers have been observed changing diapers, feeding the baby, using electric carpet sweepers and even helping the wife with the dirty dishes. Those changes are observable not merely among specific educational groups, nor among certain socio-economic classes, but are general among ex-farmers and village dwellers, long considered bastions of traditional attitudes and orientations towards these issues, as well as among city and town dwellers, who are perhaps more adaptable to new conditions.

An explanation of the changes taking place in the Polish family structure and relationships is not possible without further in-depth study but it may be suggested that the processes, both psychological and sociological, associated with migration, the decision to "uproot," separation from the old community, the initial shock of the new environment, the ensuing efforts of learning new skills and language, and establishment in the new society, have left little room for the continuation of traditional familial attitudes and values. It was easier to adapt and change than struggle with overwhelming odds in the new context. It is likely that the children also serve as unwitting agents of socialization, forcing the parents to learn new values, norms, and even the language, just to be able to communicate with them. Perhaps by exposing their parents to the ideas and styles of the Canadian society, and by urging them to abandon the "old fashioned" values and attitudes of the Old Country, they have effected some shifts in their parents' views. Canadian attitudes towards economic achievement, desire for acceptance by the host society, higher education, travel, and other experiences of life may be other important factors contributing to this change. Lack of clear aims in the preservations of family traditions, or means of achieving them, and the factor of permanency of residence in Canada may also play important roles in this process.

New patterns of family interaction and new attitudes and beliefs are plainly discernible not only among the post-war immigrants but also among the whole Polish aggregate in Canada. Nuclear family[37] orientations are slowly replacing the traditional extended family values. There is a generally greater permissiveness and very little authoritarianism on the part of the father; equally noticeable is the abandonment of previously rigidly held attitudes and values. It is likely that the Polish family in Canada is fast becoming indistinguishable from the Anglo-Saxon urban Canadian family, sharing many of its values and attitudes in parent-child and husband-wife relationships. The changes have taken place here while much traditionalism still seems to remain in Poland.[38]

All this does not suggest that the Polish family is facing exceptional problems or difficulties or is on the verge of fragmentation and dissolution. There is little to hint at marital breakups or other less desirable issues. The Polish family has successfully adjusted to the new situations, conditions and demands following migration and will be able to face other situations and problematic conditions in future without many problems.

NOTES

1. For historical background on the Polish family see C.R. Barnett, *Poland* (New Haven, 1958), and Jan Szczepański, *Polish Society* (New York, 1970). For a more recent portrayal see F. Adamski, "Funkcjonowanie Katolickiego Modelu Małżeństwa i Rodziny w Środowisku Miejskim," *Znak* xxv (8), 1050-1069, and D. Markowska, "Family Patterns in a Polish Village," *Polish Sociological Bulletin* 2 (8), 1963, 97-110. A less formal but factual account is provided by Reymont, *op. cit.*

2. Defined as more isolated, encouraging or stressing greater respect for the existing moral and social precepts, and characterized by the traditional division of labour.

3. Szczepański, p. 182.

4. Zygmunt Bauman, "Economic Growth, Social Structure, Elite Formation: The Case of Poland," *International Social Science Journal* 16 (1964), 204.

5. Quoted in Wańkowicz, p. 24, author's translation.

6. Barnett, p. 348.

7. Quoted in Wańkowicz, p. 279.
8. See Reymont, *op. cit.*,; W. Witos, *Jedna Wieś* (Chicago, 1955).
9. J. Turowski, "Changes in the Rural Areas under the Impact of Industrialization," *Polish Sociological Bulletin* 1 (13), 1966, 123-131.
10. This is not to say that everyday relations always followed such a pattern.
11. Witos, *op. cit.*, claims that even a mature son would not light a pipe or a cigarette in front of his father and had to have permission to go to dances or to meet with friends. It was noted that the sons showed little rebellion.
12. Reymont, *op. cit.*
13. F. Radecki, "Notatki" (Toronto, 1973).
14. Barnett, p. 348.
15. *Ibid.*, p. 351.
16. This is one of the persisting values even in contemporary Poland as suggested by one study where 95% of village respondents denied the freedom of choice of occupation for their children if such choices conflicted with the family's business or farm. About half of the sample studies held that parents should have a veto power over the choice of occupation and education for their children. See D. Markowska, "Family Patterns in a Polish Village," *Polish Sociological Bulletin* 2 (8), 1963, 97-110.
17. Wańkowicz, *op. cit.* In Canada the study of the family has been generally neglected and only in 1964 was a Canadian text published. See F. Elkin, *The Family in Canada* (Ottawa, 1964).
18. Census statistics. See also *Report of the Royal Commission*, Book IV, pp. 279-98.
19. Recently, the post-war Polish families in one city have been subject to a survey. See H. Radecki, "POLISH-Canadian, CANADIAN-Polish, or CANADIAN?", Mimeograph, 1970, York University, Toronto.
20. Okołowicz, *op. cit.*
21. Despite the fact that land was the most treasured possession for a peasant in Poland, not all claimed the almost-free homesteads in Canada even before 1914, when both the quality of the land and the geographical locality were comparatively good. Many Polish families remained in urban centres and no explanation can be provided for this development.
22. Jean R. Burnet, *Ethnic Groups in Upper Canada*, Ontario Historical Society Research Publication No. 1, 1972.
23. The classical study by W.I. Thomas and F. Znaniecki, *The Polish Peasant in Europe and America*, 2 volumes, (New York, 1958), found that among Polish families in Chicago, "obedience is the most persistent of all attitudes."
24. The radio arrived in the 1920s and television only in the 1950s.
25. Extended family, which includes three or more generations and might include grandparents, the unmarried or married children with their spouses and children.
26. See, for example, Foster, *op. cit.*; Gibbon, *op. cit.*
27. While some Canadian sources, in particular Anderson, *op. cit.*; Bridge-

man, *op. cit.*; Woodsworth, *op. cit.*, raise the problem of juvenile delinquency, the claims are not well documented. Drunkenness and brawling were prevalent among some Polish male emigrants, especially in the 1900-1914 period, but this was characteristic of the urban settler and those who came to Canada without their families. See, for example, James H. Gray, *Red Lights on the Prairies* (Toronto, 1971). The heads of the households had little money to spare for drinking and consideration of the wife and children was an effective barrier to others.

Thomas and Znaniecki, *op. cit.*, discovered high rates of family breakup, juvenile delinquency and a high rate of prostitution among Polish immigrants in Chicago, but to extend those findings to Canadian cities is not appropriate. The Polish community in Chicago was extremely large, containing some of the worst slums in the city, stable both geographically and occupationally, and open to the influences of corrupt politicians and criminal elements. None of the Canadian cities can be compared to Chicago; the Canadian society had entirely different conceptions of law, order, morals and politics than the United States, and this reflected on the Polish immigrants in Canada. In memoirs and other sources there are no hints that Polish families experienced the problems noted by Thomas and Znaniecki.

28. P.J. Giffen, "Rates of Crime and Delinquency," in W.T. McGrath, ed., *Crime and Its Treatment in Canada* (Toronto, 1965).

29. One study holds that arranged marriages among Eastern Europeans ceased after World War I. See Palmer, p. 246.

30. But not Anglo-Saxon. Hurd, p. 151, finds that "less than four per cent of the married Poles had wives of British origin," according to the 1921 census.

31. For all Canadian women few occupational categories were available until recently and the vast majority looked forward to (or were resigned to) the position of wife and mother.

32. Examples can be found in Anderson, *op. cit.*; R. England, *The Central European Immigrant*; Woodsworth, *op. cit.*

33. See K. Danziger, *The Socialization of Immigrant Children*, Part I (Toronto, 1971), for problems of socialization faced by the Italian traditional families.

34. E.V. Stonequist, *The Marginal Man* (New York, 1937). See also E.L. Child, *Italians in America: The Second Generation Conflict* (New Haven, 1943); M.M. Goldberg, "A Qualification of the Marginal Man Theory," *American Sociological Review* 6, 1941, pp. 52-8; A.S. Green, "A Re-Examination of the Marginal Man Concept," *Social Forces* 26 (2), 1947, 167-171.

35. Radecki, *POLISH-Canadian*. The study involved 60 Polish families living in Toronto for at least five years and with at least one school-aged child. The area chosen was one whose Polish ethnic residential concentration was documented by A. Richmond, *Immigrants and Ethnic Groups*

in Metropolitan Toronto, York University, Ethnic Research Programme, 1967, and the sample included both urban and rural residents in pre-war Poland. The sample was randomly selected and represented all levels of occupations and education.

36. There are Polish Senior Citizens' Homes in Montreal, Winnipeg, Edmonton and Vancouver and one is in the advanced planning stages in Toronto.

37. A family composed of parents and their unmarried children.

38. See D. Markowska, *op. cit.*

EIGHT

Religion

For from the rising of the sun even unto the going down of the same my name shall be great among the Gentiles; and in every place incense shall be offered unto my name, and a pure offering; for my name shall be great among the heathen, saith the Lord of hosts.

Malachi (1:11)

BACKGROUND

Poland was Christianized in 966 and has remained overwhelmingly Roman Catholic since. The Reformation and religious wars did not affect Poland greatly and the majority of Poles remained loyal to Roman Catholicism. The state has always tolerated the religions of its minorities, and Judaism, Greek Orthodoxy or Greek Catholicism and Protestantism flourished among Polish citizens of Ukrainian, Byelorussian, Jewish, or German background. Monasteries and religious orders contributed significantly to the rise of Polish civilization and the Church has played an important role in the political and intellectual life of Poland since the Middle Ages.

During the periods of partition, from 1795 to 1918, the Catholic church was the only intact institution and, while besieged or persecuted, became the spiritual mainstay of the subjugated Polish people. The church served as the main force in the preservation and maintenance of the Polish language and traditions and thus provided the only distinct source of Polish national identity. The hardships suffered by the Poles and the Roman Catholic Church under Orthodox Russian and Protestant Prussian rule reinforced and deepened the identity of the Polish nationality with the Catholic faith to the extent that to be a Pole was almost synonymous with being a Roman Catholic. Common suffering, persecution, and resistance during World War II against the German occupiers reinforced the ties

141

between the church and the people further. The ties did not lessen percep-tibly as an aftermath of concentrated efforts of both the Polish and Soviet Communist parties to eradicate or at least undermine the position that the church occupies in Poland.

Poles of all social strata accepted the Catholic faith although the middle and upper classes were less likely to follow all pronouncements and teach-ings of the Catholic dogma or the clergy, and were more likely to question the authority and influence of the church. For the peasants and less edu-cated city dwellers, the church and religion had a strong impact on every-day life, and religious beliefs were an integral part of daily existence. One writer[1] notes many examples of the extent that religion permeated the language, customs, and everyday relationships with friends and neigh-bours, and even the perception of self.

For the Polish peasant all celebrations and festivals, local occasions, collective social life, not to mention christenings, weddings, funerals, and all activities providing richness and colour to the otherwise drab and unexciting life, were connected with the church, religious customs and traditions. Religous paintings were the main decorations of the peasants' houses, prayers were said morning, noon and night, the sign of the cross was made over a loaf of bread before it was cut, time was often measured by so many lengths of prayers,[2] the house, livestock and fields were blessed by the priest yearly, and all religious days were scrupulously observed. A pilgrimage to the shrine of the Madonna of Częstochowa was held in similar esteem among the Polish peasants as a pilgrimage to Mecca by the Muslims.

Polish Catholicism was characterized by national and local peculiari-ties. It was more ritualistic than in many countries, strongly infused with long-forgotten pagan customs and beliefs. Rites of passage such as bap-tisms, weddings or funerals were celebrated in church but all had their counterparts at home. Special services were performed for the dead; the baptized child was subjected to rituals performed by the parents or the village 'wise woman.' There was a widespread belief in witchcraft, evil spirits and ghosts, and superstitions were often interjected into purely religious beliefs. The local priests repeatedly thundered from the pulpit for the abandonment of such practices and beliefs but generally with little effect.[3]

As in other agricultural societies, each Polish community had its patron saints who were effective in certain areas of human problems, but greatest importance was attached to the worship and powers of the Virgin Mary. Paintings of Madonnas, in a cathedral, monastery or church named after the city or the locality, were declared special protectors over the districts, ascribed special powers and influence over the faithful, and venerated above all. It was acknowedged that some Madonnas were more influential or powerful than others and the "Black" Madonna of Częstochowa was recognized as the Queen of Poland and therefore the most influential; other Madonnas had to defer to her position.[4]

In addition to satisfying the spirtual and emotional needs of the people, the church in Poland played an important social role. It was during the Sunday service that individuals and their families could demonstrate visibly and to all concerned their social status or place in the community. The manor had special pews and local dignitaries sat in the very front. The most prosperous farmers had seats near the altar and they assisted the priest during processions, carrying the canopy or walking directly behind it. The less prosperous farmers had seats farther back and participated less in the church rituals. The rentiers or landless peasants and workers stood in the church. Their role was to note and acknowledge the position of the more prosperous farmers.

Following the service, all gathered outside the church to debate, discuss and exchange news and gossip. This custom brought outsiders from the outlying smaller communities without their own church into contact with others, allowed for important debates among the farmers on outstanding issues of the community and generally served to promote community identity and cohesiveness. The social function of the church and religion is emphasized by an eminent student of Polish society, who found that the larger proportion of Polish population was "more interested in the social than in mystical aspects of religion."[5]

Catholic churches in Poland were generally built and richly endowed by prosperous landowners, nobles or bishops. Protected by the Episcopate, supported by manors and estates as by the state, the local churches were financially independent of their parishioners. Many of the more concerned clergy utilized the resources of their churches to aid those in need.

For the peasants, the priests were the representatives of God, Jesus Christ, and the Virgin Mary; they were the intermediaries between the sinner and salvation of the soul. With deep religiosity it was only natural that high respect, even attachment, was felt for the parish priest, the only educated person willing to talk to the peasant, advise him on secular matters, and provide him with reassurance in times of trouble. The resident priests, assured of economic security, could devote all their efforts to the needs of their parishes and parishioners.

/The religion, the church, and the local priests played a significant role in the lives of all members of rural communities, from birth to death. The religion provided richness and spectacle but, more importantly, meaning and explanation for the very existence of man, his successes and failures, trials and tribulations. It also offered hope for eternal rest and salvation in the afterlife. The church served as a locus where social position was established and reaffirmed weekly, where people gathered to renew ties and bonds.

Undoubtedly, there was a strong dependence and close relationship between the members of communities and the church in Poland. 'Those Poles who came to Canada brought their faith and loyalty with them, expecting a liberal climate and freedom to practise their beliefs. But the

143

special relationship was not to be fully re-established at any time after their arrival.

THE NEW SETTING

The Polish immigrants arriving in Canada before 1895 were deeply concerned with the maintenance of their religious values and practices. The chapel in Berlin (now Kitchener) and the first church in Wilno, Ontario, clearly demonstrate the importance that they attached to worship in a familiar language, with familiar rituals, and with their own Polish priests. The same need was felt by the later arrivals from Galicia and other parts of Poland.

Having secured work or settled down on the land, their attention turned next to spiritual needs. Roman Catholic churches, established by the French Canadian, Irish, or German people, could be found in the larger communities in all provinces. The Mass in Latin did not differ from that in Poland, and the priests, whether of French, Irish or German background, followed the universal pattern of the liturgy. But this was all that the Polish immigrants found familiar. The churches seemed bare, devoid of the rich decorations and colour familiar to them in the past. During the service, they stood or knelt at the wrong times. The hymns were strange, foreign and incomprehensible. The sermons, advice, announcements, or even admonitions could not be understood. They brought their faith with them but found strange rituals, an absence of close relationships with the priest, and a gap of communication with the other faithful. More important, they could not confess their sins and partake of the Holy Communion, even at very special times like Easter and Christmas. The guilt of sin remained for months and years, adding to other problems facing them in the new environment.

A few of the more understanding or concerned local parish priests, with numbers of Polish immigrants in their congregations, communicated the difficulties of their Polish charges to the bishops who made requests to have Polish-speaking priests visit from the United States. The parish priest would offer the use of his chapel or a room in the basement where the visitor would celebrate Mass for the Poles. This was very welcome to the immigrants, but the visits were infrequent and irregular. This solution was never satisfactory to people who saw in the church much more than a place of worship. Leaving behind the whole complex, age-old system which regulated their lives and provided meaning to their beliefs and values, they now wanted more than ever to re-establish their special relationships with the church and other Poles. They concluded that only in founding their own parishes with Polish priests could they find again the essence of the missing community and self-identity.

Wherever a large number of Polish families were to be found, there was also found a concern over the absence of Polish-speaking priests and their own places of worship. Church building committees were organized to erect Polish churches, settlers in rural areas built log chapels or small churches in hope that a Polish priest would be found to serve them. The chapels or churches were built at first on the same pattern as settlers' houses, cheaply and quickly, without style or beauty. Later, when the missionary priests provided guidance and encouragement, the edifices were larger, better planned and built more solidly.

Polish parishes, with their own churches and resident priests and missions[6] where the priests visited the faithful only periodically, grew in number as more immigrants came from Poland. By 1921 Manitoba alone had 44 chapels or churches for Polish immigrants. By 1926 there were 29 Polish parishes across Canada. By 1929 the number had increased to 33 parishes and 157 missions. In 1938 there were 52 Polish parishes and 120 missions. A number of sources[7] note the generosity of the hard-working and seldom prosperous Polish immigrants in contributing their time, effort and money to church building. The beautiful churches in Winnipeg, Manitoba and in Wilno, Ontario, were built within a few months through the efforts and sacrifices of Polish immigrants and priests.

Having erected a log chapel or a church, the earliest settlers sent petitions requesting Polish clergy to bishops in Poland and the United States while making representations at the same time to the local sees. The Catholic hierarchy, especially Bishop Langevin of Manitoba, were generally sympathetic towards the petitions. Their sympathy may have stemmed in part from concern about the missionary activities of the Protestant churches among the new arrivals. Efforts were made in the late 1890s to secure Polish priests for the larger concentrations of immigrants from Polish-American parishes, which were adequately staffed and receiving new priests through Polish seminaries in the United States and through immigration. The results were disappointing: there is no record of any Polish-American priest coming to the western provinces before 1900.[8]

The bishops' attention turned next to Ottawa where an Oblate seminary was preparing priests for missionary work in Canada and elsewhere. Among the Oblate Fathers were three brothers of Polish background. One of them, Adalbert Kulawy, came to Winnipeg in May of 1898 and was given the task of organizing a Polish parish in Winnipeg as well as ministering to the scattered settlers in other parts of the province. He was joined a year later by his brother John Wilhelm; a church was built in 1899 serving not only the Polish immigrants but other immigrant Catholics, among them Ukrainians, Slovaks, Lithuanians, Hungarians, and Germans. John Wilhelm Kulawy was appointed parish priest while his brother Adalbert began missionary activities to the scattered Polish (and other) settlers and workers in Western Canada. In time other Polish priests began to arrive from the United States and from Poland[9].

While the number of churches and chapels grew yearly, there were continuous problems of finding sufficient Polish priests to staff the parishes. The 29 parishes in 1926 were not all staffed. In 1929, for the 33 parishes and 157 missions there were only 42 priests, of whom 20 served in cities, leaving the rest to perform the missionary work in scattered communities of the three western provinces and Ontario.[10] In 1938, the 62 parishes and 120 missions were served by 75 priests, still insufficient to provide regular service to all the established missions.

THE CLERGY

The activities of the Polish clergy began early in the history of Polish settlements in Canada. One source[11] notes that a Polish Jesuit priest was serving isolated communities without priests or churches in 1855 in Ontario. The Polish Congregation of the Resurrection began its work in Canada on August 14, 1857, when two priests arrived at St. Agatha, Ontario. Since that day the Polish Resurrectionists in Canada have been active in parishes and schools, "chiefly among the German settlers throughout the province of Ontario,"[12] but also among Polish parishes in Kitchener, Hamilton, Brantford, and Montreal, Quebec. Others[13] discuss the arrival of Polish priests at Wilno, Ontario, in the early 1860s. From 1896 the Polish Oblate Brother Kowalczyk devoted his life in the service of Indians and Metis in Alberta. His life and activities have been the subject of two biographies[14] and processes are under way to have him canonized. Activities of the two Oblate Fathers Kulawy were recorded elsewhere[15] and the service of "Father Joe," L.J. Kręciszewski, a Polish-American priest active in Manitoba beginning in 1921, is described in yet another biography.[16]

These and other outstanding individuals were among the small number of Polish clergy serving the immigrants and their descendants in Canada. Demands on them were extremely heavy. The pioneer priests had to be hardy, without concern for comfort and personal well-being, and constantly on the move. They had to earn their own living, organize parishes, build and maintain churches or chapels, and retain the loyalty of the faithful under proselytization efforts of other churches. They had to be young, healthy, and dedicated to face the hardships, discouragement and poverty of their charges. The greatest problem for many of them was isolation from other priests. For months they travelled without the company of other clergy, without the consolation of retreats or encouraging words from their supervisors. Even those priests assigned to a parish often had responsibility for four or five missions. They had to travel, to divide their effort and attention between their parishioners and others without their own priests.

The handful of Polish priests travelled great distances to hear confessions, baptize, marry and celebrate mass. Where no chapel or church existed, the services were performed in the open or in a private home. That many more Polish immigrants did not withdraw from active participation in the Roman Catholic Church or join other religions is in no small measure due to the efforts of the Polish missionary priests; if infrequent and irregular, their visits and services were able to sustain for years the faith of the bewildered and isolated Polish immigrants. The missionary period lasted well into the 1920s. When roads and communications were improved and people began to feel more financially secure, the visits became more regular and funds were available to support the clergy and to build or renovate churches and chapels.

For many decades Polish priests occupied a special position within the Polish aggregate in Canada. Their role went beyond spritual concerns. The only educated people in any numbers until 1939, the priests were aware of the many difficulties of adjustment facing Polish immigrants in Canada. It was within parishes, and usually through the advice and efforts of the parish priest, that the first mutual aid associations emerged, giving the members their only protection and security.[17] When time allowed, the Polish priests taught not only religion but the Polish language and history as well. Realizing the growing need for this education a few invited teaching nuns from the United States to settle in Canada and take over parish schools. Aware of the need for communication among the scattered and isolated immigrants, they began to publish the first Polish-language newspaper in Canada in 1904.

In the cities the social life of the Polish immigrants went at times beyond the parish and its facilities, but in rural areas the parish organizations and parish halls or church basements served as the centres of social life. Celebrations, dances, theatrical performances and religious anniversaries were either led or encouraged by the parish priest. Concerns and activities ranged further. In 1927, with lay activists, the Polish priests established a central organization. With headquarters in Winnipeg, it advised the new Polish arrivals on the best areas of settlement, where conditions, land for farming, or chances of finding work were suitable, where other Polish settlers or workers were already present, and where Polish parishes or organizations were established. In times of difficulty or financial crisis they "fed the hungry, found employment for the jobless, lifted the hopes of the discouraged."[18] The Polish clergy were able to recreate and maintain some of the traditions and customs of communities left behind in Poland, through familiar religious practices and observances in an understandable language. This role will remain important in the maintenance of cultural distinctiveness for the people of Polish descent in Canada.

PROBLEMS

The positive contribution in easing the adjustment for Polish immigrants to Canada has to be balanced with some less positive developments, stemming from the attitudes and relationships between individual priests and Polish immigrants. The problems that arose are difficult to categorize or isolate and have a number of causes. One of the more important was the continuous shortage of Polish priests who were suitable to the special conditions of pioneer life. Demands made by the Polish immigrants for their own priests could not be easily satisfied, and the clergy that were found were not always acceptable to the Polish Roman Catholics.

The first major problem arose in Winnipeg at the turn of the twentieth century. According to one source[19] the main difficulties between the Fathers Kulawy and the Polish immigrants were the inability of both parties to communicate fully. These two Oblate priests, as some other Oblates who came to Canada in later years, were educated in German or other non-Polish seminaries. The brothers Kulawy were from Polish Silesia where people spoke with a distinct dialect[20] not easily understood by immigrants from other parts of partitioned Poland. The gap in communication was difficult for the Polish parishioners who had hoped for a 'real' Polish priest to come to them.

Another development relates to conditions in Canada. Polish immigrants, struggling to establish themselves in the new society, had little cash to spare, but it was seldom stinted for the church building or other needs of the parish. Contributions in time, effort and money in building, renovating or expanding churches and priests' residences were generous.[21] Having made contributions, the people were no longer prepared to remain passive in decisions affecting their parish. They felt that their sacrifices entitled them to some voice in the control and disposition of parish finances. The Polish parish priests were loath, as a rule, to abandon their traditional position of total independence from the control of parishioners. They did not look kindly on any attempts at 'interference.' The response to such claims was that "you trust us with your sins, why should you not trust us with a few of your paltry pennies."[22]

Yet another source of problems was found in the clergy's attitude towards the parishioners. The relationship between the peasant and the priest in Poland was strongly characterized by obsequiousness on the former's part. The local parish priest, whether kindly or severe, was condescending towards his uneducated charges, and he expected deference from them. In Poland this was accepted without question. The more open society in Canada and the widespread egalitarianism quickly undermined the established relationship between the priest and the faithful. The Polish peasants in Canada experienced democratic ideals in their contacts with civil servants, members of the police and other 'figures of authority.' The immigrants were called Sir or Mister, treated with respect and seeming equality, and were not expected to show excessive deference. Soon many began to chafe at and resent the traditional position of superiority maintained by a number of Polish priests. To the Polish clergy these issues were petty misunderstandings and small problems, but on occasion they led to suspicion, antagonism, and deep conflicts. They eventually resulted in the establishment of a number of Polish National Roman Catholic parishes, composed primarily of dissident Roman Catholic faithful. They also made the task easier for the missionaries from the Protestant churches who treated potential converts with dignity and respect.

148

In Winnipeg, the Polish Roman Catholics were disappointed that the communication between their priest and themselves could not be fully developed, while at the same time the Fathers Kulawy had a close *rapport* with the German segment of the parish. Resentment and acrimony followed. The Oblate priests were labelled Teutonic Knights (Krzyżacy), while the more outspoken referred to them as German Monks, both terms of censure with highly negative connotations in the Polish frame of reference, relating to the pride, cruelty, and abuse of power by the Teutonic Knights in their attempts to convert the pagan Prussians and Lithuanians.[23] Polish immigrants repeatedly sent petitions to their bishop for a replacement but to no avail. By 1904 Father Kulawy was replaced in Winnipeg by another Polish priest, but not before a large segment of the Polish parish left, more or less permanently, to establish a new parish independent of the Vatican.

A more significant development occurred early in the century which, for some decades, deeply affected the Polish aggregate in Canada. While concern with the re-establishment of their own religious life was paramount in the minds of the majority of Polish immigrants, others were equally concerned with establishing associations whose goals and aims would stress Polish culture, political developments in Poland and other non-religious interests.[24] The organizers and advocates of such associations immediately met stiff resistance from the Polish clergy.

The opposition seems to have been based on two issues. Firstly, any organizations adhering to the then-popular socialist doctrine would seemingly detract from the religiosity of those joining, and could result in hostility towards the church and the clergy. The Polish clergy were vehemently opposed to the Polish People's Association (referred to by some as the Polish Communist Party),[25] which attracted significant numbers of followers in the 1930s, but even prior to World War I, Polish socialists were considered areligious or anti-clerical despite the fact that the majority of them were deeply religious and practising Catholics. Thus, organizations with political or ideological connotations were opposed as potentially or in fact detrimental to the Roman Catholic Church.

Secondly, the traditional position of the clergy in Poland was adopted in Canada and the resident parish priest claimed exclusive direction of organizational activities. The priests were in fact the only professionals among the masses of unskilled, uneducated (or poorly educated) Polish immigrants. It was natural that they saw themselves as leaders, organizers, sponsors, and arbiters of right or wrong. The undermanned Polish clergy was primarily concerned with the maintenance of Roman Catholicism in Canada and could give little attention to the non-religious needs of Polish life. Thus, certain priorities were established and they did not include concern with the events taking place in Poland, nor with the maintenance of the broader aspects of Polish culture.

The leadership or guidance of the Polish clergy would, undoubtedly, have been accepted if it had shown more flexibility towards the non-religious needs of their Polish parishioners, if it had been able to accept compromise on non-crucial issues, and if it had demonstrated an awareness that a Polish Roman Catholic was often a Pole first and only then a Catholic. In reality, not all Polish clergy possessed the characteristics necessary to cope with the situations facing their compatriots in the new society. Sources note that "the moral and educational standard of the Polish priests . . . was not of the highest calibre,"[26] and the intellectual level of the clergy was much lower than was found generally in Poland.[27] Their conduct was not always exemplary and their unbending position on sharing power and authority did not allow even the most concerned and qualified individuals freedom to start much needed organizations or activities without the express approval or supervision of the parish priest.

Realizing that the pursuit of certain activities was not possible under the auspices of the Polish clergy, lay activists began to establish associations and organizations. Others, unwilling to accept any guidance or leadership from the clergy, organized independent bodies and by the 1920s the Polish aggregate was split into two (later three) camps; the clerical and parish affiliated bodies, a variety of independent organizations, associations and clubs, and, in the 1930s, the leftist-radical organizations. The last were rejected and condemned by the first two, but the sharing of a 'mutual enemy' did not provide sufficient grounds for a harmonious relationship. The Polish clergy, faced with the defection of some of their organizations and individuals to the secular side, mounted a campaign of recrimination against the independent organizations and those who joined them. Some were labelled 'leftist,' 'radicals,' or 'anti-clerical'; others were termed 'disruptive' or 'anti-social' elements within the parishes and disloyal to the Church and its representatives.

The Oblate Order, representing the largest, best organized and most cohesive group of Polish priests, was the most vocal in its opposition and condemnation of the independent camp, refusing to heed pleas by the representatives of the Polish government in the 1920-1939 period for unity and harmony of all Polish organizations in Canada. Attempts to persuade Polish parishes and parish affiliated organizations to join the World Association of Poles Abroad was met with a counter-proposal to establish a Canada-wide federation of all Polish organizations under the auspices of the Roman Catholic Church. This in turn was rejected by the independent camp and the struggles and conflicts for influence and membership continued. To counteract the recruiting drives by the Alliance Friendly Society and The Polish Workers' and Farmers' Association, the clerical camp founded its own organization in 1933, the Associated Poles in Manitoba (since 1946, of Canada). This organization was led by Polish priests and Catholic laymen, their goal being to offset what were considered the secularizing influences of other Polish organizations, especially the two named above. The stated aim of the new organization was Catholic action, designed to strengthen the Catholic life and values of Poles in

Canada, and to exchange ideas reflecting this concern.[28] The Associated Poles organization never achieved prominence among Polish immigrants outside Western Canada.

During some periods, especially in the 1930s, the verbal conflict between the three camps was bitter. The clerical camp, through its press organ and from the pulpit, attacked 'anti-clerical free thinkers,' socialists and communists alike. There is no evidence to suggest that anti-clerical material was published in Canada but such tracts were widely available from the United States[29] to Polish immigrants in Canada. The most heated polemics between the clergy and the independent organizations were conducted in the pages of the Polish-language press, since each camp had its own press organ by 1933.[30]

During World War II a truce was observed and all activities focused on the events in Europe and the war effort. The conflicts did not resume on any scale after the war, but mutual distrust persisted for some years. The Oblates and other Roman Catholic clergy remained unconvinced that closer co-operation among all Polish organizations in Canada would benefit individual members of this aggregate. The Associated Poles in Canada still remains unaffiliated with the Canadian Polish Congress, an umbrella organization which represented, until 1972, all other associations and a majority of smaller independent organizations.

What effects the struggles and acrimonies between the clerical and other camps had on the orientation of Polish immigrants and their descendants cannot be stated with any accuracy. It may well be that for most individuals the alternatives were clear-cut, and remaining loyal to one side or joining another posed no problems, but for many others such a decision created difficulties. Those who saw many positive values in the goals and activities of the independent organizations were hesitant to join for fear of being labelled as socialist, communist, or anti-clerical. Others disregarded the advice and urgings of the clergy and did join while remaining practising Catholics, but such decisions were not easy for the deeply religious people.

The effect on the Polish youth, especially those born in Canada, was without doubt of great consequence. Unaware or unconcerned with the issues which created this turmoil, witnessing the bitterness and divisions created by the struggles, they could only conclude that the institutional structure of the Polish aggregate in Canada served as an arena for battles rather than for co-operation. The more positive aspects of organizational activity in Polish parishes, through cultural and social pursuits or education, were in their eyes overshadowed by the intolerance of other points of view or other faiths, by the hostility voiced against individuals and groups, and by the factionalism, intrigues, and accusations. Proportionally, an insignificant number became active themselves in one or another of the organizations. The majority preferred to abstain from involvement outside the Polish parishes. The inter-group hostilities of the 1920-1939 period undoubtedly soured many people's perception of the organizational structure.

Conflicts, accusations, acrimony, and struggles have largely ceased in the last decade or two. The Polish clergy and especially the Oblates are not formally affiliated with the Canadian Polish Congress, but there is evidence of increasing co-operation and tolerance by all concerned.[31] The Polish clergy is invited by various organizations to participate in activities and celebrations. The influence of the priests is no longer as pronounced as it was before 1939, but the members of the clergy continue to elicit respect and deference for their roles, not only as caretakers of souls, but as organizers, initiators, teachers, and custodians of Polish culture and traditions.

THE OBLATES

Among the Polish Roman Catholic clergy in Canada, the Oblates occupy a special position in the religious as well as socio-cultural life of Poles in Canada.[32] This was the only group of Polish priests who managed to coordinate the efforts and purposes of their work, and to co-operate among themselves. An Oblate, Brother Kowalczyk, was active among the Indians and Métis in Alberta as early as 1896, but the activities of the Oblates officially began with the arrival of Father Kulawy in Winnipeg in 1898. Other Oblates followed, becoming active and influential in parish organizations, education, and aspects of Polish cultural life in Canada. Aware of the need for means of communication and ties to the church among the scattered and isolated Polish settlers, the Oblates began a weekly publication in the Polish language in 1904, which, under different names, continued for the next 44 years.[33] The newspaper served not only as a pulpit for religious pronouncements but also as an organ for other information of value to immigrants, and provided for many years the only forum for the literary endeavours of talented individuals.[34] Other activities and interests of the Oblates have been already discussed in this monograph.

After 1926, the Polish Oblates were members of the St. Mary Canadian Province which also included German priests. In 1956, a separate vice-province was established, named Assumption Province, with its own Father Provincial, which primarily represents Polish Oblate Fathers. The province encompasses 26 parishes and 22 missions from Vancouver to Ottawa. The vast majority of these parishes and missions are territorial rather than distinctly Polish national organizations, serving mixed congregations of whom only a proportion are of Polish descent. According to one source,[35] the parishes are served by 60 priests, one brother and six fratrers scholastics. The background of the clergy is predominantly Polish (there are five Italian priests and one French Canadian). New priests are invited from the Oblate seminary in Poznań, Poland. Seven priests came to work in Canada in the years 1968 to 1973 and two more are expected to join them soon.

THE POLISH NUNS

The religious life of the Polish aggregate in Canada also includes the presence and activities of the Polish Orders of Nuns. The Benedictine Sisters, invited from the United States to teach at the Polish Holy Ghost parish in Winnipeg in 1904, are still active in education, orphanages, charity work and hospitals in Manitoba. The Felician Sisters came from the United States to Toronto in 1937 and immediately assumed responsibilities for education, orphanages, care of the poor and visits to the sick in Polish parishes in Toronto, Hamilton and Oshawa.[36] The Redemptionist Sisters remain active in Montreal and Vancouver, and the Nazarene Sisters in Windsor, Ontario. At present there are about 100 sisters in these four religious orders. The Polish nuns have been and remain active in many parishes, maintaining close contact with the Polish people.[37] The focus of their activities is shifting towards teaching in Roman Catholic (separate) schools, and their charitable activities range beyond the Polish aggregate. It is probable that the orders are slowly losing their distinctly Polish character for lack of recruits of Polish background.

OTHER DENOMINATIONS

Historical sources concerned with the Polish group in Canada generally tend to equate Polish background (Polishness) with Roman Catholicism, and claim that the Polish immigrants to Canada were almost exclusively Roman Catholics.[38] This is not accurate, for there were always significant numbers of representatives of other churches and religions – Lutherans, Baptists, Greek Orthodox, and Jewish. It is probable that about 80% of the Polish immigrants arriving prior to 1939 were Roman Catholic, and a number of factors in Canada further affected the religious composition of this group.

Only a minority of Polish immigrants found themselves in larger communities where there was a Roman Catholic church. Most were scattered over the vast expanses of the western provinces and totally isolated from all institutions. Some settled in communities where only Protestant churches were present. Others lived among the Ukrainians who were able to build their Greek Orthodox churches quickly and had few problems with staffing them with Ukrainian priests. Without churches or priests, other immigrant people consoled themselves by reading the Bible. For a number of reasons, the Bible was never popular reading among the Polish Roman Catholics and there was little other material of a religous nature.[39] But then not all of the earlier Polish immigrants could read. For the illiterate, only the pictures of their patron Madonnas and daily prayers served to remind them of their faith. These conditions were favourable to the proselytizing efforts by various Protestant missionaries active in the Prai-

TABLE 9

RELIGIOUS AFFILIATION OF THE POLISH ETHNIC GROUP IN CANADA CENSUS DATA FOR YEARS 1941, 1951, 1961, 1971

	1941		1951		1961		1971	
	#	%	#	%	#	%	#	%
Anglican	3,374	2.0	6,457	2.9	11,626	3.6	12,285	3.9
Baptist	2,994	1.4	3,151	1.4	4,172	1.3	3,670	1.2
Greek Orthodox	5,039	3.0	7,741	3.5	9,752	3.0	5,565	1.8
Jewish	29	–	7,608	3.5	27,204	8.4	–	
Lutheran	7,674	4.6	8,248	3.7	10,586	3.3	9,425	3.0
Mennonite and Hutterite	265	0.1	391	0.1	466	0.1	515	0.2
Pentecostal	895	0.5	not given		2,006	0.6	1,860	0.6
Presbyterian	1,812	1.0	2,257	1.0	3,120	1.0	3,345	1.1
Roman Catholic	135,405	80.0	153,059	69.6	210.271	65.0	224,430	70.9
Ukrainian (Greek) Catholic*			11,361	5.2	10,681	3.3	7,205	2.3
United Church	6,304	1.1	13,077	6.0	25,229	7.8	26,445	8.4
Salvation Army	62	–	not given		not given		440	0.1
Other	3,632	2.2	6,459	3.0	8,404	2.6	7,659	2.4
No Religion or Not Stated	242	0.1	not given		not given		13,545	4.3
Totals	167,485		219,845		323,517		316,430	

* Ukrainian (Greek) Catholics were included with the Roman Catholics in the 1941 Canadian Census.

rie provinces at the time, and the Canadian census data suggest that the Protestant denominations made inroads into the Polish Roman Catholic group. There are now adherents to various fundamentalist denominations and churches which had few or no followers in Poland.[40]

The numbers of Anglican or United Church adherents among the Polish group may be the result partly of intermarriage but to a greater extent of the Protestant missionary work among the earlier phases of Polish immigration to Canada.[41] One source notes that "determined efforts were made by the Presbyterians and Methodists of the East to turn those people (Polish and Ukrainian immigrants) away from Catholic faith,"[42] while another mentions numerous individuals who posed as priests or even bishops, who confused people and created difficulties in fulfilling work by the Roman Catholic clergy, adding that some Polish parishioners "succumbed to evil influences and their faith did not stand the test."[43] The Polish clergy and the Catholic bishops considered this activity an unfair assault on the faith of the new and confused arrivals, but the proselytization efforts of the Protestant missionaries and the seeming success of their work was applauded by one Canadian writer who noted that the only 'redeeming' feature of the otherwise undesirable people is their willingness to break away from Rome where the "leavens of western enlightenment were at work."[44] For a variety of reasons the Protestant missionary activities among the Polish newcomers abated after World War I and only the Jehovah's Witnesses still conduct campaigns, publishing religious tracts in Polish and urging them to 'see the light.'

Inroads into the Polish Roman Catholic group took yet another form. It is widely accepted that the most efficient means of maintaining the religious affiliation of an ethnic aggregate is through endogamy, or marriage to members of the same group sharing the same religion. Alternatively, exogamy is acceptable if the outsider is of the same faith. For the Polish people this was seldom possible. Until recently, the number of males was greater than that of females. Intermarriage with other ethnic groups was a necessity. Further, Polish people were not strongly opposed to exogamy, having intermarried with the Ukrainians and others in Poland for centuries. And the Polish immigrants and their descendants intermarried in Canada.

In 1941 51% of the Polish people married other Poles and a total of 19% married non-Catholics.[45] In 1951 the rates of exogamy, or marriage with non-Polish, were 44.3% for males and 43.3% for females. By 1961 the rates of exogamy had increased to 51% for males and 46.9% for females. There is no data on the rate of religious retention provided by this source for 1951 and 1961, but if the 1941 figures are accepted as an illustration, a great many Polish Roman Catholics leave their religion on marriage.[46]

The majority of the adherents of Polish descent in the various Protestant, Greek Orthodox, and Jewish[47] denominations have not maintained distinct or separate churches or synagogues, but there are some exceptions.

THE POLISH EVANGELICAL CHURCH

Very little is known about the Polish Lutherans in Canada, who numbered 9,425 persons according to the 1971 census. The adherents are dispersed and resort to the institutions of other ethnic groups or participate in the Canadian Lutheran congregations. There are two small Polish Lutheran congregations in Canada, determined to maintain their religious and cultural distinctiveness. Polish Lutherans at Inglis, Manitoba, established a separate church in 1905 and since 1911 have had a resident pastor. This congregation is still active but no other details are available at present.[48]

The second Polish Lutheran church was founded in Toronto in 1954 by about twenty-five families. The congregation experienced problems of financing and accommodation but has recently been sharing a building with a Slovak Lutheran church and is served by a Polish pastor who visits monthly from London, Ontario. The Polish Lutheran congregation in Toronto is a part of the Lutheran Synod of Missouri.

THE POLISH BAPTISTS

The first Polish Baptist church in North America was established in Buffalo, New York, in 1894 and a religious handbook in Polish was published in 1897 for the use of other Polish congregations.[49] In Canada a missionary Baptist church was established in Toronto in 1910 which served Polish and other Slavic people. The first exclusively Polish Baptist church was established in 1921. By 1930 there were two Polish Baptist congregations in Toronto, one in Hamilton, one in Brantford and missions in Kitchener and St. Catherines, all in Ontario. There was another Polish Baptist congregation in Winnipeg, Manitoba.[50]

All of these congregations were active in educating the Polish youth, and in conducting classes on religion, language, and music. The Baptist churches provided aid and advice to new Polish immigrants and the Toronto congregations published a monthly, *Głos Prawdy* (*Voice of Truth*), between 1923 and 1943. The Baptists' further development was retarded by the geographical mobility of their members and by an acute shortage of ministers. The congregations were numerically small, representing only a portion of the Polish Baptists in Canada. The majority were participating in non-Polish Baptist congregations. In the early 1940s the various congregations began to dissolve and the two congregations in Toronto amalgamated in 1944. The small number of adherents, combined with a number of socio-economic factors, precluded continuation of a distinct religious organization.

The Canadian census for 1971 shows 3,670 people of Polish descent claiming the Baptist denomination but today the Polish Baptist church in Toronto is the only surviving congregation. According to its spokesman[51]

156

the congregation represents about fifty Polish families and is led by a Polish resident pastor. The First Polish Baptist Church maintains a ladies' organization, and is concerned with the issues of Polish culture and identity as well as with other needs of people of Polish descent in Toronto. The pastor is actively involved in the Wawel Villa, a home for the Polish aged which is in advanced stages of planning. The church services and Sunday instruction in religion are in Polish and this poses problems, for members who marry non-Poles are usually lost to this congregation. The church is a member of the Polish Baptist Association of North America and the members subscribe to the journal *Przyjaciel* (*Friend*), published by this association in Polish.

THE PENTECOSTAL CHURCH

The 1971 Canadian census found 1,860 people of Polish descent claiming the Pentecostal denomination. The Full Gospel Tabernacle in Toronto is the only organization led by a Polish pastor and has, among other, Polish members, whose number varies between fifteen and twenty-five at any service.[52] New members are solicited through leaflet distribution, newspaper advertising and by 'word-of-mouth,' but the response has never been great and the membership from among the Polish people remains small.

The activities of this religious body centre around the pastor. A Polish immigrant to Canada in the 1920s, a devout Roman Catholic, a member of parish organizations, he became interested in the Pentecostal Church by attending tent revival meetings in Peterborough, Ontario, in 1930. His interest led him to further study of theology and he began his religious activities first in private homes, and for the last ten years in a tabernacle in Toronto. The tabernacle has four services weekly with worshippers coming from various parts of Metropolitan Toronto. Services and hymn singing are in Polish and in English. The pastor stresses 'faith healing' as an important part of the services. Church members are forbidden to drink alcoholic beverages or smoke. The membership is not limited to Polish people and the organization does not stress Polish cultural or traditional values.

THE POLISH NATIONAL CATHOLIC CHURCH

The Polish Roman Catholic parish established in Winnipeg in 1899 was soon plagued by internal problems. The Polish parishioners were not happy with their priest and requested a replacement or the establishment of another Polish parish. The bishop did not wish to split the congregation, which at that time included large numbers of non-Polish Roman Catholics, and there was no replacement easily available. Aware that the Polish Roman Catholic churches were well established and staffed in the United States, the Winnipeg parishioners sent a request there for a Polish priest. In 1904, one arrived and began to organize a separate Polish par-

157

ish. Much to the surprise of the Winnipeg parishioners, the priest was not a Roman Catholic but a member of an independent Catholic church, no longer acknowledging the authority of the Vatican. Because of the charismatic qualities of this priest[53] the dissident group of the Roman Catholic parishioners joined the newly established parish but still considered themselves Roman Catholics. They were automatically excommunicated anyway. Problems emerged in the new parish and the parishioners sent petitions to the bishop for readmittance to the Roman Catholic fold and for appointment of a Roman Catholic priest for their new parish. The bishop was uncompromising and the separate church remained. The independent parish continued with some success and in 1909 joined the Polish National Catholic Church (PNCC) of the United States, headed by Bishop Hodur, who appointed the first PNCC priest to the Winnipeg parish. The PNCC movement in Canada originated in Winnipeg but its sources were Polish American.

The numerous Polish immigrants to the United States, settling primarily in the northwestern cities, quickly established an extensive organizational network, with their own mutual aid societies, parishes and parish schools. A number of concerned and patriotic Polish priests soon became alarmed over relationships with the Episcopate and with the seemingly threatened future of the Polish parishes and schools. The issues stemmed from a number of factors. Firstly, the deeds to the church property acquired by the Polish immigrants were under the control of the bishop and this property could be transferred to other Roman Catholics for their use. This was alarming to the Polish immigrants who contributed much effort and money in acquiring or building their own institutions. The second issue revolved around the position of the Irish and German Roman Catholic hierarchy towards the maintenance and preservation of cultural distinctiveness in the United States. Under the ethos of 'Americanization' or 'Melting Pot,' the bishops discouraged the continual use of the Polish language, posed obstacles to Polish schools and generally stressed the goals of rapid assimilation. Lastly, concern among the Polish clergy grew because of a lack of representation of their nationals within the higher ranks of the Roman Catholic hierarchy in the United States. Many felt that they were discriminated against in favour of Irish, German, or Anglo-Saxon groups in appointments to bishoprics or other positions of responsibility.

Frequent appeals were made and the Vatican agreed to consider their concerns, but was slow to do so. Further appeals to the Vatican for the creation of an independent Polish Episcopate, subject directly to the Holy See, were strenuously opposed by the American bishops. Dissatisfaction and resentment among the Polish clergy and parishioners grew and in 1895 about 145 clerical and lay representatives and over 20,000 church members declared themselves independent of the authority of Vatican.[54] A number of independent parishes were established, Latin was replaced with Polish for all church liturgy, and rules were introduced which stipulated the full control of church property and income by the parishioners. Other changes in liturgy were introduced later and the priests were permitted to marry. One of the most active Polish priests in the independence movement was Rev. Hodur, who in 1897 established the Polish National Catholic Church, becoming its first bishop.

To return to Canada and the PNCC parish in Winnipeg, the possibilities of the independent church increasing its following and establishing new parishes in Canada were good, since control over church property and finances was attractive to the Polish immigrants and the use of vernacular appealed to the national sentiments of the newcomers. But the PNCC, even more than the Roman Catholic Church, suffered from a shortage of qualified priests and the parish remained static in its membership and activities. The parish experienced internal difficulties in the years 1913 to 1922 with the arrival of an ambitious priest[55] who, disappointed at not being made a bishop, broke away from the PNCC, founding a new organization, the Apostolic Catholic Polish Church, and was elected bishop by his parishioners.[56] The parish reverted back to the PNCC in 1922 and later the church extended its influence outside Winnipeg, establishing parishes in Brandon, Beausejour, and Libau in Manitoba and Mikado, Saskatchewan.

The establishment of the PNCC parish in Toronto in 1933 followed conflicts between the parishioners and their pastor at St. Stanislaus Polish Roman Catholic Church. From a number of accounts[57] the main difficulty stemmed from the personality of the pastor,[58] whose authoritarian attitude towards his charges combined with an undignified treatment of the simple working people led to confrontations, dissent, and conflicts. The accounts hold that the pastor did not brook any suggestions of sharing in the decisions on financial matters of the parish, the parishioners were not informed of the use made of their contributions, and many were referred to publicly as 'ignorant peasants' and rebuked from the pulpit for offering coppers at Sunday collections. Those who protested were labelled 'communists.' Delegations were sent to the bishop but the pastor was only replaced after a segment of the parishioners broke away. The dissenting group invited a PNCC biship from Buffalo, New York, to discuss the establishment of a PNCC parish and about fifty families joined the new organization. Other PNCC parishes in Ontario were established later in Hamilton in 1949, Oshawa in 1961, and Oakville in 1971. There is also one PNCC parish in Montreal, established in 1951. The total membership of this church in Canada is around 6000. The clergy consists of one bishop and five priests.

The PNCC is a viable and active organization maintaining a parish credit union and five part-time Polish-language schools. Each parish has its committees and ladies' religious organizations. Only the Winnipeg parish has a formal youth club. There are also three choirs which perform at times for the general public. The PNCC publishes a bi-monthly socio-religious bulletin in Polish. According to its spokesman[59] the PNCC has possibilities of establishing over twenty more parishes since the problems giving birth to the parish in Winnipeg and Toronto remain, but such growth is precluded through a lack of clergy and material resources. The PNCC bishop and the clergy are active in various functions of the Polish aggregate in Canada, and are invited to celebrations by various lay organizations. The Roman Catholic clergy waged polemical campaigns against this organization and its members until the 1950s, but at present there is a climate of mutual tolerance.

ROMAN CATHOLIC PARISHES

In spite of the ten PNCC parishes, the Lutherans, Baptists, and the Full Gospel Tabernacle, the fact remains that the people of Polish descent in Canada are still overwhelmingly Roman Catholic, and the religious organizational structure clearly illustrates their affiliation. Statistically, 70.9% or over 224,000 individuals were members of the Church in 1971. They maintain about 75 parishes and there are about 100 Polish Roman Catholic priests to serve those organizations.[60] A number of parishes in the larger urban centres have very large congregations. St. Casimir and St. Stanislaus in Toronto have about 4,000 and 2,000 families respectively, St. Stanislaus in Hamilton and Holy Mother of the Rosary in Edmonton well over 1000. Polish Roman Catholic parishes in Montreal, Ottawa, Brantford, Kitchener, Thunder Bay, Winnipeg, Regina, Vancouver, and other larger urban centres attract hundreds of families. Each parish is served by one or more Polish-speaking priests. Churches with resident priests celebrate a daily mass and from one to eight masses on Sundays depending on the size of the parish and its special needs. Even the largest exclusively Polish parishes celebrate at least one mass on Sunday in English for the younger generations who no longer speak Polish. Administration of the parishes and parishioners is well organized. Each head of the family is registered and all details such as address and other vital statistics noted. Envelopes for weekly donations are sent to each parishioner and a receipt is given for tax purposes.

Nearly all Polish parishes maintain church choirs of various age groups. Some of these choirs achieve high levels of quality and perform at various celebrations of the Polish community. Altar boys serve at the celebration of the mass. The parish committees of each church serve in an advisory capacity to the parish priest, and have charge of collections, seating, and other functions. A number of the larger parishes have auxiliary organizations for men, women and youth[61] and sponsor parish credit unions, and thirteen parishes conduct Polish-language and religious instruction schools.

The Polish Roman Catholic clergy in Canada has been represented in the higher echelons of the church hierarchy only once, during the years 1909 to 1918, by the Archbishop Joseph Weber, CR.[62] In the opinion of the Polish clergy a number of individuals from among its ranks have been and are qualified for appointment as auxiliary bishops but this is unlikely to take place in the near future. The Polish aggregate in Canada expressed on a number of occasions a wish for a Polish-Canadian bishop, sending petitions to the representative of the Vatican in Canada and to the Canadian Synod of Bishops, but thus far without success.

The clergy are concerned with religious matters, emphasizing Catechism and religious instruction for the younger generations and Catholic ethics for adults, and are also involved in wider social issues, helping the Polish newcomers with finding work or accommodation, advising them on their duties, rights and privileges. The clergy from Polish parishes in cities are also concerned with the maintenance of Polish culture and traditions. Polish priests visit the sick and the aged, and in Toronto and Edmonton there are priests assigned exclusively to minister to the needs of imates in prisons, hospital patients and residents in senior citizens' homes.

BELIEFS, VALUES AND TRADITIONS

The information on the development of Polish religious institutions and organizations, and the efforts to maintain Polish Roman Catholicism, is fragmentary at best. Sources concerned with religious issues of the Polish aggregate in Canada focus largely on the establishment and maintenance of churches and parishes, and on the activity of the clergy. Much information lies buried in parish records which contain vital statistics on baptisms, confirmations, communions, marriages and deaths. The numbers of parishioners is known but there are few details on the 'religiosity' of the faithful or the strength of their religious convictions. No one has yet studied in depth what traditional customs were maintained and have survived to the present, but there are suggestions and some evidence of changes in the relationships with clergy and in religious beliefs and practices.

As the number of Polish immigrants to Canada grew, Polish parishes were formed, chapels or churches built, and a number of Polish priests began their work. But the religious life, as it existed in Poland, could not be recreated fully in the new setting. Many religious holidays, observances and customs had to be abandoned and the whole complex of rituals and beliefs was, by necessity, modified or forgotten. It is likely that religious traditions and customs survived longer among the larger concentrations of rural settlers. One example of such a concentration is at Wilno, Ontario, where residents have retained the customs of greeting each other by the traditional 'Praised be Jesus Christ' with the response 'For ever and ever.'[63] In other areas this form of greeting was exchanged with a priest but quickly fell into disuse in other situations. The Kashubs also retained the custom of all-night prayers over the dead and some beliefs in the supernatural.[64]

Two Polish traditions that are known, liked, and practised by all members of the Polish community in Canada are the Christmas and Easter festivities. They play an extremely important role in the life of every Pole and are universally and continually adhered to even after all other traditions of the Old Country are lost and forgotten. Christmas, or more accurately Christmas Eve, is especially important; it usually unites scattered members of the family, and forces the forgiveness of differences and animosities among the family members by tradition and ritual bread-breaking. The festive supper consisting of traditional foods brings back memories of Poland, of relatives long deceased, of Polish cuisine and other customs. The wife must retain some knowledge of the Polish kitchen in order to prepare this supper. The carol singing, taking place after supper, reintroduces some Polish language to children who do not use it in other contexts. The widely practised gift exchange enforces a certain degree of obligation and maintenance of contacts among all family members. This ritual and traditional day concludes with the midnight Mass in which even non-practising individuals make an effort to participate.

Easter is celebrated by attending a morning Mass, when once again everyone makes an effort to be present, and when all practising Catholics are strongly urged by the Roman Catholic Church to go to confession and take Holy Communion. Following the Mass, there is a festive and elaborate breakfast consisting of various Polish sausages, hams, other cold meats, special breads, painted eggs, cakes and pastries. A small portion of every kind of food is taken to the church on the preceding Saturday to be blessed and this food is then shared and consumed by all members of the family, after which the rest of the breakfast is eaten, washed down with glasses of fruit juices for the younger members and wine or other alcoholic beverages for the adults.

Easter is festive, but the various traditions still observed in Poland during Easter Sunday and Easter Monday have now largely fallen into disuse. The two special occasions more than anything else may serve the function of maintaining family cohesion for some generations in the future.

A number of other religious festivals and holidays retain at least something of their traditional character. The veneration of the Virgin Mary and patron Madonnas retains its importance for a great many, as demonstrated by the annual pilgrimage to Midland, Ontario, in August to coincide with the celebrations of the Madonna at Częstochowa in Poland. This annual event draws pilgrims not only from Ontario but from other parts of Canada and from the United States as well. Special rosary services are celebrated and one of the most popular among parish organizations is a rosary society. Vespers remain a part of traditional Polish religious custom, the litanies and special May services regularly draw large numbers of worshippers. Polish hymns for all occasions, Lenten songs and carols are sung. Processions, if only within the confines of the church, are part of the traditional service on such feasts as Corpus Christi. On the other hand, most of the religious beliefs and practices permeated with traditional customs and folklore have largely disappeared. Christenings, funerals, marriage ceremonies and other festivities differ little from those generally observed in Canada. The Canadian-born generations find it increasingly hard to understand and relate to the traditional practices of their parents. There are other changes as well.

For lack of other studies we will once again resort to the findings of a small study[65] to illustrate the religiosity of one group of sixty Polish immigrant families. The study found that the vast majority of the post-war immigrants attend church on a regular basis and the Polish church is considered important to the extent that over 55% gave proximity to this institution as the most important reason for satisfaction with the area where they reside. At the same time even the regular church-goers no longer adhere to all teachings stressed by the Roman Catholic Church. Less than half of those questioned believed that a good Catholic should obey all teachings of the church; a significant number approved of artificial birth control methods, and over half saw divorce as the best solution in certain circumstances.[66] Such beliefs, if they were held or expressed thirty years back, would label the individual a heretic at best and would be sufficient to send a 'good, practising Catholic' to hell forever.

It was found that about one-quarter of regular church-goers never prayed before or after meals, even on special occasions such as Christmas and Easter. Only 55% sent their children to separate Roman Catholic schools because they believed that their children would learn higher moral standards than are taught in the public school system. Only 58% would strongly want their children to marry other Roman Catholics and nearly one-third were very disappointed with their own children's attitude towards the church, which is considered by the youth to be an institution with little meaning or importance in daily life. For the mature respondents the church and the clergy were no longer sacrosanct and a number of criticisms were levelled at both. Among the older generations church holidays and holy days were still known and observed, but the younger generation was far more familiar with such holidays as Dominion Day, Valentine's Day, or even St. Patrick's Day.

The findings of this study cannot be generalized; however, the trends towards greater secularization and the quest for relevance voiced by the youth today are universal and not limited to one or another group. The people of Polish descent in Canada are experiencing changes which are affecting other people. The Catholic church, with nearly 2000 years of history and experience, is aware of the changes in attitudes and beliefs and is coping with the changing situation. The spokesmen for the Polish religious institutions are confident that the Polish people in Canada will retain their attachment to the churches, the Polish clergy, and to religious values in the foreseeable future.

CONCLUDING OBSERVATIONS

In 1938 there were 172 Polish parishes and missions, served by seventy-five Polish priests, in a population of about 160,000 people of Polish descent in Canada. By 1973 the population had increased to over 316,000 while the number of parishes and missions had shrunk dramatically. In the larger urban centres, Polish parishes remain centres of social life, cultural activities, and education, and are "pivotal elements in Polish substructure within the general Canadian community."[67] In many other cases the parishes having Polish clergy are Polish in name only. They are composed of Roman Catholics of various ethnic backgrounds, and English is used more and more as the means of communication. Such 'Polish' parishes may celebrate a mass in Polish once each Sunday or even less frequently. The presence of a Polish-speaking priest assures the older Polish immigrants of confession in their own language. Certain services such as marriages, baptisms, and funerals are conducted in Polish and this may be the full extent of distinctiveness of such a Polish parish.

The geographical mobility of Polish immigrants in Canada is important in the 'anglicization' of previously Polish parishes. In 1941, 54.5% of the Polish ethnic group was found in the three Prairie provinces. It was in these provinces that the largest number of parishes and missions was established before 1939. By 1971 the three provinces represented only 36.3% of the total Polish ethnic group. More significantly, the rural population in 1941 was 50.7% of the total group;[68] by 1971 the rural group was only 19.5% of the total.[69] Beginning during World War II, people of Polish descent began to move East and to the cities, leaving behind their chapels and churches, which remain staffed by Polish clergy and retain their Polish names, but are used by other Roman Catholics.[70] The few remaining Polish parishioners have had to reconcile themselves to the fact that they are a minority and no special Mass can be said for them.

Christian churches generally complain of 'estrangement' and lack of meaningful communications with the youth, and this problem is accentuated in relationships between the Polish priests and the youth of Polish descent. Those born in Canada are no longer familiar with distinctly Polish religious traditions and customs and see little relevance in their continual practice. Speaking Polish inadequately, if at all, they attend English-language Mass, or else to go another church. For the young people the Polish church is serving the same role as other Canadian religious institutions and is not necessarily equated with Polish culture and traditions.

It cannot be ascertained how many of the seventy-five parishes in Canada remain distinctly Polish. A guess can be hazarded that no more than twenty fall into this category, as others are experiencing various stages of 'anglicization.' Should this trend continue it will have important implications for the Polish aggregate in Canada. Religion and Polish parishes provide a setting where different phases of immigration meet, linking generations and socio-economic classes. From among the whole organizational structure of the Polish aggregate in Canada, religious organizations are given the best chances of survival. The survival of Polish parishes is thus closely related to the maintenance of cultural distinctiveness for the Polish ethnic aggregate as a whole, and should these institutions be transformed in time into Canadian parishes the Polish aggregate will lose one of the main agencies assuring retention of Polish culture and tradition among the Canadian-born generations. The prognosis for the future is not optimistic.

NOTES

1. Barnett, pp. 64-8.
2. "Za Parę Pacierzy" (in so many prayers), a term of time measurement probably unique to the Polish people.
3. The best illustration of such practices and beliefs is to be found in Reymont's *Chłopi*. See Also Perkowski, *op. cit.*, and Wańkowicz, *op. cit.*
4. As noted by Wańkowicz, *ibid.*, among the few possessions brought over by a family, the district Madonna was most treasured.
5. Florian Znaniecki, "The Poles," in H.P. Fairchild, ed., *Immigrant Backgrounds* (New York, 1927).
6. A mission represented between 20 and 50 Polish families, with a chapel or a church, but without a resident priest. The area was considered too isolated from other Polish or other Roman Catholic families and thus unable to maintain a permanent priest.
7. See for example Głęborzecki, *op. cit.*; E. Hubicz, *The History of Our Lady of the Lake Church, Winnipeg Beach, Manitoba, 1911 to 1956* (Winnipeg, 1956), and *Father Joe*; Turek, *Poles in Manitoba*.
8. Hubicz, "Early Polish Priests."
9. Hubicz, *ibid.*, discusses the early pioneer priests in Manitoba.
10. Mazurkiewicz points out that the 22 missionary priests had a territory of many thousand square miles to travel and reach all the scattered settlers.
11. Kos-Rabcewicz-Zubkowski, *The Poles in Canada*.
12. Iwicki, p. 141. The Resurrectionists of the Ontario-Kentucky Province conduct four colleges in Canada, one high school, two novitiates and nine parishes, of which only three, in Kitchener, Hamiton, and Brantford, are Polish.
13. Głęborzecki, *op. cit.*; Makowski, *History and Integration*.
14. Breton, *op. cit.*; Jan Sajewicz, OMI, *Nasz Brat* (n.p., 1972).
15. Józef Pielorz, OMI, *Oblaci Polscy 1920-1970* (Rome, 1970); *Silver Jubilee, Oblate Fathers* (1960); Turek, *Poles in Manitoba*.
16. Hubicz, *Father Joe*.
17. What is now the largest parish credit union in Canada began through the efforts of Father S. Puchniak, OMI, in 1945.

18. *Silver Jubilee, Oblate Fathers* (1960).
19. Rev. Puchniak, in an interview with H. Radecki, August 29, 1973.
20. Gwara Śląska.
21. Turek, *Poles in Canada*, p. 166, terms this generosity "astonishing."
22. Paraphrased from Hubicz, *Father Joe*, p. 84.
23. The reputation of the Oblates as a 'foreign' or 'German Order' persisted, without justification, into the 1930s. See Jacek Rolnik, "Wycinanki Prasowe," *Związkowiec*, No. 8 (Toronto, 1935).
24. The association Sokofs, established in Winnipeg in 1906, illustrates well such an organization.
25. See pages 69-71 of this study.
26. Turek, *Poles in Manitoba*, p. 167.
27. Mazurkiewicz, *op. cit.*
28. K. Buchwald, OMI, "25-Lecie Stowarzyszenia Polaków Manitoby," *Czas*, October 25, 1959.
29. See for example L.O., *Polskie Duchowieństwo w Amercye – Jego Zasługi, Patriotyzm i Moralność* (Toledo, Ohio, n.d.). The publishing firm of A.A. Paryski in Toledo, Ohio, issued anti-clerical material.
30. Details of these conflicts can be found in the files of *Gazeta Katolicka, Głos Pracy*, and *Związkowiec*, and this task awaits further research.
31. With the exception of the Polish Democratic Association, which is shunned by all other organizations and institutions.
32. The activities of the Oblates have been documented in a number of sources: Makowski, *History and Integration*, Pielorz, *op. cit; Silver Jubilee, Oblate Fathers*, 1960; Turek, *Poles in Manitoba*, Złote Pokłosie Parafii Św. Stanisława Kostki, Toronto, 1911-1961 (Toronto 1961), and are the subject of a forthcoming in-depth historical study by Rev. Puchniak, OMI.
33. See Turek, *The Polish Language Press*, pp. 100 *et passim*, for further details.
34. Yars Slavutych, "Slavic Literature in Canada," *Slavs in Canada*, Vol. I, Proceedings of the First Conference on Canadian Slavs, June 9-12, Banff, Alberta (Edmonton, 1966).
35. Pielorz, *op. cit.*
36. *Archives*, Mother House (1937-1973).
37. Among other activities, the Felician Sisters in Toronto teach in all-Polish parish schools, run a nursery, conduct two school choirs, distribute Christmas wafers to parishioners of the St. Stanislaus parish and annually have an Open House at their convent for all parishioners, attracting hundreds of families to this event.
38. See, for example, Buchwald, *op. cit.*
39. A search through various archives discovered only one small booklet containing prayers for the dying and at funerals where a priest was not available. See *Trzy Prześliczne i Bardzo Skuteczne Modlitwy Przy Umierającym* (n.p.,n.d.), probably published at the turn of this century in Galicia.

40. With one exception which will be discussed later, there is no evidence to suggest that any have established separate Polish churches or congregations.
41. It is also certain that some changed their religious affiliation for convenience, expediency, or else through social or economic pressure. An example is Sir Casimir Gzowski, who became an Anglican after coming to Canada.
42. Rev. Boniface, p. 49.
43. Hubicz, *The History of Our Lady*, p. 20.
44. Woodsworth, p. 141. The leavens referred to the Protestant missionaries.
45. *Report of the Royal Commission*, Book IV, *op. cit.*, Table A61, p. 300.
46. *Ibid.*, Tables A61, A62, p. 291.
47. There were 27,204 Jews, or 8.4% of the total Polish ethnic group, in 1961, but the 1971 Canadian census failed to record any Jews claiming membership in the Polish aggregate. The disappearance of this group from the Polish ethnic category awaits further explanation.
48. Even Turek, *Poles in Manitoba*, provides few details of this congregation in his thoroughly researched study.
49. Rev. T.W. Jakimowicz, *Podręczniki Dla Użytku Polsko-Baptyjskiego Kościoła* (Buffalo, 1897).
50. Lubicz, *op. cit.*
51. Rev. A. Pashko in private correspondence with H. Radecki, November, 1973.
52. The information is based on a telephone interview with Pastor F. Berezowski by H. Radecki, November, 1973.
53. Rev. W. Blazowski. For further details see Turek, *Poles in Manitoba*, pp. 178-9.
54. Helena Lopata, "The Function of Voluntary Association in an Ethnic Community: 'Polonia'" in E.W. Burgess and D.J. Bogue, eds., *Contributions to Urban sociology* (Chicago, 1964); Wytrwal, *op. cit.*
55. Rev. A. Markiewicz.
56. This church ceased to be active in 1949.
57. *Echo; Dwumiesięcznik* (No. 1-4, Vol. 5, 1973).
58. Rev. Col. Dekowski.
59. Rt. Rev. Bishop Niemiński in an interview with B. Heydenkorn, August, 1973.
60. The figures are provided by Rev. Capiga, the chairman of the Conference of the Polish Roman Catholic Priests in Eastern Canada.
61. The St. Stanislaus parish in Toronto has the following religious organizations: Towarzystwo Żywego Różańca (Living Rosary), Towarzystwo Imienia Jezus (Holy Name), Trzeci Zakon (Terciaries), Sodalicja Mariańska (Marian Sodality), two church choirs and altar boys.
62. Archbishop J. Weber (1845-1918) was consecrated Auxiliary Bishop of Lwów, Poland, in 1895 and was appointed Archbishop in 1904. He

arrived in Canada on February 10, 1909, to assume the duties of Novitiate Master in the Resurrectionist Novitiate in Kitchener, Ontario. See Iwicki, *op, cit.*, pp. 172, 261. It was noted in *Złote Pokłosie* that Archbishop Weber officiated at the opening of the first Polish church in Toronto in 1911.

63. Głęborzecki, *op. cit.*
64. Perkowski, *op. cit.*
65. Radecki, "POLISH-Canadian."
66. The 1971 census found 3,800 (1.2%) divorced individuals in the Polish ethnic group in Canada.
67. Turek, *Poles in Manitoba,* p. 183.
68. R. Kogler, "A Demographic Profile," Table 3, p. 16.
69. Census of Canada, 1971.
70. Rev. M. Szwej, "Cząstka Polskiej Całoséi," *Związkowiec* (Toronto), No. 14, February 20, 1973, provides a good example from Krydor, Saskatchewan, of this very process.

NINE

Work and Occupational Mobility

They were good for Canada, Canada was also good for them.

Report CR-2 (1961)

Thus far we have dealt with a number of topics relating to the experiences of all Polish immigrants and their descendants in Canada. Another such topics includes work, occupations and economic mobility. While this study has previously raised issues of work and related conditions to some extent, further elaboration will now be undertaken, and occupational mobility and work conditions will be discussed.

An overwhelming majority of Polish immigrants to Canada before 1939 came in search of land, employment and economic improvement. They were the type of people that Canada wanted; strong, healthy, in the prime of life, willing to claim the land or work on it, or to perform any physical labour in mines, forests, factories and on roads or railways. Canada did not solicit tradesmen or professionals but farmers, farm workers, and domestics. These were the categories of immigrants recruited by the shipping company agents. After 1926 the Canadian consular inspectors in Poland subjected applicants to a visual inspection to determine if they 'looked like farmers' and examined their hands for signs of physical toil.[1] Others were not barred but they were never encouraged. The only professional people that accompanied the large numbers of peasants and manual workers were a small number of Polish priests.

Poor to begin with, the Poles brought few material resources with them. Many did not even have the $25.00 per family demanded as proof of solvency by the Canadian immigration officials.[2] But they did possess physical endurance or what was often termed 'strong backs.' They came willing to undertake any work, under any condition, and they were determined to succeed. They were thrifty, or perhaps more accurately they were extremely careful with their money, food, and other possessions, for a 'bad year' could mean privation and suffering. They were able to 'make do' on very little, to sacrifice for the future, to postpone gratification and minimize considerations of comfort for their families and themselves. These resources served them well during the first years of their life in Canada or during the economic crises. In Canada, the new arrivals were directed to the western provinces where some claimed their homesteads and settled on land. Many others remained in towns and cities, or moved to other parts of Canada and worked at whatever was available and most rewarding.

SETTLERS

It is said that if a farmer is given land in sufficient quantity, he will proceed to cultivate it, feeding not only his family but others as well. This is true to some extent, but each geographical environment and each society poses a number of challenges to a newcomer which have to be mastered before work on land can begin: different soil and climatic conditions, suitable seed, and proper farming techniques. In time these obstacles were mastered by the Polish immigrants who learned by working for others, from advice, or by bitter experience.

The earliest arrivals from Poland were able to select land suitable for immediate ploughing, close to towns and to means of communication and transportation. Others, less fortunate or less wise in their choice, settled on marginal or less suitable land, but all had their 160 acres or more and immediately became unbelievably rich. No peasant in Poland could boast of having so much land. No matter that it was virgin land, only forest perhaps. It was or would soon be theirs completely. The forests would be cleared, the wood used for buildings and fences or sold for cash, and the soil would be broken. No matter that the only food was a bag of flour and a sack of potatoes, and the only farm implements they possessed were a spade, an axe, and a scythe. Established neighbours and the government helped with food[3] during the first two or three winters.

The whole family pitched in. The men built shelters for the first winter and cleared some land for vegetables. When nothing else could be done they left their wives and children for a time and went in search of work. Any work – clearing the bush, working on the railroad, performing odd jobs – and every cent possible was saved towards the seed, a plough and a pair of oxen. Their situation improved slowly. More land was cleared and ploughed, the oxen were replaced by a team of horses, a cow or two were purchased. In time, the wife had some pigs and chickens to look after as well. The farmer had less and less time, or need, to hire himself out for seasonal work, devoting all his efforts and attention to his own land. The wives worked as hard as their husbands, looking after the family, the livestock, and the garden, selling whatever they could to supplement the family savings.

Inevitably, there were failures and disappointments. Some found the conditions too harsh, found nature with its mosquitoes, grasshoppers, and severe winters too hostile, and abandoned their land. But most remained. Within a few years the first shelter, the log cabin or mud shack, was replaced by a larger home, farm equipment and more livestock were purchased and the poor landless peasants or petty farmers were proud possessors of a large piece of producing land, with bright hopes for the future.

Those who were determined and enjoyed some luck survived the first few years under adverse conditions and soon began to prosper. The demand for Canadian wheat on the world market was growing and the prices reflected its popularity. In 1908, a bushel of wheat sold for eighty cents; in 1909 the price increased to ninety-five cents. World War I was a period of great prosperity for the western farmers as well as the Polish settlers who had established themselves by 1914, and all reaped the rewards. In 1914, a bushel of wheat sold for $1.15, it jumped to $2.10 in 1916 and there were further price increases in 1917. By 1918, a bushel of first grade Canadian wheat fetched $2.35, an unbelievable price at that time. The prices fell drastically again to eighty cents a bushel in 1921 but by that time most debts were paid off, new and better farm implements were purchased and the farmers had some savings in the bank. The years of toil and hardship were not in vain. By the mid-1920s Polish immigrants owned nearly 4,000 farms worth over $27,000,000 with total yearly incomes of nearly seven million dollars.[4]

This success may be explained by a number of factors. The families were large as a rule, and it was customary for all to have duties and responsibilities with the livestock, farm implements, land or the house. Noting that little children worked, Canadian social activists accused their parents of exploitation, but in reality they did not overburden their children. The fathers were not satisfied to remain on their own land but sought work during winter months among the established farmers or elsewhere. By working for others they learned not only the best techniques, methods and conditions of farming but also the language and Canadian values and standards. The farmers saw little value in higher education for their children and at the age of fifteen sons and daughters became full working members of the family farm, or else were sent out to find work elsewhere to supplement the family earnings. The pride of owning so much land provided the necessary motivation for all struggles. And finally the popular saying that "behind every successful man stands a woman" is certainly applicable to the Polish immigrants whose wives contributed numerous skills, physical help, and money saved through sale of vegetables, dairy products, and such.

Of all Polish immigrants who came to Canada prior to 1929 the Great Depression affected the established farmers the least. They had shelter and food and some income from their grain and livestock, and their accrued savings helped out as well. As with other Canadian farmers, a number of the Poles could not survive the long economic crisis, but had to abandon or sell their farms and move to towns and cities in search of better conditions. The trend, established on a small scale in the late 1930s, continued

TABLE 10

FARMS OWNED BY POLISH IMMIGRANTS – 1926

	No. of Farms	Cultivated Acres	Worth of Farms	Yearly Income
Manitoba	1,642	272,611	8,800,000	1,950,000
Saskatchewan	1,337	492,665	11,800,000	3,300,000
Alberta	994	258,247	6,600,000	1,600,000
Total	3,973	1,023,523	$27,200,000	$6,850,000

From R. Mazurkiewicz, *op. cit.*, p. 44.

TABLE 11

SIZE OF POLISH FARMS IN THE THREE WESTERN PROVINCES IN 1926

	Manitoba		Saskatchewan		Alberta	
	#	%	#	%	#	%
Under 51 acres	284	17.3	12	0.9	28	2.8
51 to 160 "	969	59.0	482	35.1	522	52.5
161 to 320 "	286	17.4	438	31.9	278	28.0
321 to 480 "	69	4.2	204	14.9	92	9.3
481 to 640 "	22	1.3	149	10.8	48	4.8
Over 641 "	13	0.8	88	6.4	26	2.6

From R. Mazurkiewicz, *ibid.*, pp. 38, 41.

during World War II and the number of people of Polish descent engaged in agriculture decreased steadily.

The 1941 Canadian census found 50.7% of the Polish ethnic group in rural areas (both farm and non-farm), and the corresponding percentages for the 1951 and 1961 censuses were 37.0% and 24.0% respectively.[5] The 1971 census registered a further decrease to 19.5% of the total group. Further, of the 61,740 rural residents, only 27,880 or 8.8% of the total were in fact farmers.[6]

It is likely that their economic position differs little from that of other farmers within the provinces where they reside. In 1971 there were only ninety-five members of the Polish ethnic group listed as farmers in all of the Maritime provinces, 165 in Quebec, 4,695 in Ontario, 6,225 in Manitoba, 7,800 in Saskatchewan, 7,840 in Alberta, and 1,055 in British Columbia.[7]

THE WORKERS

Polish immigration to Canada, which began in 1895, went in two directions in almost equal numbers up to 1939.[8] The land seekers claimed their homesteads, or remained in towns and cities only long enough to save some money for equipment and livestock and then claimed or purchased their farm. Other people came in search of non-agricultural work and money.

The latter group came expecting the going rate of pay, little realizing that they were not average workers by Canadian standards. They were hard-working and willing but they did not speak English and were unfamiliar with Canadian methods and techniques. Their occupations and remuneration reflected their shortcomings. They were generally welcomed by the Canadian employers as a source of steady, reliable, and cheap labour. They were inarticulate and thus could not make many demands, and their rates of absenteeism were extremely low. Willing to take any work, the Poles formed "a part of every construction gang, engaged in road-making, street paving, excavating and other forms of manual labour."[9] The former farmers and farm workers turned to work in mines, factories and lumber camps.

Few jobs lasted more than one season. Projects were completed and all workers were dismissed. Then there were the winter layoffs. Unaware of conditions, not conversant with the language, they were susceptible to rumours and exaggerated claims of 'better' work elsewhere. For the men without families the life was frequently one of constant travel in search of better conditions or more pay. The movement was not limited to one area or one province. Individuals traversed Canada from British Columbia to Nova Scotia in search of economic security or improvement. By the mid-1920s Poles could be found in every community where an industry was present or a natural resource was being extracted.[10]

The remuneration for the type of work available to them was not designed to make them rich quickly. Before 1914, the new arrivals who contracted to work for a farmer received between $250 and $300 yearly with their food and accommodation. During the harvest a man working from sunrise to sunset could earn between $3.50 and $5.00 a day, depending on his previous experience. In the factories the hourly wages were between twenty-five and forty cents. In steel mills the worker earned between $4.00 and $5.00 for a shift of eleven or twelve hours. Railroads paid their workers between thirty and forty cents hourly and men were paid from $1.75 to $2.15 for ten hours of clearing stumps or cutting wood. Various other types of work applied pay scales wherein a tradesman was worth about seventy cents hourly, unqualified labourers received between thirty and forty cents, and the new arrivals, the 'greenhorns,' were only worth twenty-five cents. Miners could earn between $5.00 and $7.00 daily and even more on a rate system, but this was dangerous work where the rate of injuries and fatalities was very high. Even here some concerns, especially the coal mines, frequently reduced their productivity in winter months and the miners could only count on a three-day work week. Despite the fact that most were inured to hard and demanding work in Poland, the jobs they found in Canada were beyond the physical capabilities of many. The former farmers and farm workers were especially affected by the strange conditions, by the pace of work, the unfamiliar instructions and demands. From the open fields and fresh air, the Poles found damp, dark, and often poisonous mine shafts and corridors, the heat of blast furnaces, or the noise of a busy factory. Some returned to Poland, other sought less rewarding but bearable types of work. The majority persisted.

A portrayal of the economic position of the Polish immigrants who entered non-agricultural occupations prior to 1939 contains a number of interesting and strange developments. While they were exploited economically, when working steadily the wages they received in Canada were sums that they could never have dreamed of earning if they had remained in Poland. The harsh and demanding conditions, decried by the trade unions and concerned individuals, were not greatly different from those under which they had toiled in the Old Country. Canada offered a range of opportunities for all new arrivals but the Polish newcomers were not able or willing to meet the conditions which would improve their economic status and earning power. Better and more permanent work was available, but such work required a working knowledge of English, and few realized the importance of fluency in the language.

The pervasive opinion was that if workers were needed language was unimportant. Those coming with intentions of returning deemed it unnecessary and burdensome. Others, working with fellow Poles or other Slavs, saw no need to speak anything but their own language.[11] There was also a rather negative attitude towards learning a language in night or part-time schools[12] for fear of ridicule, derision, or laughter from their fellow immigrants, where it was popular to refer to those who took this step as "little children going back to school." Their attitude towards formal education has been already discussed but it can be re-emphasized that very few realized the value of education as a prerequisite to higher occupations and more rewarding work for themselves and for their children.

Naive or unaware of Canadian conditions and terms of work, they were open to abuse and exploitation by unscrupulous agents, entrepreneurs, and at times by their own countrymen. Their memoirs note that it became accepted to buy work from agents, and to insure continual employment by bribing the foremen or supervisors with gifts, drinks or money. In time this became a widely practised custom, probably introduced by immigrants themselves, anxious to find steady employment.[13] One source notes that in the late 1920s work was available in Windsor, Ontario, paying forty-five cents hourly (both unusual occurrences) but newcomers were warned that "half of the earnings had to be spent drinking with a foreman to avoid difficulties."[14] In Windsor employment agents charged a commission of between $50 and $75 for finding work in factories. During periods of economic prosperity contractors were able to withhold their wages for months to prevent them from leaving for better paying work, especially at the harvest.

Like many "non-preferred" immigrant groups, they were subject to a variety of socio-economic conditions in Canada. In 1914, those who came from the Austrian or German parts of Poland and were not yet Canadian citizens were dismissed from their jobs as enemy aliens. The wartime conditions and demands for all the available manpower necessitated a reluctant acceptance of aliens[15] but with the cessation of hostilities and the return of Canadian soldiers from Europe, large scale dismissal of the foreign workers took place in 1919 and 1920.

The Canadian economy was always plagued by seasonal changes. The unemployment rate in winter months was two or three times as high as in August. The Polish immigrants were especially susceptible to seasonal fluctuations in employment. Work in mines and factories was frequently reduced, building and road construction ceased altogether, and there was little work on farms in winter months. Without skills and trades it was not easy to find any type of work at that time.

They learned quickly that savings were the most important and best means of insurance, and every earned dollar meant better chances of survival through periods of unemployment. Those who came before 1914 and soon after the cessation of World War I generally fared well. The economic crises were short-lived and the war effort created an intensified demand for labour. Working for wages unacceptable to an average Canadian, they managed to save substantial sums of money.

One of the first concerns of practically every immigrant from Poland to Canada before 1939 was to pay off debts which were incurred when obtaining passage money or when taking out mortgages on land back home.[16] One example illustrates the thrift of the new arrivals. A son, sent to Canada to help his parents, earned over $100 working at harvesting in his first six weeks in Canada. He sent the whole sum to his parents in Poland to pay a part of the family debt. Contracting to remain with a farmer for two years at $50 a month in summer and $10 in winter, he was able to save $800 in this period. His yearly expenses were $70 for clothing and another $20 for such luxuries as tobacco and postage stamps.[17] Thrift characterized not only the Poles but all Slavic immigrants, and their savings allowed most of them to survive the economic crises of 1929-1939 comparatively well.

The Polish immigrants arriving after 1925 had barely managed to establish themselves when the economic crisis ended or postponed all their plans and hopes. Those coming to Canada in the years 1918 to 1939 experienced the greatest problems of economic insecurity. Memoir writers complained that the foremen and supervisors treated them like animals. On gangs and in factories men were fired for stopping to light a cigarette

175

or talking to fellow workers. Labour was plentiful and dozens were ready to fill any vacancy. At the time of economic crisis, even qualified tradesmen could not obtain work in their own fields, but had better chances of getting some kind of work than the unskilled new arrivals. The single men were often in dire straits for there was little work and no welfare was available to them.[18]

A very small number of Polish immigrants were union members, and the Canadian trade unions were not sympathetic towards their plight. The unions saw immigrants as a threat to the prevailing wage rates in their willingness to undertake any work, under any conditions and with minimal remuneration. At best, they represented competition for the Canadian workers. The trade unions seldom encouraged immigrants to join their ranks, and there were no attempts to create a united front of native Canadians and immigrants in demands for better conditions and wages. The antipathy continued for many decades and survives to some extent to the present, where the unskilled immigrant labourer is considered a threat to the Canadian worker.[19]

The professional and trade associations have also maintained barriers, precluding an easy acceptance of immigrants into their fields of speciality. Each provincial professional and trade organization regulates the entry of new members by licences to practise. The rules are not uniform across Canada, but generally the professional, technical, or trade status of the Polish-trained doctors, dentists, pharmacists, architects, electricians, carpenters, plumbers, sheet metal workers, and many others are not recognized by certain provincial professional and trade associations. In a number of occupations, further training or examination is a condition of acceptance and licensing to practise in Canada. In others, training obtained abroad is of little use in Canada. This especially affected Polish lawyers, career officers, and some teachers.

World War II once again created a demand for all categories of workers and the Polish immigrants were by that time more experienced and fluent in the English language. Much of the heavy manual labour was performed by machines, and the ditch diggers and casual labourers moved into steady and remunerative work in factories and other occupations. Their children, born and educated in Canada, joined the Canadian armed forces[20] or entered the Canadian economic structure according to their educational or professional qualifications.

The post-war immigrants generally began on the lowest occupational levels of the Canadian society, but their background and qualifications allowed them to seek better and more rewarding jobs within few years of their arrival. A comparatively small number acquired their own farms or remained on the land. The vast majority joined the crafts and production occupations, while a significant number established their own concerns, or entered into professional or technical fields.[21] The occupational distribution of the Polish group in Canada in 1971, shown in Table 12, is

contrasted with the occupational composition of the groups in the last three decades.
Table 13 shows that people of Polish descent in Canada are now represented in most of the major occupational categories.[22]

SOCIAL MOBILITY

All available historical sources suggest that the vast majority of Polish immigrants to Canada before 1939 were from the rural, agricultural part of Polish society and from the lower socio-economic classes. The earlier phases of immigration were composed of a significant proportion of illiterate or poorly educated people. They came penniless and with few skills in demand by the Canadian economic structures. They arrived with definite ideas of achievement, which was measured in terms of ownership of land or a city house, and regular, remunerative work in some economic enterprise. They did not come with images of becoming managers, estate owners, bankers, or even white collar workers. It would be sufficient if they could provide well for their families and assure some comfort for their years of retirement.

For the peasants and their children, opportunities for socio-economic mobility were extremely limited in pre-1939 Poland, and a father's greatest hope was to see one of his sons becoming a teacher or a priest. It is not surprising that upward socio-economic mobility was slow, and very few individuals achieved prominence in the business or financial spheres for many years after coming to Canada.[23] They came without the traditions or the experience of having their children move to better and higher positions, and the middle class of recognizably Polish origin grew but slowly. A number of individuals of the first phase did achieve prominent positions in Canada.[24] One Canadian writer proudly portrays the achievements of an individual who came as a young boy to Canada from Poland, was first enrolled in a Canadian school at the age of 14, enrolling later in a university, becoming a respectable teacher in Canadian schools.[25] The same writer found that "in the western cities there are prominent lawyers, doctors, and educators whose parents were born in Austrian Poland."[26]

Scattered and brief references in various sources indicate that a proportion, albeit a small one, of the children of Polish immigrants were enrolled in Canadian universities and a larger number completed high school, becoming eligible to enter middle class occupations. Except for few individuals[27] they disappeared as members of the Polish aggregate either by emigrating from Canada or by anglicizing[28] their names and moving away from the concentrations of the Polish immigrants. This was a necessary step for the ambitious and qualified individuals since the economic positions and chances for upward socio-economic mobility were for decades the functions of "being a member of Masonic Order, not being a Roman Catholic, having an ethnic background largely Anglo-Saxon or

TABLE 12

OCCUPATIONAL COMPOSITION OF THE POLISH MALE AND FEMALE LABOUR FORCE – 1971

Occupational Category	Polish Group – Number				Total Canadian Labour Force – Number			
	Male	%	Female	%	Male	%	Female	%
All Occupations	95,770	100.0	52,510	100.0	5,665,715	100.0	2,961,210	100.0
Managerial, Administrative and Related	3,375	3.52	750	1.42	313,935	5.54	58,305	1.97
Natural Sciences, Engineering, Mathematics	4,395	4.59	425	0.80	217,025	3.83	17,905	0.60
Social Sciences & Related	510	0.53	475	0.90	49,525	0.87	29,525	0.99
Occupations in Religion	180	0.19	40	0.07	19,880	0.35	3,710	0.12
Teaching and Related	1,805	1.88	2,585	4.92	138,170	2.44	211,125	7.13
Medicine and Health	1,170	1.22	3,555	6.77	83,865	1.48	242,690	8.20
Artistic, Literary, Recr.	750	0.79	290	0.55	58,585	1.03	21,895	0.74
Clerical and Related	6,190	6.46	14,905	28.38	433,380	7.65	940,180	31.75
Sales Occupations	6,740	7.04	4,010	7.63	567,985	10.02	247,760	8.37
Service Occupations	8,955	9.35	10,385	19.78	521,935	9.21	447,985	15.13
Farming, Farm Management	8,675	9.05	3,185	6.06	405,305	7.15	106,845	3.61
Fishing, Hunting, Trapping	50	0.05	5	–	26,655	0.47	525	0.01
Forestry and Logging	715	0.75	20	–	65,850	1.16	1,415	0.04
Mining and Quarring	1,620	1.69	10	–	58,780	1.03	380	–
Processing Occupations	5,810	6.07	1,260	2.40	275,180	4.86	59,565	2.01
Machining and Related	5,775	6.03	320	0.61	227,260	4.01	13,675	0.46
Product Fabricating, etc.	9,830	10.26	3,310	6.30	484,145	8.54	150,210	5.07
Construction Trades	9,815	10.25	110	0.21	563,440	9.94	5,130	0.17
Transportation	4,105	4.28	110	0.21	330,240	5.83	8,190	0.27
Material Handling	3,330	3.47	935	1.78	165,390	2.92	40,450	1.37
Other Crafts, etc.	1,320	1.38	210	0.40	95,390	1.68	13,540	0.46
Other Occupations	3,085	3.22	456	0.87	145,900	2.57	21,730	0.73
Occupation not stated	7,570	7.90	5,245	10.08	418,000	7.38	319,275	10.78

Source: Radecki, Table 2.9.

TABLE 13

OCCUPATIONAL COMPOSITION OF THE POLISH MALE LABOUR FORCE – YEARS 1941, 1951, 1961

Occupational Category	1941			1951			1961		
	Number	% of Polish Canadian Total	% of Canadian Category	Number	% of Polish Canadian Total	% of Canadian Category	Number	% of Polish Canadian Total	% of Canadian Category
All Occupations	54,846	100.0	1.63	78,780	100.0	1.9	96,100	100.0	2.0
Agriculture	20,547	37.4	1.92	18,434	23.4	2.3	13,466	14.0	2.3
Fishing, Hunting, Trapping	129	0.2	0.2	103	0.1	0.2	86	0.1	0.2
Logging	1,122	2.0	1.4	1,386	1.7	1.4	966	1.0	1.2
Mining and Quarrying	2,709	4.9	3.8	2,853	3.6	4.4	2,369	2.5	3.7
Labourers	6,957	12.7	2.8	10,047	12.7	3.0	7,240	7.5	2.5
Construction	2,702	4.9	1.3	5,635	7.1	1.9	Not available		
Manufacturing	10,864	19.1	1.9	17,162	21.8	2.5	33,695	35.1	2.5
Service	2,948	5.4	1.5	4,422	5.6	1.6	7,011	7.3	1.7
Clerical	864	1.6	0.5	2,553	3.2	1.0	4,962	5.1	1.5
Financing	65	0.1	0.2	233	0.3	0.7	Not available		
Professional	103	0.1	0.1	2,082	2.6	1.0	6,458	6.7	1.8
Managerial	Not available			4,433	5.6	1.2	8,813	9.1	1.8

Modified from Isajiw and Hartmann, Tables I, II, III, pp.106-9.

Germanic."[29] Changing one's family name and religion was a major decision, but there is evidence that many did so in order to be more 'acceptable' or to be less 'strange' and 'different.'[30] To the extent that they no longer identified themselves as members of the Polish aggregate it is difficult to include them in discussing the emergence of a middle class in Canada.

The establishment of enterprises by Polish immigrants in Canada had auspicious beginnings. By 1788, Globenski started an apothecary store in St. Eustache, Quebec, and two years later received a licence to practise medicine, becoming the first Polish doctor in Canada. The next enterprise was established by Gzowski in 1853 (Gzowski and Company, Canadian Contrators), the firm that built the railway from Toronto to Guelph, Ontario. Gzowski also headed the Toronto Rolling Mills and was involved in a number of other business enterprises.

The succeeding phases were not able to follow in the footsteps of those two predecessors for some time. In Winnipeg, which contained the largest concentration of Polish immigrants well into the 1930s, the growth of any business concerns was slow. A shoe repair store was opened in 1850, two grocery stores in 1880, a forge in 1904, and another shoe repair store in 1905.[31] In Saskatchewan the first store, a grocery, was opened with a capital of $34 in 1907. In Alberta the first store was probably opened in 1908. In British Columbia the first enterprise, a carpentry shop, was opened in 1907.[32] Beginnings were slow in Ontario as well. The first business enterprise is considered to be a jewellery store which was opened in . Toronto in 1906 but it is likely that the Polish groups in Wilno-Barry's Bay area, and in Berlin, Ontario, had established some business concerns before 1906. In Toronto, a tailor shop followed in 1910, a bicycle store in 1913, a bakery in 1915, and a mattress factory in 1919.[33] In Hamilton, Ontario, there were food stores by 1913 as well as a movie theatre, a winery, and a hotel owned by Poles. In Montreal, where the main concentration of Polish immigrants in the Province of Quebec was to be found, entrepreneurship was more active. In 1915 there were twenty-eight business concerns run or owned by Polish individuals. These were small restaurants, groceries, travel, real estate, and insurance agencies, two bakeries, billiard halls, and other small service concerns. There was also a branch of the Galician Financial Company of Canada with a capital of $50,000.[34]

There were grocery stores, repair shops, small restaurants, 'general' stores and a few small manufacturing concerns in other towns and cities where such enterprises could rely on the support of Polish and other Slavic immigrants. Another type of business enterprise which allowed the owners substantial profit was the boarding houses. Most were crowded, with low standards of hygiene, and some of the owners or managers became widely known to social workers for their callous concern with money to the detriment of care for their boarders.[35] The total number of all such enterprises was small until 1920, but with the influx of new arrivals from Poland, the numbers grew steadily and by 1934 there were about 1,000 small businesses run by Polish immigrants, with largest numbers in Winnipeg and Toronto. Few achieved significant economic prosperity. There are only two known cases of Polish immigrants becoming millionaires before 1939. The owner of the Sisco Mine in Amos, Quebec, was one of them,[36] the other, a contractor of steel and concrete building materials.[37] Other sources report a Polish colliery near Edmonton whose owners were two Polish immigrants,[38] and a successful meat packing plant in Kitchener, Ontario.[39]

The enterprises were generally small and the rates of failure or bankruptcy were high. The Poles had little previous experience in business and even when a venture was successful those who saved extra capital had little business acumen to undertake growth or expansion. An awareness of these problems led to the establishment of Polish businessmen's associations, first in Hamilton in 1928, later in Toronto in 1932 and Winnipeg in 1933. The aim of these associations was to strengthen their members by providing mutual aid, contact, information and advice.

The socio-economic conditions in Canada prior to 1940 did not allow the majority of Polish immigrants and their descendants to attain the levels of prosperity enjoyed by the Canadian population at large. During the economic crisis of 1929-1939 some just managed to hold on to menial and low paying jobs; many were unemployed for months and years. Only those who achieved economic stability or even relative prosperity by 1929 were able to cope with the economic problems. These were generally the established farmers. Even after 1940 the Polish elite was mainly comprised of small business owners and the more successful farmers. They were missing in trade unions, civic service, and all levels of government. There were few professionals and white collar workers.

In 1941, Canada welcomed a number of Polish scientists, technicians, engineers, and skilled tradesmen, and their arrival was felt almost immediately. Polish scientists organized a Department of Aeronautics at the University of Montreal, there were six Polish professors teaching at Canadian universities, and within five years of their arrival the newcomers established twelve industrial corporations employing more than 800 people.[40] The post-war years saw the arrival of large numbers of Polish immigrants with professional, technical, highly skilled and white collar occupations. To escape the refugee camps many of these qualified individuals volunteered for farm work or for domestic service,[41] but such status dislocation did not last long.[42] More suitable work was found, the new arrivals began to establish new businesses and corporations and enter into new ventures, bringing new ideas and initiative.

By 1961 there was 267 new businesses established by the Polish immigrants within three to six years of their arrival in Canada. There were also 229 farms purchased after the immigrants had been in Canada for five years or had worked for someone else,[43] in what was termed a cycle –

from field worker, to share crop producer, tenant operator, and finally, owner.[44] An occupational profile of Metropolitan Toronto provides a further illustration of the occupational distribution of the Polish ethnic group. In 1961, of the 58,578 in the Polish ethnic origin category, 17,931 were in the labour force, and of these 40% were in white collar occupations and about 50% in blue collar jobs. The study[45] distinguishes between the pre-1946 and post-1946 arrivals from Poland and provides the following information:

TABLE 14

POLISH ETHNIC GROUP (MALE) LABOUR FORCE
(METROPOLITAN TORONTO)
1961

Pre-1946 arrivals from Poland	White-collar	42.6%
(and their descendants)	Blue -collar	57.0%
TOTAL 7,411	Farm	0.4%
1946-1961 arrivals from Poland	White-collar	30.8%
TOTAL 10,392	Blue -collar	68.9%
	Farm	0.3%

Source: Turrittin (1972: Tables 7.4 and B1).

The data above indicate that the post-war Polish immigrants have not reached levels as high as had the earlier Polish immigrants and their descendants, but between 1951 and 1961 the Polish aggregate 'shook off' their long-held entrance status as agricultural workers and unskilled labourers. The arrival of a large number of better-educated and highly qualified people and the entrance into higher occupations by the second and third generations totally changed the occupational composition of the Polish group in Canada. There are now significant proportions[46] of the Polish labour force in Canada who are doctors, dentists, lawyers, professors, engineers, scientists, architects and highly skilled technicians. There are a number of civil servants in municipal, provincial and federal offices. Thousands have established their own businesses while others are managers or executives for larger concerns. "They are consumers of Canadian products but also producers of wealth and employers of labour."[47] The Polish group is now well represented in the higher socio-economic occupations.[48]

The Polish middle classes are constantly growing and are realizing more and more the importance of higher education for their children. The doors to the corporate elite remain at present closed to them, as they are largely closed to many other immigrant groups,[49] and this has been to some extent responsible for the establishment of many new economic concerns, for as one researcher found, "it has been easier for an immigrant to create something than to penetrate the higher levels of the Canadian social structure."[50] But even this is changing. In the last few years, those appointed or promoted to various executive positions of the larger Canadian business firms have no longer exclusively Anglo-Saxon or French names and a number of individuals with distinctly Polish names have begun to appear. The elite of the trade unions has now also been penetrated by at least one individual of Polish descent.[51]

In comparison with their predecessors, the post-war Polish immigrants made a significant and quickly visible contribution to the Canadian economy. Yet it needs to be stressed that the earlier Polish immigrants also played a very significant part in the Canadian economy, helping to conquer virgin land for cultivation, introducing or inventing new farming methods and techniques, and improving strains of wheat. They "have performed much of the necessary tough work in connection with the opening up and development of a new country,"[52] building roads and bridges, digging ditches, extracting mineral resources, or clearing the bush. They had to struggle physically for all they achieved and Canada owes much to those anonymous toilers of the earlier years.

NOTES

1. The examination for the 'desirable characteristics' was continued by the Canadian recruiters among Polish soliders and refugees from 1946 to 1948.
2. Smith, *op. cit.*, found that in 1899 the average Polish immigrant arrived with $10.37 in his possession. But this was typical of all immigrants, for even the British newcomers could only boast of $38.90 on the average per family, and Italians were even poorer than the Poles, coming with $8.70 per family.
3. For a time in the early 1900s the Canadian government helped the new settlers on homesteads by providing one cow for four families and ploughing one acre of land for potatoes. There are very few references to this from the Polish sources and it is uncertain if the immigrants from Poland received this service. There are records of food allocations to needy families on homesteads.
4. According to Mazurkiewicz, p. 44, these statistics only relate to the foreign-born. The author estimates that the number of properties and their worth would be 2½ times as large if the descendants of Polish immigrants were included in these figures.
5. R. Kogler, "A Demographic Profile," Table 3, p. 16.
6. 1971 census of Canada, Catalogue 92-723.
7. *Ibid.*
8. After 1945, the agriculture-bound segment became a mere trickle.
9. Foster, p. 43.
10. Lubicz, *op. cit.*

11. Some expressions and common terms were learned, and the majority of Polish workers could communicate to a degree in English but seldom sufficiently to allow them to occupy a position of responsibility or authority.
12. Courses in English were offered in some cities in the 1910s and a returnable fee of $2.00 was charged for 40 lessons to assure that the students completed the course. See Anderson, *op. cit.*
13. This was strongly suggested by at least one memoir. See *Pamiętniki Emigrantów*, No. 8, p. 242.
14. Lubicz, p. 290.
15. The shortage of manpower resulted in the introduction of "anti-loafing" laws in April, 1918. See D.H. Avery, "The Immigrant Industrial Worker in Canada 1896-1930: The Vertical Mosaic as a Historical Reality," Paper presented at the Conference of the Canadian Ethnic Studies Association, Toronto, October 26, 1973.
16. The money was always available from money lenders at exorbitant rates, and the Polish 'honour system' could not allow not meeting such an obligation. Borrowed money was scrupulously repaid if at all possible.
17. *Pamiętniki Emigrantów*, 1970, No. 9, p. 256. According to Isaac A. Hourwich, *Immigration and Labor* (New York, 1922), records in Russian Poland in 1903 showed that 37 Polish workers in an American city sent home in that one year the sum of 47,863 rubles ($424,605, or $665 per person), demonstrating the saving capabilities of Polish immigrants, as well as concern with the families left behind.
18. The Depression years have been the subject of inquiry by a number of Canadian writers, in particular Barry Broadfoot, *Ten Lost Years, 1929-1939: Memoirs of Canadians Who Survived the Depression* (Toronto, 1973) and M. Horn, *The Dirty Thirties* (Toronto, 1972). But for the Polish immigrants the best portrayal is presented in their memoirs. See *Pamiętniki Emigrantów*, 1971.
19. *Toronto Daily Star* Forum on Immigration, October 17, 1972, Position of R. Bell, Director of Research, Canadian Labour Congress.
20. Canadians of Polish descent served in all branches of the Canadian armed forces during World War II and a son of Polish immigrants, Mynarski (Młynarski) was awarded the Victoria Cross for bravery. Many others were distinguished for their sacrifice and bravery.
21. For a further elaboration of economic experiences of this phase of Polish immigration to Canada see Heydenkorn, "Emigracja Polska;" "Polonia Kanadyjska;" "The Social Structure."
22. W.W. Isajiw and N.J. Hartmann, "Changes in the Occupational Structure of Ukrainians in Canada," in W.E. Mann, ed., *Social and Cultural Change in Canada*, Vol.1 (Toronto,1970), and A.H. Turrittin,"Ethnicity and Occupational Stratification in Metropolitan Toronto, 1961," Mimeograph, York University,1972, discuss occupations in which the Polish ethnic group is "over-represented" and "under-represented."
23. In the United States ethnic minorities were able to utilize three important

routes of upward social mobility: labour leadership, crime, and ethnic politics. Such modes were not as developed, accepted or practised in Canada and certainly were not used by the Polish aggregate.

24. See pages 18-20 of this study.
25. Anderson, Chapter XV, devotes an entire chapter to the experiences of Louis Niemczyk.
26. *Ibid.*, p. 81.
27. *Canadians All: Poles in Canada* lists seven Polish doctors and five lawyers in all of Canada in 1938.
28. According to Mazurkiewicz, *op, cit*, university graduation forms allowed the candidates to change their names for their graduation diplomas.
29. M. Dalton, "Informal Factors in Career Achievement," *American Journal of Sociology* LVI (1951), pp. 407-15.
30. R.B. Klymasz, *A Classified Dictionary of Slavic Surname Changes in Canada* (Winnipeg, 1961), discovered over 2,000 name changes from Slavic to Anglo-Saxon for the Province of Manitoba in the years 1937-1957.
31. L.S. Garczyński, *Handel, Przemysł Naszą Przyszłością*(Winnipeg, 1934), p.7.
32. *Ibid.*, p. 8.
33. *Księga Pamiątkowa*, 1962.
34. *Pierwszy Kalendarz.*
35. There are few references to the notorious boarding houses after 1920 but the Poles, like many other immigrants, continued the practice of renting out a part of their own homes to help with the mortgage payments and thus allow them to become full owners of their property much sooner than their regular earnings would allow.
36. His name was Stanisław Szyszko.
37. Mazurkiewicz, *op. cit*, provides few other details about this individual.
38. *Kalendarz Czasu, op. cit.*
39. B. Heydenkorn, "Emigracja Polska."
40. Admission to Canada of Members of the Polish Armed Forces, "Brief Submitted to the Standing Committee of the Senate of Canada on Immigration and Labour by the Canadian Polish Congress in Ottawa," June 25, 1946.
41. As was said elsewhere, "for a time they could not exchange all their battle decorations and honours for better jobs or working conditions." See Heydenkorn, 'Związkowiec.'
42. According to Richmond's hypothesis, immigrants who initially experience lower socio-economic status but regain their previous level within a few years tend to be more satisfied with general conditions in Canada and identify more readily with their adopted country. See A. Richmond, *Post-War Immigrants*, pp. 118, 191.
43. Department of Citizenship and Immigration, 1961.
44. Palmer, p. 228.
45. Turrittin, *op. cit.*

46. See Table 12 for details.
47. Fairclough, p. 19.
48. For an in-depth portrayal of certain professions and occupations see A. Wołodkiewicz, *op. cit.* For Polish Canadian scholars and scientists see T. Krychowski, *The Register of Persons Actively Engaged in Scholarly Pursuits or Scientific Research* (Toronto, 1970).
49. This has been well illustrated and documented by J. Porter, *op. cit.*, and M. Kelner, "Ethnic Penetration Into Toronto's Elite Structure," *Canadian Review of Sociology and Anthropology* (1970), pp. 128-37.
50. Hawkins, p. 359.
51. See B.C. Hughes, "The Seafarers' New Strongman, " *The Canadian Magazine*, October, 1973.
52. Foster, p. 50.

TEN

Relationships

They talk; occasionally to each other, sometimes about each other, and most often at each other.

Only in a few, rare cases did the Polish immigrants find themselves among other people from Poland, forming a community where little contact needed to be established or maintained with members of other ethnic groups. Generally, only a few families were to be found living in close proximity and contact with different people was inevitable. What kind of relationships did the Polish immigrants experience with other immigrant groups and with the host population? How did they get along among themselves?[1]

THE HOSTS

An earlier chapter[2] dealt with some aspects of the relationships of the Polish immigrants with their hosts, especially in economic areas. Here it may be added that while a proportion of the native Canadian population expressed hostility in times of socio-economic problems, the larger society's attitude was indifference, reflected in the absence of broader social contacts. Personal and friendly relations were established slowly and were largely limited to the work place. This has been experienced by most first generation immigrants; their children, born in Canada, found comparatively few problems in being accepted or in entering into Canadian social life.[3] As the Polish aggregate emerged from its entrance status in the 1950s, its members became more readily acceptable to their hosts and at present there are harmonious, often close and co-operative relations between people of Polish descent and the Canadian population of either Anglo-Saxon or French descent.

The relationships with the institutional structure of Canadian society[4] were extremely good. The Polish immigrants were immediately impressed by the politeness and respect received from the immigration and other

187

officials and were largely satisfied with the reception given to their representations in Ottawa or the provincial capitals. Canadian laws were accepted as impartial and just, the political and law enforcement agencies were considered as legal representatives of the Canadian nation. The new arrivals from Poland were never faced with legal, political or social obstacles in their efforts to re-create aspects of their life left behind, or in the maintenance of their cultural distinctiveness.

Since the mid-1960s, the relationships between the Canadian government and the Polish (and other) aggregates have become even closer and more harmonious. The recommendations of the Royal Commission on Bilingualism and Biculturalism are known to all, and Canadians are aware of the positive and encouraging attitude adopted by the federal and some provincial legislatures towards ethnic minorities. The appointment of a minister[5] responsible for these policies demonstrates the commitment to, and concern with, ethnic diversity within the context of the two founding cultures. The people of Polish descent have welcomed those developments and their organizations are eager to co-operate with all levels of governments in implementing the policies.

RELATIONSHIPS WITH OTHER ETHNIC GROUPS

Prior to 1939, about 35% of the population of Poland was composed of Ukrainians, Byelorussians, Jews, Germans, and others. The Lithuanians, whose nation, until the last partition in 1795, formed an integral part of the Kingdom of Poland and Lithuania, were an inseparable part of the Polish nation. Poland fought against both Germany and Russia and there were bitter struggles against the Ukrainian independence movements in the 1650s and again in the early 1920s. There were periods of peace, mutual tolerance, even harmonious relationships, but there were also numerous conflicts, struggles and acrimony between the Polish people and the national minorities and political neighbours.

On crossing the Atlantic and coming to Canada, the Polish people have seemingly shed all animosities towards others who were their political or geographical neighbours. The involvement with events taking place in Poland remained. The political developments taking place in Europe in 1914-1918 and later from 1939 onwards deeply concerned the majority of Polish immigrants in Canada but this concern was not reflected in changed attitudes towards the representatives of nations affecting Poland in the Canadian context. Germans, Russians, Ukrainians, Jews, and others all were fellow immigrants, all shared the same problems and difficulties, all were a part of Canada. European political developments in the early 1920s affected relationships between the Polish and some other ethnic groups in Canada, but since the 1940s there is nothing to suggest that relationships, where they exist, are based on anything but mutual tolerance, understanding, or co-operation.

Despite the fact that a significant proportion of the Jewish group in

Canada were born in Poland, and many close contacts were maintained in Poland, the relationships that were established in Canada were at best peripheral. The two groups seldom settled on the same streets in urban areas or together on land. The only contacts that were established stemmed from the patron-client interaction in which the Polish Jews opened enterprises near concentrations of Polish (and other Slavic) immigrants, providing goods and services in a common language. There were few social contacts on the individual or organizational level, and this situation remains to the present.

There is little concrete evidence to determine the relationships between the Polish and the Russian and German groups in Canada. Until 1881, the Poles were counted with the Russians in the Canadian censuses but there is little to suggest that the two people lived in close proximity, or that frequent or close relationships existed. It is likely that the two groups had in fact few contacts outside of working together in certain occupations and only in the last decade or so was closer co-operation established within the context of the Canadian Slavic Committee.[6]

The relationships with German immigrants is illustrated in memoirs[7] and in a novel,[8] and it would appear that contacts, where they existed, were generally friendly. The Germans, who came to Canada earlier than the Poles and were quick to establish themselves successfully, were helpful to the Polish immigrants on many occasions. There are no references to incidents of hostility or even unfriendliness between the two peoples at any time, a surprising development in the context of the historical relationships between Poland and Germany.

Relationships with the Hungarians, largely on an individual basis, were always good – a continuation of very close and harmonious relationships that existed between the two countries for centuries. Even closer contacts were established and maintained with the Slovaks. Individuals from the two groups settled near each other in many areas, the Slovaks joined Polish parishes where no church of their own was established, and the clergy helped the nationals from both groups. For example, "a Polish prelate, Msgr. Vincent Helenowski provided the leadership for the Slovaks in establishing their own parish in Montreal, in 1928."[9] Roman Catholic Slovaks were members of a Polish parish in Toronto until 1929.[10] The Toronto Polish Lutheran congregation shares the church facilities with the Slovak Lutherans.[11] The close affinity between the Polish and the Slovak people stems from the many similar experiences shared in Canada and is due in part to the ease in communications which is possible since the two languages are closely related and easily understood or learned by each side.

There seem to have been fewer contacts with the Czechs, except for certain occasions such as the United Polish-Czech "tag day" in Toronto in 1943 to collect funds for the two fighting nations. It is likely that contacts were established on an individual basis at the place of work, through

189

residential proximity, or through membership in the same church. Co-operation with other Slavic groups is illustrated by the case of the Croatians, whose parish in Toronto is under the jurisdiction of the bishop of the Polish National Catholic Church. Roman Catholics and other denominations are members of Polish parishes just as people of Polish descent belong to other non-Polish parishes.

Very close relationships were maintained between the Polish and Lithuanian immigrants, who lived and worked closely together until 1920. Polish-Lithuanian clubs were established, the two people shared the same parishes and priests, and many Lithuanians spoke some Polish. In 1918 Lithuania won her independence and the dispute with Poland over the city of Wilno (Vilnius) and neighbouring territory ended the previously friendly relationships between the two people. The Lithuanians withdrew from all association with the Polish people and only some individual contacts remained. Since 1940, the Lithuanians have no further political 'grudges' against Poland but the relationships between the two people have not recovered their previously friendly level.

More than any other ethnic groups in Canada, the Poles and the Ukrainians were tied together through a number of circumstances. The two people lived for centuries in close geographical and residential proximity. Large numbers of them left at approximately the same time, from the same geographical areas, travelled together, and the numerically smaller numbers of Polish rural settlers tended to drift close to the Ukrainian settlements and concentrations in the Prairie provinces. Occasionally the process was reversed and Ukrainians settled among larger concentrations of Polish people. The many cultural similarities they shared were a great attraction to the confused and lonely people. Their relationships in Canada reflected those that existed in the old communities. They lived and worked together and intermarried often. "The result of the close coexistence of the two Slavic groups, was, among others, extensive Ukrainization of the numerically smaller Polish people."[12]

Events taking place in Poland once again affected established relationships. The proclamation of an independent Ukrainian Republic in November, 1917, led in time to military confrontations with the newly re-established Polish Republic, and the militarily stronger Poles were able to maintain control over disputed territories. The Ukrainians in Canada, alarmed at the alleged mistreatment of their nationals by the Polish authorities, appealed to the Canadian government to intervene. The accusations and hostilities were largely limited to the Ukrainian-language press and focused on the Polish government and its policies and not on Poles in Canada. The Polish-language press felt obliged to defend the policies and actions of the Polish government and attempted to justify its position. The majority of Polish immigrants were in agreement with their press, a stand which led in time to degeneration of individual relationships.

In the early 1920s numerous Ukrainian political activists, veterans of the Ukrainian army, and others who were imprisoned by the Polish government for some outlawed political activity, arrived in Canada. The strong nationalistic feelings among the earlier Ukrainian immigrants were further strengthened and were reflected in intensified unfriendliness towards Polish immigrants. Undoubtedly, there were many individual confrontations and co-operation was frequently replaced by friction, but there is only one reported incident of premeditated hostility, taking place in Oakburn, Manitoba, where a verbal campaign by Ukrainian nationalists led to the destruction of roadside crosses built by the Polish settlers.[13] The relationships between the two Slavic groups remained cool well into 1940s, and until that time only the Polish Leftist Radicals maintained close ties with their Ukrainian political counterparts.[14]

Faced with post-war political developments (the disputed territories are now a part of the Ukrainian Soviet Socialist Republic), enlighted individuals from both Slavic groups sought ground for common understanding leading to improvement in relations. In this the editors of the respective presses played a significant role, ignoring contentious issues and stressing a need for co-operation and the formation of a common front to face common problems. The relationship between the two groups has now largely improved and among the academicians, scientists, and some organizational leaders, has become co-operative and close.

Today, the older generations are becoming more mellow and the memories of the past are losing much of their bitterness. For the new generations of the Polish group in Canada, the Polish-Ukrainian problems are incomprehensible or irrelevant.[15] There are new challenges in Canada which demand close co-operation and the presentation of a common front to the Canadian authorities, and concerns related to the maintenance of the respective cultures provide grounds for harmonious relationships and co-operation.

Relationships between the Polish immigrants and other ethnic people in Canada, where contact was established and maintained, were generally co-operative and harmonious. The conflict with the Ukrainian aggregate has never assumed explosive proportions. Both the Polish and Ukrainian groups were politically and economically weak, fragmented internally, and without any encouragement, concern, support or even recognition of their claims by the host society and the Canadian government. The unfriendly, occasionally hostile attitudes between the Polish and Ukrainian immigrants here stemmed from developments which took place in Europe. Once this situation was eliminated the two groups began to re-establish the lost ties. This trend will, it is hoped, continue.

RELATIONSHIPS WITH POLAND

In the historical perspective the relationships of Polish immigrants in Canada to Poland were strongly related to the socio-economic and political developments taking place there, and were subject to the arrival of new phases of immigrants. The attitudes to and perception of Poland among the earlier arrivals to Canada, prior to 1914, largely exhibited themselves in concern and interest in the old communities, their friends and relatives. Poland, as an independent nation, did not exist.

World War I kindled a much deeper concern with the events taking place in Europe, and with the struggles of the Polish people attempting to re-establish an independent nation. There were relatively few individuals who travelled to Europe to fight for Polish independence, but those remaining in Canada participated by sending food, clothing, money, and later by buying Polish government bonds. Some returned to live in the independent state. In the immediate post-World War I years, Polish patriotic feelings were aroused and the immigrants were most likely to consider themselves as Poles abroad. Organizations were established which were counterparts of those in Poland and developments and activities in the old country were followed avidly.

After nearly 125 years of foreign domination, Poland faced a tremendous task of rebuilding and reorganization, a legacy of misrule and destruction during the war. By 1919, the Polish government had established a consultate in Montreal,[16] but the nation had few resources which would allow it to be concerned with Polish immigrants in Canada and elsewhere, and there were few attempts to lead or influence the Polish aggregate in Canada.[17]

It was not until 1927 that an organization[18] was formed in Poland which had as one of its main goals the maintenance of ties with Polish emigrants. By 1933 a federation[19] was established in Canada which was affiliated with the central body in Warsaw to promote closer ties between the immigrants and Poland. By 1938 there were over 80 Canadian-Polish organizations as members of this federation.

The immediate post-war patriotic fervour abated by the 1930s, and the perception of Poland as a source of identity, guidance and reference was no longer shared by all. Some organizations and institutions, especially the Polish parishes and parish organizations, chose to remain outside any influences from Poland. On the other hand there were two associations voicing their criticism or opposition to the Polish government. The Polish Friendly Alliance in Canada criticized the Polish government in strong terms for the mistreatment of Polish peasants and workers and the persecution of their leaders. The press organ *Związkowiec*, which carried those condemnations, was eventually barred from circulating in Poland. The Polish Workers' and Farmers' Association (The Polish Peoples' Association after 1936) was strongly opposed to the Polish government, terming it fascist, exploitative and repressive. The press organ of this organization was also barred and the leaders faced imprisonment should they ever venture to Poland. Finally, there were increasing numbers of Polish immigrants who were becoming progressively less interested in matters related to Poland, intent on the socio-economic issues facing them in Canada. The

Canadian-born generations of Poles were largely unaware or unconcerned with Poland.

The attack on Poland in 1939 and World War II brought ethnic loyalty to the fore, and evoked deep concern for the fate of the Polish people and the Polish armed forces. The suffering of the nation united many of the warring or dissenting factions, eliciting an intensification of activities aimed at helping occupied Poland. But the years spent in Canada had their effect. In the early years of the war, the Polish military mission attempted to recruit Polish Canadians for military service in the Polish army which was being formed at the time in France. Despite the permission of the Canadian government to recruit Canadian citizens of Polish background, the mission was not successful: the Polish Canadians preferred to serve in the Canadian armed forces.

The immediate post-war years saw the activities of the Polish organizations intensified to aid the Polish people, but the relationships with the official representatives was in a state of confusion, for now there were two Polish governments, the government in Poland which came on the heels of the liberating Soviet armies and was fully sponsored by the Kremlin, and the wartime Polish government in London, England, which was recognized by the Allies and other free nations as the only government until 1945. The government, first in Lublin and later in Warsaw, took control of Poland while the government-in-exile retained a powerful influence over the thousands of post-war refugees, political exiles and armed forces veterans who fought by the side of the Allies in Italy and Western Europe. The existence of two governments, each claiming legality, led to some confusion among the Poles in Canada well into the late 1940s. Only the Leftist Radicals immediately recognized and supported fully the government in Warsaw. Others awaited further developments, stressing in the meantime the need for a stronger orientation to Canada as the permanent home.

The arrival of a large number of Polish refugees and veterans from 1946 to 1950 had a strong impact on the attitudes of the Canadian Poles towards Poland and the two governments. The ensuing Cold War politics and the East-West confrontation left little doubt in the minds of the uncommitted that the government in Warsaw, now officially recognized by all major nations, was merely a puppet body imposed by Moscow on the Polish people. The Polish government in exile in London, now isolated and no longer effective diplomatically, was given moral and financial support by various organizations and individuals in Canada. Until 1956 the majority of the Poles in Canada considered the members of the Warsaw regime as nothing but servants of Stalin and strongly condemned anyone travelling to Poland or having any contacts with the representatives or officials of the Warsaw government. This is not to say that concern with the Polish people diminished. Contacts were maintained through the mail, and according to various shipping documents between 1945 and 1956, parcels of medicine, food and clothing, to the value of $4,000,000 or $5,000,000, were sent annually from Canada to Poland.[20]

In 1956, the rigid Stalinist Polish government was replaced by a more moderate leadership under Gomułka, ushering in reorientation and a change in attitudes among Polish people in all parts of the world. Visits to relatives in Poland resumed the same year on a small scale, and each succeeding year saw larger numbers going to Poland to see their families, friends, or merely to visit their place of birth. More recently young people, born in Canada, have begun to show an interest in visiting the land of their fathers, and for the last two or three years, large groups of Canadian-born students go to Poland to attend summer courses in the Polish language, history, geography, and literature. Polish-Canadian dance and song groups and other individual artists attend cultural festivals in Poland, academicians and scientists travel for discussions with their colleagues in Poland, editors of the Polish-language press visit to gain first-hand knowledge of conditions in Poland, and many others make the journey for purely sentimental reasons.

The movement of people occurs in both directions. Close relatives are able to visit Canada. Since 1956 world-famous song and dance ensembles, such as Mazowsze and Śląsk, have entertained in Canada. Polish films are shown in various Canadian cinemas in areas where large concentrations of Polish-speaking people reside. Theatrical, revue, and other cultural groups visit certain Canadian centres a few times each year. Polish academicians, scientists, and journalists come to lecture and meet Polish immigrants and their descendants. Economic contacts are now also established by businessmen and some organizations and a number of Polish products – handicrafts, food, records, and books – are now available in Canada. It appears that emotional and family ties and feelings are able to override the strong political and ideological considerations for many, though not for everyone.

Not all the Poles in Canada support or even condone these developments and practices. The loyal supporters of the Polish government in exile in London, England,[21] maintain that the present Polish government, despite the political relaxations, is imposed on a Polish people who are not free to voice their true choice and are powerless to change the existing political structure. In their view, it is the sacred duty of all Polish immigrants to inform the free Western world of the true conditions behind the Iron Curtain. The pro-London adherents were always concerned with the activities and potential influences of the Warsaw government on Polish immigrants, especially in Europe and North America. They have argued that the Polish state propaganda machinery has been and is employed to neutralize the activities of the Polish immigrant organizations and associations through seemingly harmless cultural exchanges, innocuous meetings with the Polish state representatives, and even visits to relatives in Poland.

It is difficult to estimate what proportion of the Polish group in Canada adheres to the emigré policies and continues to support the government in exile in London, but it is likely that their numbers are relatively small.[22]

The 'average' Polish immigrant in Canada is unconcerned with those issues, or else feels that since the Cold War has ended, and there is little likelihood of any significant changes in European politics in the near future;[23] reconciliation with the present situation is the only logical alternative. Some publicly adhere to the stance acceptable to the 'Londoners,' others openly dismiss them as no longer relevant. Yet the issue remains the most contentious problem facing the Polish aggregate today.

The debate on these issues has been carried on in the Polish-language press for some years now, and a very distinguished gathering of Polish academicians and scientists from Canada and elsewhere devoted a few days in a special conference to those questions.[24] Within the last decade the Polish group witnessed the emergence of an articulate and significant body of adherents who no longer exclude contacts with Poland 'at all costs.' This faction began stressing a need for renewed and broad contacts with Poland. It shares the opinion that the present government in Poland is not elected by democratic criteria as in Canada, but stresses relationships with the Polish culture and the Polish people, not with the government and its representatives. This faction supports such endeavours as aid to school buildings, restoration of national treasures or monuments, material help in time of calamity, and similar concerns.

The activists and some prominent individuals or organizational leaders adopt one or another position with relation to Poland, but the vast majority of Polish immigrants and their descendants are unaffected. Those who have relatives in Poland travel there to visit them. The appearance of certain performing groups from Poland is well-attended, even by those who profess deep enmity towards the Warsaw government and all its representatives. Under the general world conditions of *rapprochement* between East and West, previously rigid attitudes are modified or abandoned and closer contacts with the Polish culture and people (if not the government) are becoming more acceptable. The trend is likely to continue.

INTRA-GROUP RELATIONS

While Polish immigrants were generally able to maintain neutral or friendly relations with almost all ethnic groups in Canada,[25] their history has been characterized by frequent and harmful internal conflicts and animosities. One of the most destructive developments has been the self-classification into the categories of 'we' and 'they.' 'We' applied to identification with certain areas of partitioned Poland. 'We' were from Galicia; 'they' were 'Russian Poles' or 'German Poles.' They were Polish people but 'not really the same as we.' This criterion ceased to play an important role after 1918 when Poland regained her independence, yet the 'we' and 'they' remained. 'We' were the older generations of immigrants, jealously guarding 'our' position against 'them,' the new arrivals, who wanted to impose their ideas and plans.

The established immigrants derived their self-identity and status from their Canadian achievements and material possessions[26] while the new arrivals most often based their claims to status on their position in Poland, or wartime sufferings and the glory of battle. 'We' were the established immigrants and descendants of immigrants who often considered Canada as 'our home' where the first loyalties rested. 'They' were the political emigrés and refugees who accepted directives from London, England, and attempted to apply their guidelines to other Polish immigrants in Canada.[27] 'We' were people adhering to democratic ideals and values, 'they' were Communists and subversives.

The division into 'us' and 'them' prevailed within religious and secular institutions and associations, and reached into the day-to-day relationships of people, creating divisions and lack of consensus on purposes and goals. Only during emergencies in Poland were the differences largely put aside. The organizational structure and individual efforts were joined in a common cause to alleviate suffering and help in any way possible. Such cooperation and unity of purpose was best demonstrated during World War II. Polish parishes, lay organizations, and prominent individuals focused their concern and activities on the victims of the German occupation of Poland, and on the Polish soldiers who escaped from Poland or joined from other nations to fight the common enemy. Funds were collected, clothing was donated, medicine purchased and parcels were sent to war orphans, to prisoners of war, and to Polish units serving beside the Allies. Continuation of this activity in the immediate post-war years focused largely on the country and at this time there was some co-operation with the Polish Leftist Radicals within the United Polish Relief Fund. The activities and concern of Polish organizations in Canada with the problems facing the decimated and economically ruined Poland was soon overshadowed by political considerations. By 1948 it was concluded that further efforts meant dealing with the Communist-imposed regime and concern was focused on the problems related to the arrival of increasing numbers of Polish veterans and refugees in Canada.

The 'we' – 'they' problems gradually diminished. The rigid Stalinist Polish government provided a frame of reference for the post-war newcomers, who gave full support to the exiled Polish government in London, England, and recognized its representatives in Canada. The pre-war immigrants generally adhered to the views of the newcomers but for them the issue was not of overriding importance, and greater emphasis was placed on matters of adjustment and acculturation to the Canadian society. Among the newcomers, especially the veterans of the Polish armed forces, the prevailing view was that the Cold War would lead sooner or later to a renewal of hostilities, and the resultant conflict would free Poland from Communist domination, allowing them to return and take their rightful place there. The pre-war immigrants stressed the permanency of residence in Canada and encouraged the newcomers to forget their dreams.

In 1956 the Polish Stalinist rulers were replaced by a strongly nationalistic and seemingly more liberal government under Gomułka. The official view of the Polish organizations in Canada towards these developments did not change greatly. Although the liberalization of the political rule was welcomed, it was argued that the new government was still Communist and under the influence of Moscow. Unofficially the Polish aggregate did not share this view. The pre-war immigrants especially welcomed the changes as significant. Despite the condemnation by the 'Londoners,' increasing numbers of individuals travelled to Poland, Polish visitors were welcomed to Canada, and attitudes towards the Polish rulers mellowed. They were "Communists," but "Polish Communists."

Gradually two Polish-Canadian factions have emerged. The first are the loyal supporters of the exiled Polish government in London who continue to adhere to the pronouncements and ideology of this body, condemning any contacts which could be interpreted as recognizing the legality of the Warsaw government, and continuing to stress the need of maintaining the 'ambassador' role for all Polish immigrants. The other faction, influenced by the pragmatic issues related to the preservation of some aspects of their culture among the successive Canadian-born generations, sees the expansion of contacts with Poland as the only feasible means of achieving this goal. Stopping short of direct dealings with the central Warsaw government and its representatives, it advocates co-operation with educational and cultural institutions, and sees the exchange of scientists, academicians, artists, and intellectuals as desirable. Its primary efforts are directed at creating situations where the descendants of Polish immigrants are exposed to the cultural and traditional richness of the Polish nation. This faction, represented by such organizations as the Polish Alliance in Canada, the Polish Roman Catholic and the Polish National Catholic Church, and various other bodies, is opposed by the leadership of the Canadian Polish Congress, combatant associations and other organizations.

The issue of broader co-operation and contacts with the Polish culture, however represented, as opposed to the avoidance of any contacts whatsoever and adherence to the position of the exiled government body in London, has been so contentious that the Polish Alliance in Canada, representing over 30 organizations, withdrew from affiliation with the Canadian Polish Congress in 1972. The withdrawal was the result of a number of earlier disagreements with the executive of the Congress on the definition of the role of the Congress. According to the Polish Alliance in Canada, the Congress subverted its original role as a co-ordinating body into a source of power, attempting to impose rules and ideologies which were previously determined by each affiliated organization. The Polish Alliance in Canada argued that it had a right to determine its own goals and to carry them out without the imposition of strict guidelines on relationships with people and institutions in Poland. This issue has created

197

much dissent and had prevented a unified effort towards solving problems facing the Polish community in Canada today.

Differences brought over from Poland and those that emerged in Canada were responsible for fragmenting the Polish aggregate for a number of decades. Differences remain to the present, preventing full co-operation, spoiling harmonious relations, and retarding the establishment of plans which would assure the continuation of a Polish cultural distinctiveness within the Canadian cultural mosaic. The improvement of intra-group relations in the near future is not likely. The organizational structure with its potentialities for the whole Polish group in Canada is undermined by a reluctance to co-operate, and by personal ambitions,[28] petty rivalries, individualism, and absence of commitment or apathy on the part of the majority of the people of Polish descent in Canada.

NOTES

1. This subject is of great interest to many, but here the authors are faced with tremendous gaps in available information.
2. See the chapter on Adjustment.
3. As is demonstrated by the rates of intermarriage between the Polish and Anglo-Saxon groups.
4. Outside of the economic structure, which has been discussed elsewhere.
5. The Hon. Dr. Stanley Haidasz, who was born in Canada from parents who came from Poland. Dr. Haidasz was very active in the organizational structure of the Polish aggregate in Canada.
6. Such as the Inter-University Committee on Canadian Slavs. For its activities see the three-volume proceedings of the National Conference of Slavs in Canada (1966, 1967, 1971).
7. *Pamiętniki Emigrantów*, 1971.
8. Wańkowicz, *op. cit.*
9. Kirschbaum, p. 143.
10. *Złote Pokłosie, op. cit.*
11. *Księga Pamiątkowa 20-lecia Polskiego Zboru Ew-Augburskiego w Toronto* (1973).
12. V. Turek, "Jeszcze o Polonii," p. 89. Hunchak, *op. cit.*, provides further proof of this process taking place before 1941.
13. W. Turek, *Poles in Manitoba*, p. 564.
14. Unlike other Canadian-Polish organizations, the Polish Workers' and Farmers' Association disclaimed all rights of Poland to the disputed territories.
15. See the editorial in *Echo*, Vol. 4, No. 2, 1972.
16. Other Polish consulates were opened later in Winnipeg and in Ottawa.

17. The efforts of the Polish consuls in Canada were largely devoted to maintaining a positive image of the political leadership in Poland, and to counteracting the disruptive organizational struggles of the Polish groups in Canada. The only known attempts to influence the Polish-language press were to ensure that the contents were not opposed to the Polish government.

18. Swiatowy Związek Polaków z Zagranicy (The World Association of Poles Abroad).

19. Zjednoczenie Zrzeszeń Polskich w Kanadzie.

20. B. Heydenkorn, "Emigracja Polska," p. 86.

21. In the terminology of the Polish community in Canada they are referred to as 'Londyńczycy' (Londoners) or 'Niezłomni' (unshaken or abiding).

22. Recently, representatives of the government in exile, interviewed by a reporter from Toronto's *Globe and Mail*, erroneously claimed the allegiance of all the immigrants of Polish descent in North America and elsewhere. Especially in North American their support is minimal and shrinking rapidly. See C. McCullough, "Polish Government in Exile Battles On," *The Globe and Mail*, July 4, 1973.

23. For those views see Adam Bromke, "Diaspory Polskiej – Ciąg Dalszy . . . . " *Związkowiec*, June 13, 1972.

24. B. Heydenkorn, "Problemy Polonii"

25. With the exception noted in the preceding pages.

26. Acquired usually after experiencing shortages, insecurity, hard toil, and great resolve.

27. See the statement by T. Glista, President of the Polish Alliance in Canada, in *Związkowiec*, No. 35, 1973.

28. Termed "self-aggrandisement" of certain individuals. See *Związkowiec* (36), 1973.

ELEVEN

The Canadian "Polonia"

Poles tend to believe that a man born a Pole cannot stop being one. The children and grandchildren of Polish immigrants are often said to have a 'Polish nature' which will come to the fore in the important moments of life.

Barnett

The growing tendency of people to think in terms of their ethnic group, even to demand a separate political status, is global in scope, and is currently changing the political divisions of Africa, Southeast Asia, and some parts of Europe. In Canada, the existence of the two founding nations and cultures precluded the establishment of something which could be accepted as a single 'ideal' of Canadian culture to provide a source for clear identity. As was argued by one Canadian historian, "Canada presents no common denominator in those profundities which normally unite, in race, language, religion, history and culture."[1] The later immigrant arrivals were expected to adapt to one or another of the two dominant cultures, but the pressures for conformity were unlike those which were present in the United States. Loyalty to one's own ethnic origin was generally acceptable, or at least tolerated, by the two founding people. Over time, this emerged with an even higher degree of tolerance for the 'strange' or different cultures and values, "to the point where pride is often taken in our culture mosaic and ethnic pluralism."[2]

It has been popular for Canadians to identify themselves in terms of the regions they live in. There are Canadians who are first and foremost Maritimers; others are Quebecois or Ontarians; then there are the Westerners who think of themselves as a special kind of Canadian, while the Rockies provide a natural border for others to define themselves as British Columbians. Finally, there are the Canadian Northerners. The regional labels provide a sense of closer identity for a relatively small and scattered population inhabiting a vast land. An even more comforting and intimate identity is available in identification with one or another of the Canadian ethnic aggregates. The Westerners or Ontarians, the Maritimers or Quebecois, also think of themselves in such terms as Canadians of German, Ukrainian, English, French, Italian, Polish or other descent, or as members of some ethnic group.

Sociological literature deals extensively with the role that membership in an ethnic group plays for its members. Such membership provides a partial substitute for the traditional community and extended family, allowing for closer and more intimate contacts and relationships which are largely absent in an industrialized and highly urbanized society like Canada. It provides an important source of reference and a sense of belonging which satisfies to some extent many psychological needs of all Canadians, but especially more recent immigrants and their descendants. It can counteract the depersonalizing or alienating conditions of the 'highrise,' mass entertainment, and impersonal life in any larger city. In the Canadian context, ethnic membership clearly establishes the individual's place within the whole society. A person is born into an ethnic group, "becomes related to it through emotional and symbolic ties,"[3] and this position serves as a platform for self-conceptualization which represents a set of psychological states as well as social roles.

The literature abounds in definitions of ethnicity and ethnic group identity, and stresses such variables as descent,[4] language, nationality, religion, customs, values and attitudes. For the purposes of this monograph ethnicity will refer to a group of people who share common ancestry, historical past, a common language or other cultural traits (of which religion is one of the more important), who identify themselves as belonging to the ethnic group, and who are so identified by others. In a special context, where an ethnic group is a minority their distinct institutions and organizations are often important symbols of cultural distinctiveness.[5]

OVERVIEW

The urban workers came quickly under the socio-economic pressures and influences of the receiving society; their identities as Poles or Galicians were assailed and condemned as undesirable by their hosts, their customs and traditions derided, their language and their family names made subjects of sharply critical comments. Many attempted to avoid the negative stereotypes and labels by blending in, becoming inconspicuous. Their "Polishness" emerged largely on special occasions, patriotic anniversaries and traditional celebrations. Their Canadian-born children adopted Canada as their own country quickly and easily, shedding their mother tongue, traditions and culture, often against the wishes of their parents who taught them the Polish language at home and attempted to instil in them an awareness of their cultural heritage.

Many who were unconcerned about or not strongly aware of their ethnicity were forced to re-evaluate their status when labelled 'enemy aliens' during World War I. Protests were made that if they were not accepted as 'Canadians,' they were not Austrians or Germans either, but Poles, and the Polish people were not in conflict with Canada and other Allies but were themselves struggling against the common enemies. The events taking place in Poland in the years 1918-1920 strengthened their previously suppressed identification with other Polish immigrants in Canada as well as with Poland. There was now an independent nation which could provide a focus of symbolic and concrete ties.

The post-1918 Polish immigrants came to Canada with a strong identification with Poland, as many had served in the armed forces and fought for its independence. Most of the new arrivals (or at least their children) had some education in Polish schools, were aware of Polish history and nationality. In Canada they were more likely to involve themselves in the activities of the Polish associations and more stress was placed on the maintenance of cultural distinctiveness for their Canadian-born children. The growth and availability of the Polish-language press, various contacts with Poland, and the presence in Canada of representatives of the Polish government were other factors affecting the self-identity of the Polish immigrants.[6]

The majority of the post-1945 arrivals were political refugees or exiles, "an army in exile with an almost messianic duty to keep alive certain ideas and cultural values that would otherwise be destroyed"[7] in the Communist-dominated Poland. They came with a highly developed self-identity as Poles, often seeing themselves as trustees of the unencumbered Polish culture and heritage, believing that it was their sacred duty to remain Poles in order to preserve and foster their values abroad since it was no longer possible in Poland itself.

The 1950s witnessed intense organizational activity under the impact of those new arrivals, focusing on Polish political issues, cultural values and self-identity. As was noted elsewhere, during this period the largest number of Polish part-time schools were established, demonstrating the concern of the parents with the preservation of cultural values among the youth. At this time, Polish ethnic identity was clearly evident in the mass participation in various patriotic, historical, and religious anniversaries and celebrations. Memories of Poland and wartime experiences were fresh in the minds of the participants in the struggles and sufferings and could not easily be put aside. The more tolerant and understanding attitude of the Canadian population provided sympathetic grounds for the display and assertion of attachment to Poland, its culture and traditions. This period may be said to represent a time of reassertion of ethnicity for some, redefinition of ethnic affiliation for others, and a general strengthening of identity as Poles or people of Polish descent. The latest arrivals, the post-1956 immigrants from Poland, form a group which is most clearly permeated with Polish cultural values and traditions. They do not necessarily share perceptions of themselves as members of the Polish group with their predecessors,[8] since they do not participate to any extent in the organizational activities of this aggregate, but their self-identity as Poles cannot be doubted.

The present political, economic, and cultural world image of Poland inevitably serves to attract the attention and interest of all who even vaguely claim membership in the Polish aggregate in Canada. Poland and Canada served together on a peace mission in Viet Nam for many years and are co-operating at present in the Middle East. Poland purchases large amounts of Canadian wheat and those and other economic agreements are well publicized. The 500th anniversary of the birth of Copernicus received attention from the Canadian mass media.[9] All this serves to remind people of Polish descent in Canada of the country of their origin, and to give them pride in its history and achievements. This is further reinforced by prominent Canadian politicians who stress the importance of Poland in cultural, political, and economic areas.[10]

Since the arrival of the Kashubs in 1858, thousands of other Polish immigrants have come to Canada. Sometimes they settled near other Polish immigrants in what were termed "Polish colonies,"[11] providing an image for their hosts by their distinct language, customs and appearance. Their ethnic affiliation and Polish identity expressed itself in the language[12] and religion, both vehicles of peculiarly Polish values and traditions. On occasion, their identity was reinforced by patriotism, focusing on the Old Country or on the Polish nation as a whole. The Polish group remained 'visible,'[13] reinforced by large numbers of new arrivals from Poland and elsewhere.

'POLONIA' TODAY

Today, members of the Polish ethnic category in Canada are no longer easily recognizable or located. Some are fully assimilated and no longer claim membership in this group except for census purposes, where their forefathers' origin is given as Poland. Others are acculturated, displaying their ethnicity on special occasions only. All are largely undistinguishable from other Canadians.

Various Polish sources referring to groups of Polish emigrants term them 'Polonias,'[14] thus the American Polonia, Polonia in France, Polonia in England or the Canadian Polonia. The term is synonymous with 'Polishness,' where the members possess some characteristics and traits that clearly denote a set of special relationships and attitudes to Poland and Polish culture and traditions. This term has been variously interpreted, denoting for some a clear identity and concern with all matters Polish and manifested through participation in activities stressing ideological or political and cultural values. Others claim that knowledge of the Polish language and Polish Roman Catholic affiliation are fundamental prerequisites for membership in a 'Polonia.' These are well defined but also narrow conceptualizations of membership in the Polish group in Canada.

TABLE 15

PEOPLE OF POLISH ETHNIC ORIGIN IN CANADA:
DECENNIAL CENSUSES OF CANADA

Year	Number	Percentage of total Canadian Population
1871	617	
1881	1,216	Insignificant
1891	695	
1901	6,285	0.1
1911	33,652	0.5
1921	53,403	0.6
1931	145,503	1.4
1941	167,485	1.4
1951	219,845	1.5
1961	323,517	1.8
1971	316,430	1.5

TABLE 16

POLISH ETHNIC GROUP IN CANADA – 1971

Total..316,430
Male...162,380
Female..154,045
Urban..254,690
Rural..61,740
Farm (included in the
    rural category)..27,880

Source: *1971 Census of Canada,* Catalogue 92-723.

TABLE 17

POLISH ETHNIC GROUP IN CANADA – 1971

(by Provinces)

Newfoundland 280
Prince Edward Island 110
Nova Scotia 3,260
New Brunswick 690
Quebec 23,970
Ontario 144,115
Manitoba 42,705
Saskatchewan 26,910
Alberta 44,325
British Columbia 29,545
Yukon 245
North Western Territories 270

Source: *Ibid.*

TABLE 18

POLISH ETHNIC GROUP IN CANADA – 1971 – BY AGE GROUPS

Under 15	76,475	(24.2%)
15 – 44	133,335	(42.1%)
45 – 64	77,965	(24.6%)
65 +	28,655	(9.1%)

Source: *Ibid.*

TABLE 19

POLISH ETHNIC GROUP – BIRTHPLACE – 1971

	%	Number
Canada	66.7%	210,920
The United States	1.2%	
The United Kingdom	1.2%	
Europe (including Poland)	30.6%	105,510
Asia	0.1%	
Other	0.2%	

Source: 1971 Census of Canada, Catalogue 92-723.

205

There are those who may no longer speak Polish nor participate in any Canadian-Polish organizations, and abstain from engaging in personal, intimate relationships with other people of Polish descent in Canada, but who at the same time retain special feelings and attitudes towards Poland and its culture, and maintain a strong conception of themselves as Polish.

A significant proportion of the descendants of the earlier Polish immigrants have experienced almost total assimilation but their ethnicity has not been totally erased if knowledge of their ancestry remains. Within the prevailing image of Canada as a multicultural society, stressing its diverse ethnic composition, few are insufficiently curious not to enquire further into the land and culture of their forefathers. Their images or knowledge of ethnicity may be acquired from the mass media, in public schools or through interaction with friends and neighbours.[15] Those individuals form what may be termed a quasi-ethnic group, and may potentially become involved and active in the interests and activities of those who retain their Polish identity to a broader and more visible degree. A test may be applied to determine one's perception of self-identity (even allegiance) in situations such as sports events, where teams representing different nations compete.[16] It may be asked for whom an individual would cheer if a Polish soccer or hockey team was playing a team from Russia, Germany, or Canada. Undoubtedly, the greatest test for defining their allegiance would come at a Poland-Canada game. The stand taken may well represent identity and membership in one or other of the two reference groups.

The discussion of self-identity and self-placement within the Canadian society leads us to ask,"What is the Canadian 'Polonia'?" Does it include the 316,430 individuals counted by the Canadian census in 1971 as members of the Polish ethnic category? Should the term 'Polonia' apply only to the 134,780 people whose mother tongue was Polish in 1971? Perhaps this term should apply only to those who are active in Polish organizations in Canada, those who are culturally visible through their names, accents, and behaviour, or those who have no doubt of their ethnicity and identity.

We do not wish to subscribe to the myth that identification for census purposes automatically denotes a person as "Polish." There are significant numbers of people who, given the choice, would identify themselves as Canadians, without any further elaboration, such as Polish Canadians or Canadians of Polish descent.[17] On the other hand the inability to speak Polish or lack of involvement in Polish organizations in Canada is equally inadequate in determining the ethnic identification of individuals, either with Polish culture or traditions, since those factors may be replaced by a thorough awareness of Polish culture and history, sufficient grounds for self-placement and identity.[18]

Activity in the organizations or cultural visibility are equally poor indicators of an individual's position within the Canadian cultural mosaic. There are many Polish immigrants and descendants of immigrants who are unable, for a variety of reasons, to participate or demonstrate their

206

ethnic identity even if they wish to do so. Residing in communities where there are no organizations, isolated from contact from other Polish people, they may express their Polishness at home, in the family context only. Others choose, for reasons of their own, to remain unaffiliated with formal organizations or activities of the Polish group in Canada, maintaining self-identity as Poles. The criterion of visibility can also be misleading. A casual observer would assume that individuals like George Stanton or John Bradley are members of the Anglo-Saxon group in Canada. In fact they, and thousands of others with Anglicized names, are Polish immigrants who came to Canada since 1945 and many of them are very conscious of their ethnicity and identity.[19]

Canadian citizenship cannot provide accurate guidelines for placing people in categories of ethnicity or nationality. In earlier periods, Canadian citizenship was sought for specific reasons; Canadian citizenship was one of the preconditions for becoming the full owner of the homestead. Others sought it to avoid discrimination and to secure work during the Great Depression. It was also noted that at some periods, "the two main political parties were not beyond producing masses of citizenship documents for immigrants so that they could vote for them."[20] Undoubtedly, there were many who could best demonstrate their appreciation of the conditions found in Canada, and their decision to remain permanently, by acquiring Canadian citizenship. By 1921, over 50% of the Polish immigrants had taken this step and by 1961, 90% of the Polish ethnic category were Canadian citizens.

The later arrivals often chose Canada after considering other possibilities, and consciously decided that this society would be their only home. Becoming Canadian citizens, they were fiercely loyal to Canada, defending its institutions and political system to visitors from Poland and elsewhere. At the same time, they did not see that giving up allegiance to Poland also required total abandonment of the Polish language, history and traditions. The feelings of loyalty to Canada did not necessarily displace the cultural and emotional ties with the Polish nation, nor did it require that they not demonstrate their 'Polishness' in Canada.

The problems inherent in self-identification are legion. Conceptualization of identity for people of Polish descent in Canada relates to such factors as time of arrival in Canada, the motive for emigrating, succeeding generations of Canadian-born children, the degree of socio-economic adjustment, availability of Polish institutions and organizations, and religiosity. Even more problematic is self-identification for the products of mixed marriages, especially with non-Slavic spouses. These issues have as yet not been a subject of research and it cannot be stated with any certainty who does or does not identify as a member of the Polish group in Canada, and more importantly, how this identity is defined.

IDENTITIES

In order to cope with this problem, a contingency model in the form of a typology is introduced, which may allow for a more accurate portrayal of how Polish ethnicity is defined and demonstrated. It must be stressed that the categories are generalizations, representing an undetermined number of individuals belonging to a group, but it is likely the categories reflect real situations and conditions of the Polish people in Canada. The typology is arbitrarily divided into five categories.

Poles in Canada

Poles in Canada are the immigrants whose main and persisting frame of reference remains Poland and Polish culture. They learn to conform to a number of requirements of the host society: Canadian norms and the English or French language are learned in order to function at work or in other unavoidable situations and in interaction with their hosts. But there is no internalization or even acceptance of the Canadian values and attitudes which are incongruent with those brought over from Poland,[21] and there is no change in the old values and beliefs.

In time, a degree of more or less satisfactory adjustment is achieved but the length of domicile in Canada, socio-economic successes, even acceptance of Canadian citizenship, do not really affect attitudes of the Poles in Canada towards 'Polishness' or towards their self-definition as exiles or 'temporary' residents, unable to return to Poland for political or other reasons. They remain transplanted Poles, dreaming of returning 'home' some day, if only to die in the country of their birth. The events and developments related to Poland and Polish people elsewhere are followed avidly through the press, correspondence, or other sources.

Individuals from this category are likely to be members of organizations and associations which stress Polish values and traditions or which emphasize experiences in the Polish armed forces. It is likely that they are also concerned with or involved in emigré politics and are well able to articulate their values, attitudes and identity. People from within this category would be extremely concerned with transmitting to their children the values and culture of Poland, and the Polish language would be used at home and in other situations wherever possible.

Polish Canadians

This category is largely composed of the post-war mature immigrants, already fully socialized into Polish norms and values, for whom it would be difficult or impossible to shed their attitudes and beliefs in favour of another set no matter how attractive the alternative might be. Recognizing the permanency of their domicile in Canada, they strive to adjust to the new society, adopting many Canadian norms and values, becoming in time loyal Canadian citizens, seeing in Canada a refuge for themselves and a permanent home for their children. In defining their identity they would likely term themselves 'New Canadians,' implying that they expect to become full members of their adopted society. At the same time they are already members of another society where they were raised, educated, lived and worked and whose characteristics and values will remain important to them throughout their lives.

They retain special feelings for Poland, its culture and traditions, and for other Polish people in Canada, all of which provides them with the satisfaction of a familiar language, customs and values, easing their period of transition from one society to another. It is likely that individuals from this category are active in the organizational structure in Canada wherever it is possible, establish and maintain a network of relationships with other Polish Canadians, but are also ready to learn about Canada and meet other Canadians. Their children would be fully aware of the cultural background of their parents, would learn to speak Polish at home and might even participate in some Polish-Canadian youth organizations.

Polish Canadians may be termed a transitory category for with time the individual's orientations turn more towards Canadian society. Contacts with Poland become less frequent and involvement and maintenance of aspects of Polish culture and traditions and emphasis on relations with other Polish Canadians are replaced with concerns of a specifically Canadian nature (education of their children, the economic situation, municipal taxes and similar concerns). Their ethnicity and self-identity as Poles will be affected strongly by Canadian citizenship, residence in a Canadian community and involvement in some Canadian pastime – hockey, football or various winter sports. In time, most may enter the next category, but a segment will likely remain Polish Canadians.

Canadian Polish

People of this category have adjusted fully to their new environment, have successfully resolved their two frames of reference, accepting Canada as their permanent home and a nation worthy of their first allegiance. Many Canadian values are readily adopted and internalized. When travelling abroad (especially visits to Poland) those people would proudly emphasize their Canadian citizenship. They are concerned with all matters affecting Canada, many being involved in some official or private capacity in working on Canadian issues and concerns. They also retain a clear awareness of their ethnic or national background, maintain in practice aspects of Polish culture, especially the language, and are able to draw on and enjoy their cultural and traditional heritage. They benefit from and have the advantages of membership in two cultures, able to utilize the best from both. In sympathetic and understanding Canadian political and social environments they can maintain a dual identity and two sets of allegiances, recognizing Canada as 'their' country and society, but retaining symbolic and emotional ties with Polish people, culture, and traditions.

Membership in the organizational structure of the Polish aggregate still provides emotional satisfaction, but people in this category are just as likely to have Canadian friends and belong to non-Polish organizations and associations. They would stress for their children the value of multilingualism (hoping that this would include the Polish language) and the richness of Polish culture, history and traditions in order that the children might become sufficiently interested to pursue and explore their ethnicity and cultural heritage.

Canadians of Polish Background

This category refers largely to those born in Canada or arriving here as very young children. Their self-identity and the main frame of reference is provided by Canadian institutions, norms, and values. Many of them would have learned to speak Polish as children, may even have attended part-time Polish schools, but the language and the information gained in their youth seldom survives at maturity.

Their notions of Poland, its history, culture, and traditions are vague, and their Polish ethnicity is derived largely from their parents and possibly a Polish parish. They are largely uninvolved in Polish organizations at maturity, few are able to read and communicate with ease in Polish, and their informal and secondary associations and relationships are seldom with people of Polish background.

Until marriage they remain in close contact with their parents and through them are involved in at least one Polish institution, the church. After marriage, which may often be with a non-Polish person, they tend to move away from Polish concentrations; the contact with their parents becomes less close and affiliation or participation in the Polish organizational structure ceases. Their children will not learn the Polish language and will be largely unaware of the Polish cultural heritage and of the organizational structure and the activities of the Polish community in Canada.

Statistical Polish Category

The people of this category are classified in the Canadian census as being of Polish ethnic origin. It is likely that most of them would prefer to classify themselves as Canadians without further elaboration. The majority are people born of Canadian-born parents who themselves acquired and retained only vague notions of their ethnic background and little awareness of the culture and traditions of Poland.

The only frame of reference and source of identity of the 'statistical Poles' are Canadian realities, norms and values. They are aware of Poland and its culture only to the extent taught in the public schools in Canada. They are unaware or uninterested in the structure and activities of the Polish community. They are in fact fully assimilated, consider themselves Canadians, often resent the government which insists on attaching meaningless labels to them. They are likely to be the third and fourth generation Polish immigrants to Canada.

Knowledge of the Polish group in Canada challenges the theory which holds that while the second generation immigrants attempt to become fully assimilated into the receiving society, the third generation seeks out and attempts to re-establish its ethnic background and identity.[22] There is little evidence of any significant number of individuals returning to claim their ethnic membership, at least for the Polish group in Canada.

It is more likely that with succeeding generations the self-classification may be totally redefined and membership in another group may be claimed. This is suggested by the fact that the 1961 Canadian census found 323,517 individuals claiming membership in the Polish group. Ten years later, following the arrival of 15,041 new Polish immigrants and a further estimated natural increase of 32,500,[23] the Polish group in the 1971 Canadian census actually shrank by over 7,000. No totally valid explanations for those incongruities can be offered at present, but the redefinition of ethnic identity is clearly seen in the 1971 Canadian census which recorded a total absence of Jewish people from the Polish ethnic category and the redefinition of ethnic membership by the Greek Orthodox and Ukrainian Catholics from Polish to other ethnic groups.[24] It is obvious that there are exceptions to the general pattern, where the third and fourth generation individuals remain closely affiliated with the Polish culture and traditions and may even be active in some organizational body. There are also those who deliberately and consciously discard all visible signs of their old identity in attempts to become fully Canadian in the shortest period possible.[25]

These and other possible exceptions are acknowledged, but the typology serves mainly as a device to allow a broader perception and portrayal of the Polish ethnic group in Canada from the basis of the self-identity of the individual members. The complexity of the problems related to the evaluation and measurement of ethnicity are illustrated in the following:

> Ethnicity . . . is not an all-or-none affair. Nor is it a logical affair. It is not at all understandable or describable in the Old World terms alone. For some it is composed of half-forgotten memories, unexplored longings, and intermittent preferences; for others it is active, structured, elaborated and constant. For some it is exclusionary and isolating; for others it is an avenue towards more authentic participation in general affairs. For some it is hidden and has negative and conflicted overtones; for others it is open, positive, and stimulating. For some it is archaic, unchanging and unalterable; for others it is evolving and creative. For some it is a badge of shame to ignore, forget and eradicate; for others it is a source of pride, a focus of initial loyalties and integrations from which broader loyalties and wider integrations can proceed. For some it is interpenetrated by religion and formal organizations; for others it is entirely secular and associational.[26]

In the final analysis it would seem that ethnic group cohesion, group solidarity and uniformity are largely myths; the Polish group, like other ethnic groups in Canada, is not in fact a whole but composed of many

211

divisions, in which criteria for self-placement and identity are one of the considerations. The group, or any person of authority within it, cannot dictate or impose rules to be obeyed, and each individual choses his own path, determines his own identity and defines his own place within the multicultural society.

BECOMING CANADIAN

The cultural distinctiveness of the Polish ethnic group in Canada rested at all times on the first generation immigrants. The post-1895 arrivals provided the foundations for the ethnic and cultural differentiation of the group by establishing a basic organizational structure designed to serve their specific needs and values.[27] They also provided an image, largely negative, for the host society. Large numbers of arrivals in the 1918-1939 period reinforced and expanded the established structure and helped to maintain the existing image of the Polish people for the Canadian hosts. This process was repeated once again in the 1946-1955 period, where the organizational structure and activities were largely responsible for maintaining the visibility of the Polish people to other Canadians. At this time the negative stereotypes weakened.

Despite the fact that Polish immigrants continue to come to Canada, albeit in decreasing numbers, the group as a whole is losing its 'Polishness.' The process is clearly demonstrated in a number of developments. Among the more significant are the rates of intermarriage of the Canadian-born ethnic category with other ethnic groups, and the retention of Polish as the mother tongue. While in 1921 only 4.9% did not have Polish as mother tongue, in 1971 this figure increased to 59.8%. More than half of the Polish category can no longer communicate in Polish, and this has significant implications for their awareness of the culture and traditions of their forefathers and for their self-identity.[28] Membership in the voluntary associations is also declining. It is estimated by one source that only between 5% and 7% of the Polish ethnic category are members of some such body.[29] There is no evidence at present to support this claim, but it is likely that the vast majority of the members are the first generation immigrants and only insignificant numbers of the Canadian-born generations are active in or belong to voluntary associations.

Parents who wanted their children to remain a part of the Polish community, or to identify with and share Polish norms and values, had to struggle not only against the rebellious character of the youth but also against the overpowering force and attraction of the Canadian mass media, peer groups, the public schools and other institutions. The outcome was to be expected. If not the second generation then the third became Canadians of Polish background or 'statistical Poles.' Many disappeared altogether through Anglicization of names, intermarriage and redefinition of self-placement. With time the immigrants themselves experienced varying degrees of acculturation, shedding some aspects of Polish culture and traditions. The process is continuing and the Polish group is becoming progressively less visible and culturally distinct.

ACCULTURATION, ASSIMILATION, INTEGRATION

The processes of acculturation and assimilation for the Polish immigrants and their descendants began soon after their arrival to the new society. Although Canada maintained an image of a multicultural society throughout its history there were always demands and pressures for conformity to the dominant group's norms and values.

For the purposes of this discussion *acculturation* will mean a more or less voluntary adaptation of the norms and values from the receiving society which were seen as superior. It involves a familiarity with and adoption of Canadian customs, history, and even traditions without a corresponding loss of Polish values and traditions, or loss of ethnic identity.

Assimilation is a process of total absorption of people of Polish descent into another culture and group. The process denotes the abandonment or absence of Polish norms, values, and customs and not merely outward conformity or even acceptance but a total adoption of the Canadian society's patterns of thinking, feeling and reacting. Individuals may retain knowledge of their original descent but such knowledge will no longer serve as a frame of reference for their beliefs and behaviour.

Both of the above concepts denote an adjustment of the immigrants to the receiving society in a one-sided process. The literature on ethnic groups in Canada frequently utilizes the term *integration* of immigrants within Canadian society. The validity of this term is questionable. Integration is defined by one sociological dictionary as "the mutual adjustment of diverse or conflicting culture traits to form a harmonious cultural system."[30] It is a mutual adaptation and exchange, and to be successful, integration demands readiness on the part of the immigrants and the hosts for change, mutual accommodation and adjustment.

This has not taken place in Canada to any extent. There are still two dominant cultures, the French Canadian and the Anglo-Saxon, and the millions of 'other' immigrants have affected the Canadian culture to a very limited extent. The processes of acculturation and assimilation are basically "Anglo-Conformity" in the sense that the newcomers adopt or assimilate to the two dominant cultures without effecting any significant changes in the Canadian society. The expectations and pressures for adjustment or conformity on the part of the immigrants to the norms and values of the Canadian society were never officially sanctioned but were no less effective. Those not complying, unable or unwilling to accede to the expectations of their hosts were, in the earlier periods, stigmatized by negative stereotypes, discriminated against in the economic market, and shunned socially.

Conformity to certain norms and expectations of the receiving society

213

was only one of the factors related to the eventual acculturation of the immigrants and the assimilation of their Canadian-born children. There are a number of other factors which facilitated both acculturation and assimilation. The values of the Polish aggregate were never strongly opposed to complete acculturation. Some concerned spokesmen urged the parents to instil in their children certain cultural values and knowledge of Poland, but the immigrants were often urged by their own press to adapt to Canada and to accept the permanency of their stay in the new society. Some organizations offered courses in the English language and provided other information designed to acquaint and prepare Polish immigrants to satisfy the expectations of their hosts.

Modern North American technology and values sooner or later overwhelmed the values and customs of the peasants and unskilled labourers. Most were fascinated by 'technological miracles,' by seeming prosperity, equality, and general well-being. If to succeed and share in the available benefits meant adoption of new norms and values, then this would be undertaken.

Residential dispersion and surrender of the mother tongue are considered the basic prerequisites for assimilation. There is no evidence of the existence of 'Polish ghettos' in any urban community.[31] There were concentrations of Polish residents in some larger cities, usually in close proximity to a Polish church. Even such concentrations were not lasting, for the immigrants were always mobile in search of work or better conditions and the Canadian-born descendants seldom remained in the same neighbourhood after marriage.

Although mature immigrants rarely forgot their mother tongue,[32] the absence of adequate schools or language and culture reinforcing agencies, combined with full exposure to the influences of Canadian schools, mass media, and peer groups, resulted in the Polish language never being learned well by the children of immigrants. Individuals could understand and speak it to some extent but found difficulty reading and especially writing in Polish. Those skills, mastered inadequately, fell quickly into disuse and in time were forgotten. A similar fate met the acquired knowledge of Polish history and various social values.

The 'Canadianized' individuals, especially those who anglicized their strange and difficult-to-pronounce names, have never been rejected by the two dominant cultural groups in Canada, for unlike the Asians, Blacks, or the Canadian Indians and Inuit, the Poles are not physically different from other Europeans and there were no problems related to colour differences. The 'Canadianized' individuals could enter into primary group relations with comparative ease. The high rates of exogamy have been noted elsewhere[33] and the products of mixed marriages have either joined another ethnic group through the father's non-Polish descent, or became "statistical Poles" if the mother was not Polish.

Other factors have some bearing on the degrees of acculturation or eventual assimilation. Satisfaction with life in Canada, in contrast with conditions experienced in Poland, and opportunities for upward socio-economic mobility for their 'Canadianized' children played a significant role. Tenuous contacts with Poland, if any, with the resulting cessation of family or community influences, often weakened the resolve to maintain a distinct cultural identity. There was always a proportion of Polish immigrants who came to Canada with weak national sentiments and self-identity as Poles, and saw little reason to reject the influences of Canadian institutions and values for themselves or their children. A weakening attachment to the Polish churches and parish organizations, geographical dispersion, absence of Polish institutions and organizations in smaller communities, further allowed an easy transition from the category of 'Polish Canadians' to 'statistical Poles' or to Canadians in other ethnic categories. People of Polish descent were assimilating or acculturating largely to the Anglo-Saxon cultural group, and to a much lesser extent to the French-Canadian culture.[34] They were also identifying as Ukrainians rather than Poles. The degree of such assimilation is recognized in one study[35] which found that of the 313,273 Ukrainians in the 1941 Canadian census, 17,675 gave Polish as their racial origin and 3,936 stated that Polish was the first language acquired in childhood.

A factor which provided the Ukrainians, Latvians, Lithuanians, Estonians, and some other ethnic groups with important motives for preservation of a strong and viable cultural distinctiveness is now largely absent for the Polish people. The ethnic groups above are deeply concerned with the struggles of the people in their homelands, which are now parts of the Soviet Union, and with the undermining of their cultures there. For a time in the 1950s, the London Polish exile government issued a slogan, "Wait for a new call to arms, be ready to return to fight for a free Poland again," and a state of readiness was maintained by a proportion of the veterans of the Polish armed services. In time, the readiness subsided and was eventually forgotten since it was realized that Polish culture, values and traditions not only survived under the ever-present influence of the Soviet Union but flourished in all areas.

In the earlier periods there were a number of factors retarding acculturation and assimilation. A proportion of Polish immigrants settled in isolated rural areas, occasionally among other Polish settlers, and under those conditions culture and ethnic identity were able to survive for more than one generation. For others the processes were retarded or made more difficult since they had to readjust not only from one sharply different culture to another, but also from a rural, traditional environment to an industrialized and urbanized society. This chasm was not easy to cross. Members of the receiving society did not always understand and welcome the newcomers into their midst and at some periods of history the dominant groups were insular if not xenophobic and indifferent to the problems of adjustment facing the newcomers.

The most important role in retarding the processes were held by the Polish organizations and the Polish-language press. The functions of the

Polish organizational structure in Canada have already been discussed. Without this structure, the Polish group would have been without any agencies of culture maintenance and sources of identity or reference for the dominant cultures, other ethnic groups, and for the unrepresented people of Polish descent in Canada. The processes of acculturation and assimilation are now accelerating, for unlike such culturally distinct groups as Portuguese, Italians, Greeks and others, the Polish group is receiving diminishing numbers of new immigrants from Poland who could reinforce ethnic consciousness for the established immigrants and their descendants.[36]

All Polish immigrants to Canada were subject to periods of readjustment, learning new symbols, norms and roles, and in the process, changing, modifying or abandoning their old cultural patterns. Many of the old customs and traditions were difficult to adapt to a modern urban society and they easily succumbed to acculturation pressures and fell into disuse, eventually forgotten among the Canadian-born generations. The present Polish group is at a crucial stage of its existence as a distinct cultural community within the overall ethno-cultural composition of Canada. The most important problem related to the continuation of the Canadian 'Polonia' rests on the recruitment of new members for the existing organizations. A small and shrinking proportion of the potential members is active in various efforts which serve to assure sources of identity and cultural visibility for the Polish group and other Canadians, but the activists and supporters are in the main the older generation.

The efforts to interest and involve the Canadian-born generations are weakened by the inability of the organizational leaders to agree upon what aspects of Polish culture and identity are to be preserved in Canada. The channels of communication are poorly developed between the generations. Confused and disillusioned by what they often consider irrelevant issues, goals and activities of the existing organizations, the children of immigrants are forced to search for their identity in Poland or among their Canadian-born peers, or else remain totally uninvolved and uninterested.

The Polish group is experiencing the rapid assimilation of its members into the predominantly Anglo-Saxon cultural group in Canada. A new development may retard or even reverse this process, however. The East-West detente, and the tacit recognition that Poland, while led by a Communist regime, still remains Polish, has eliminated for most previous reservations about contact with their place of birth. The revolution in transportation, especially the advent of charter flights, combined with the general prosperity of the Polish immigrants and their descendants, makes it feasible to travel to Poland frequently and also to sponsor relatives for visits to Canada. The Canadian-born are demonstrating an increasing interest in the land of their forefathers.

The re-establishment of such contacts with Poland and its culture may have lasting and significant influences on the people of Polish descent in

Canada, on their future self-identity and cultural distinctiveness. The contacts may well replace the position and influences of the threatened organizational complex, assuring the survival of the Canadian 'Polonia' in the foreseeable future.

NOTES

1. Lower, p. 564.
2. W.E. Mann, ed., *Social and Cultural Change in Canada* (Toronto, 1970), p. xiv.
3. R. Breton and M. Pinard, "Group Formation Among Immigrants: Criteria and Processes," *Canadian Journal of Economics and Political Science* XXVI (1960), p. 474.
4. The Canadian census bases ethnic origin classification on the paternal ancestry, and thus "ignores entirely the maternal lines of descent, the extent of intermarriage within society, the effects of English or French-language assimilation over generations and cross-cutting effects of birthplace and religion on ethnic group formation and identity." From A. Richmond, "Language, Ethnicity and the Problem of Identity in a Canadian Metropolis," Paper Presented at the IXth International Congress of Anthropological and Ethnological Sciences, Chicago, August 28 to September 8, 1973.
5. See R. Breton, *op. cit.*, for those views.
6. Even at this time some of the new arrivals, after a few years of residence in Canada, no longer claimed or admitted their ethnic origin. See Lubicz, *op. cit.*
7. Sheila Patterson, "This New Canada," *Queen's Quarterly* LXII (1955), p. 88.
8. Only one writer devoted some attention to the post-1956 arrivals. His findings are thus far inconclusive. See A. Matejko, "The New Wave of Polish Immigrants," *Migrant Echo* II (3), 1973, pp. 113-29.
9. CBC telecast a special one hour programme at prime television time to commemorate his birthday on October 21, 1973.
10. The address of the Hon. M. Sharp, Minister of External Affairs, at the biannual meeting of the Polish Congress, October 7, 1972, held at Thunder Bay, Ontario.
11. Wallace, p. 131.
12. For the Polish people, the language served as the main vehicle for providing a common identity "for a hundred and fifty years under Russian, Austrian, and German domination." See C.F. Ware, "Ethnic Communities," in E. Seligman, ed., *Encyclopedia of the Social Sciences*, Vol. V (New York, 1963), p. 609.
13. Visibility in the sense of both the cultural distinctiveness on the part of

the immigrants, and in the stereotypes and images that were prevalent in the receiving society to identify members of this group.

14. A Latin term for Poland.

15. It is interesting to note that enquiries as to one's ethnic background generated by signs such as physiognomy, a strange-sounding name, or an accent are common even at casual meetings between strangers. It appears to be acceptable to ask, "Where are you from?" meaning, "What is your ethnic background?"

16. This is suggested in a telephone interview with Mr. Peter Gzowski, who never identified with Poland or with the Polish group in Canada. He asserted that he was very pleased when Poland was victorious at the 1972 Olympic Games, or when a Polish team or individual of Polish background excelled in some performance. (March 8, 1973.).

17. A. Richmond, "Language, Ethnicity and the Problem of Identity," Table I, p. 28, notes that in the Metropolitan Toronto 9% of the Polish respondents chose Canadian as their ethnicity.

18. Wojciechowski, *op. cit.*, raises this problem and concludes that language is not the most important prerequisite for an individual's self-identity as a member of an ethnic group.

19. *The Toronto Daily Star*, June 6, 1969; *The Toronto Telegram*, January 18, October 18, 1969.

20. Mazurkiewicz, p. 100.

21. Attitudes and values represented in ostentatious and visible material possessions, preoccupation with work or occupation to the exclusion of other interests, difficulty in the establishment of close and intimate personal relationships with Canadians, are some examples of Canadian reality decried by those people.

22. See E.L. Bender and G. Kagiwada, "Hansen's Law of Third Generation Return and the Study of American Religio-Ethnic Groups," *Phylon* 29 (1960), pp. 360-70, and M.L. Hansen, "Third Generation in America: The Problem of the Third Generation Immigrant," *Commentary* 14 (1952), pp. 492-500, for a further discussion of the third generation return to ethnicity.

23. R. Kogler and B. Heydenkorn, "Poles in Canada, 1971," in B. Heydenkorn, ed., *Past and Present* (Toronto, 1974).

24. There were 27,294 Jewish members of the Polish ethnic group in the 1961 Canadian census and none in the 1971 census. At the same time the Greek Orthodox segment shrank from 9,752 in 1961 to 5,565 in 1971 and the Ukrainian Catholic from 10,681 to 7,205. See Table 9 of this study.

25. As was noted by A. Schutz, *Collected Papers*, Vol. II (The Hague, 1964), they may be willing and able to become a part of the group they aspire to belong to and may be accepted, but they will remain strangers to the extent that they cannot share in the history or intrinsic values since "graves and reminiscences can be neither transferred nor conquered."

26. J.A. Fishman *et al.*, *Language Loyalty in the United States* (The Hague, 1966), p. 390.

27. What was created were not transplants of cultural and linguistic entities brought over from Poland, but rather a partial reflection of their culture and traditions.

28. Loss of language is not irreversible, as was illustrated by one observer who found that "one woman I know spoke no Polish as a child, is now fluent and directs Polish-language schools simply because there is a desire to return to one's own roots." From S. Burke, "Canada: Multicultural," Report Published by the Citizenship Branch of the Provincial Secretary of Citizenship, Government of Ontario. Conference held at the University of Toronto, August 7, 1970.

29. B. Heydenkorn, "Problemy Polonii," p. 138. This figure does not include parish affiliation.

30. G.A. Theodorson and A.G. Theodorson, *Modern Dictionary of Sociology* (New York, 1969), p. 209.

31. Rapidly growing cities, the influence of Canadian institutions, and modern communications generally precluded the establishment and survival of homogeneous ethnic enclaves for any length of time. See A.G. Darroch and W.G. Marston, "Ethnic Differentiation: Ecological Aspects of a Multi-dimensional Concept," *The International Migration Review* IV (1969), pp. 71-94; A. Richmond, *Ethnic Residential Segregation in Metropolitan Toronto* (Toronto, 1972).

32. Sir Casimir Gzowski lost the ability to communicate freely in Polish in his later years. See Turek, *Sir Casimir Gzowski*, pp. 96-7.

33. See page 155 of this study.

34. Polish Ethnic Group by Mother Tongue, 1971

English	164,525	(52.0%)
French	4,360	(1.4%)
Polish	121,420	(38.4%)
Other	26,120	(8.3%)

Source: *1971 Census of Canada*, Catalogue 92-731.

35. Hunchak, pp. 26-30.

36. A. Jaworski, "Wynarodowienie Się Polonii Kanadyjskiej," *Kultura* (Paris, 1974), 1/2, pp. ; 79-192.

TWELVE

Conclusion

A Canadian citizen is privileged to live in a land where he is not
only allowed but also encouraged to perpetuate the language,
religion, and culture of his forebears.

Citizenship Programme Circular

Ours is a story largely without heroes, remarkable deeds or great
achievements. Official reports, dry statistics, dusty records, memoirs, and
weather-beaten graves tell of arrival, search for work, claims of land,
marriages, births, and finally death. It is a simple story of people who
came with courage and perserverance, who experienced very difficult
beginnings and harsh struggles for their existence, but who came with
determination to succeed and provide their children with chances for a
better future in a society which had much to offer.

They came haggard, confused and tired after their long journeys, but
possessing thrift, industry, strong hands and a willingness to work. They
did not expect a soft life or charity but were prepared to earn their place in
the new society. Social positions or economic riches were hard to grasp for
those toilers on land, in factories, on roads or in mines and forests. Each
new arrival had to discover, interpret and adjust to the new world he
found himself in, for he could not take it for granted that others would
share his understanding of the nature of the world as he knew it. For
generations and decades the new arrivals experienced economic and social instability and isolation, not only from their old communities, friends,
and relatives but also from other Polish people in Canada. They faced an
environment of different values, customs and techniques and they had to
cope with it from a socio-economic position, dictated by their 'entrance
status,' which was somewhere near the bottom of the Canadian scale.
They came as a 'non-preferred' category of immigrants, but on the whole
they were good, law-abiding people and very few were found undesirable

220

and deported. They strove to meet their obligations as 'landed immigrants' or as citizens of Canada, and attempted to satisfy the requirements of their hosts by adopting new values and standards.

Despite the many problems and difficulties, comparison with the conditions left behind could not but result in a very favourable image of Canada for most of them. Canada was not only the land of economic opportunity but also a political or ideological haven, and the Polish immigrants attempted to demonstrate their appreciation through loyalty to their new home. Their children were accepted fully and limited only by their own potentialities from a complete entrance into all spheres of the Canadian society or from achievement of fuller satisfaction for themselves and their families.

Unlike the small number of prominent early Polish arrivals who left a lasting imprint on the Canadian society and history, the masses of later immigrants, the land settlers and unskilled labourers, remained largely anonymous. In their unrecognized efforts they have contributed their share to Canadian development as co-builders of the West and other parts of Canada. The survivors from among the early pioneers and their many children who are now reaching retirement ages are justifiably proud of their achievements.

In retrospect, they were the people that this society needed at the time; people of physical strength, endurance, and lasting hope in the future. Through their unrecorded and forgotten efforts they helped to lay the foundations of our modern Canadian society. Their followers from Poland aided in the expansion and improvement of what was begun over 100 years ago and the present Polish ethnic group is adding its contributions to the Canadian whole, to the new tempo and vitality of the simmering pot which may produce in time a new type of society.

Canada grows, prospers, and changes. The dominant ethnocultural groups have moved from prejudice and indifference to tolerance and more recently to greater understanding of the many ethnic minority groups and their cultures in this society. The dominant groups have moved away from paternalism and condescension to a greater sensitivity for the feelings and values of the new arrivals. The attitudes are now more constructive and all newcomers are more readily accepted on their own merit, not because of established stereotypes or images. There is an appreciation not only for their training, education and skills, but also a recognition of their distinct cultural heritage.

In the increasingly sympathetic environment and greater range of socio-economic opportunities for all ethnic groups, the Polish people have lost their entrance status and the accompanying negative stereotypes, and have moved from the status of farmers, farm workers and unskilled labourers to become merchants, manufacturers, highly skilled technicians and professionals. Today, members of this group can be found not only in the poorer areas of Toronto, Montreal or Winnipeg but also in the most exclusive and expensive residential areas of those cities. They still farm, work in mines and perform unskilled work but the proportion of owners, managers, white collar workers, technicians, intellectuals and professionals is now significant and is increasing yearly.

They lead normal family lives, enjoy freedom to worship in their own churches, pursue their cultural and traditional interests and also claim their full place in the Canadian society. Canada is their permanent home and the only country for their children. Aware of the privileges, obligations and duties of Canadian citizenship, considering themselves an integral part of Canadian society and nation, they are not relinquishing their sentiments or a special place in their hearts for Poland, Polish people and culture.

The people of Polish descent have generally adjusted and prospered and are happy to be in Canada and we believe that Canada has been enriched by their coming and settling here. Canada is indeed unique among the nations of the world and the members of this society, be they 'New Canadians' or 'old immigrants,' are proud of being a part of this country. These observations made by R.S. Browne in 1916 are truly appropriate today:

> Canada is a type of nation where many nationalities live together in concert, each maintaining the flavour of its original heritage and its interests in its original homeland, at the same time, combining to form a richer, more cosmopolitan culture and providing a lesson of international amity for other countries.

APPENDIX I

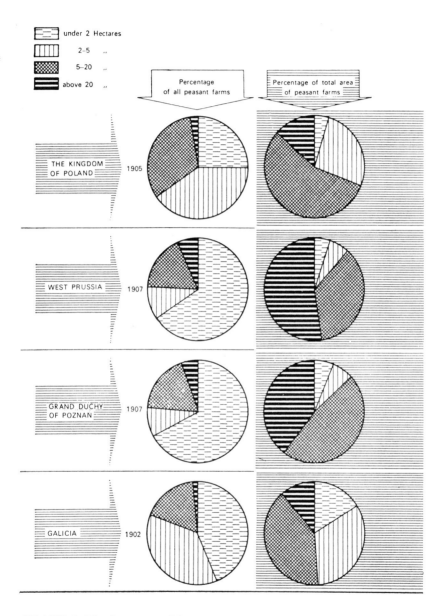

under 2 Hectares
2–5 „
5–20 „
above 20 „

Percentage of all peasant farms

Percentage of total area of peasant farms

THE KINGDOM OF POLAND — 1905

WEST PRUSSIA — 1907

GRAND DUCHY OF POZNAN — 1907

GALICIA — 1902

GRAPH 1: The Structure of Peasant Farms in Poland

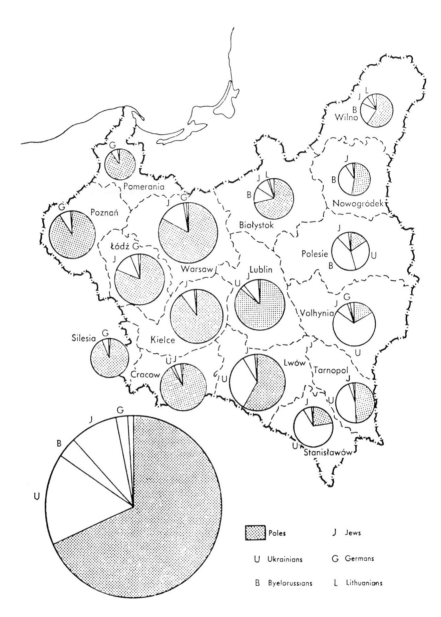

GRAPH 2: *Nationalities in Poland according to the 1931 Census*

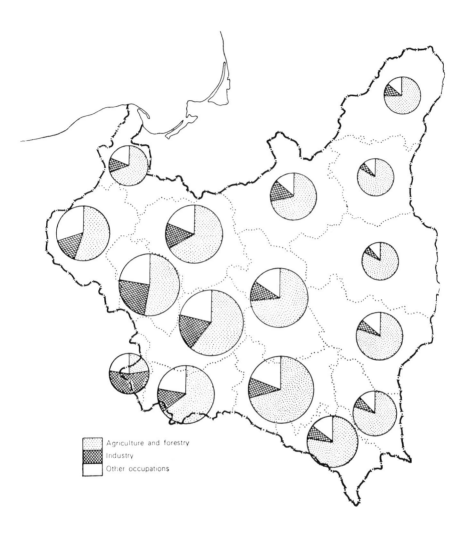

Agriculture and forestry
Industry
Other occupations

GRAPH 3: Population of Poland according to Occupation, 1936

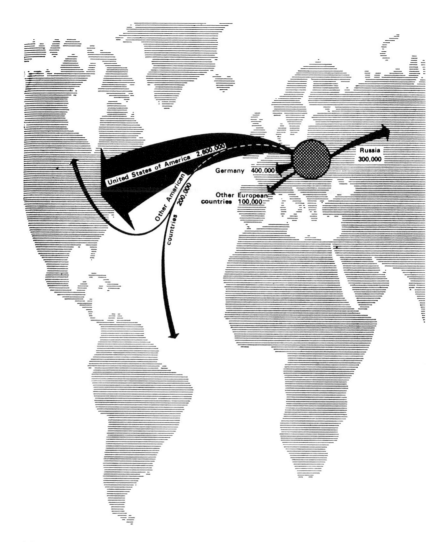

GRAPH 4: Emigration from Polish lands, 1870-1914

Bibliography

Abbott, Edith. *Historical Aspects of the Immigration Problem.* Chicago: The University of Chicago Press, 1926.

Adbank, Zbigniew. "Jednak Wracam z Kanady," *Kultura* (Paris), 57/58, 85-92.

Adamski, Franciszek. "Funkcjonowanie Katolickiego Modelu Małżeństwa i Rodziny w Środowisku Miejskim," *Znak*, XXV (8), 1050-1069.

Admission to Canada of Members of the Polish Armed Forces. Brief Submitted to the Standing Committee of the Senate of Canada on Immigration and Labour by the Canadian Polish Congress in Ottawa, June 25, 1946.

Adolf, Jacek. "The Polish Press in Toronto." York University, Mimeograph, 1970.

Anderson, J.T.M. *The Education of the New Canadians.* Toronto: J.M. Dent & Sons, 1918.

Angus, H.F. "The Future of Immigration into Canada," *Canadian Journal of Economics and Political Science*, XII (1946), 379-386.

Archacki, Henry. "America's Polish Gift to Canada." 24th Annual Meeting of the Polish-American Historical Association, Toronto, December 28, 1967.

Avery, D.H. "The Immigrant Industrial Worker in Canada, 1896-1930: The Vertical Mosaic as a Historical Reality." Paper presented at the Conference of the Canadian Ethnic Studies Association, Toronto, October 26, 1973.

Balch, Emily. *Our Slavic Fellow Citizens.* New York: Charities Publication Committee, 1910.

Bargiel, Jan. *Amerykańska Pula; Organizacja Zbytu Amerykanskich Rolników* Warsaw: Związek Spółdzielni Rolniczych i Zarobkowych Gospodarskich Rzeczpospolitej Polskiej, 1937.

Barkway, Michael. "Turning Point for Immigration," *Canadian Institute of International Affairs*, XVII (4), 1957.

Barnett, C.R. *Poland.* New Haven: HRAF Press, 1958.

Bauman, Zygmunt. "Economic Growth, Social Structure, Elite Formation: The Case of Poland," *International Social Science Journal*, 16 (1964), 203-216.

Bender, Eugene L., and George Kagiwada. "Hansen's Law of Third Generation Return and the Study of American Religio-Ethnic Groups," *Phylon*, 29 (1960), 360-370.

Biblioteczka Nauczyciela Szkół Polskich a Kanadzie; Zeszyt I. Toronto: Związek Nauczycielstwa Polskiego w Kanadzie, 1973.

Boniface, Rev., OFM. *Pioneering in the West.* Vancouver: Evergreen Press, 1957.

Borhek, J.T. "Ethnic Group Cohesion," *American Journal of Sociology*, 76 (1970), 33-46.

Breton, O.E. *Kowal Boży.* London: Veritas, 1961.

Breton, R. "Institutional Completeness of Ethnic Communities and the Personal Relations of Immigrants," *The American Journal of Sociology*, LXX (1964), 193-205.

Breton, R., and M. Pinard. "Group Formation Among Immigrants: Criteria and Processes," *Canadian Journal of Economics and Political Science*, XXVI (1960), 465-477.

Bridgeman, Rev. W. *Breaking Prairie Sod.* Toronto: Musson, 1920.

Broadfoot, Barry. *Ten Lost Years, 1929-1939: Memoirs of Canadians Who Survived the Depression.* Toronto: Doubleday, 1973.

Broda, Józef. *W Cieniu Kanadyjskiego Klonu.* Ottawa: Private Edition, 1966.

Bromke, Adam. "Diaspory Polskiej – Ciąg Dalszy . . . ," *Związkowiec*, Toronto June 13, 1972.

Buchwald, Kazimierz, OMI. "25-Lecie Stowarzyszenia Polaków Manitoby." *Czas*, Winnipeg, October 25, 1959.

Burke, Stanley. "Canada: Multicultural." Report published by the Citizenship Branch of the Provincial Secretary of Citizenship, Government of Ontario. Conference held at the University of Toronto, August 7, 1970.

Burnet, Jean R. *Ethnic Groups in Upper Canada.* Ontario Historical Society Research Publication No. 1, 1972.

Canada Year Book, 1905 – . Second Series. Ottawa: Government Printer, 1905.

Canadians All: Poles in Canada. Winnipeg: Acme Advertising Agency, 1938.

Child, E.L. *Italians in America: The Second Generation Conflict.* New Haven: Yale University Press, 1943.

Chrypinski, Vincent C. "Unity and Conflict Among Canadian Slavs: Two Examples of Alien Infiltration," *Slavs in Canada*, Vol. I. Edmonton: Inter-University Committee on Canadian Slavs, 1966.

Ciołkoszowa, Lidia, and Barbara Wysocka. *Informator Polski.* London: Światowy Związek Polaków z Zagranicy, 1945.

Citroen, H.A. *European Immigration Overseas, Past and Future.* The Hague: Martinus Nijhof, 1951.

Clark, S.D. *The Social Development of Canada.* Toronto: The University of Toronto Press, 1942.

Connor, Ralph. *The Foreigner.* New York: n.p., 1909.

Corbett, David C. *Canada's Immigration Policy: A Critique.* Toronto: The University of Toronto Press, 1957.

Crowfoot, A.H. *The Life of Isaac Hellmuth, This Dreamer.* Toronto: Copp Clark, 1963.

Cultural Contribution of Newcomers to Canada. Ottawa: Citizenship Branch, Department of Citizenship and Immigration, 1965.

Dafoe, J.W., *Clifford Sifton in Relation to His Times.* Toronto: Macmillan, 1931.

Dalton, Melville. "Informal Factors in Career Achievement," *American Journal of Sociology,* LVI (1951), 407-415.

Danziger, Kurt. *The Socialization of Immigrant Children, Part I.* Toronto: York University Ethnic Research Programme, 1971.

Darroch, A. Gordon and Wilfred G. Marston. "Ethnic Differentiation: Ecological Aspects of a Multi-Dimensional Concept," *The International Migration Review,* IV (1969), 71-94.

Dawson, C.A. "Group Settlement: Ethnic Communities in Western Canada." in W.A. Mackintosh and W.L.G. Joerg, eds., *Canadian Frontiers of Settlement,* Vol. VII. Toronto: Macmillan, 1936.

Dawson, C.A., and R.W. Murchie, "The Settlement of the Peace River Country," in W.A. Mackintosh and W.L.G. Joerg, eds., *Canadian Frontiers of Settlement.* Toronto: Macmillan, 1934.

Dawson, C.A., and Eva R. Younge, "Pioneering in the Prairie Provinces," in W.A. Mackintosh and W.L.G. Joerg, eds., *Canadian Frontiers of Settlement,* Vol. VIII. Toronto: Macmillan, 1940.

Department of the Secretary of State. *Our History.* Ottawa: Information Canada, 1970.

Dwudzieste Ósme Sprawozdanie. St. Stanislaus Parish (Toronto) Credit Union. Toronto: Głos Poski, 1972.

Eisenstadt, S.N. *The Absorbtion of Immigrants.* London: Routledge & Kegan Paul, 1952.

Elkin, F. *The Family in Canada.* Ottawa: Vanier Institute of the Family, 1964.

Emerson, Hugh. *The Sowing.* Winnipeg: Vanderhoof-Gunn Col. Ltd., 1909.

England, Robert. *The Central European Immigrant in Canada.* Toronto: Macmillan, 1929.

_____. "Disbanded and Discharged Soldiers in Canada Prior to 1914," *The Canadian Historical Review,* XXVII (1946), I, 1-18.

Estreicher, S. "Galicia in the Period of Autonomy and Self-Government, 1849-1914," in W.F. Reddaway *et al.,* eds., *The Cambridge History of Poland,* Vol. II. Cambridge: University Press, 1941.

Fairclough, Ellen. "What Immigration Means to Canada," *Migration News,* 8 (1959), 2, 19-20.

Fishman, J.A., *et al. Language Loyalty in the United States.* The Hague: Mouton & Co., 1966.

Foster, Kate A. *Our Canadian Mosaic.* Toronto: The Dominion Council YWCA, 1926.

Francis, E.K. "Variables in the Formation of So-Called 'Minority Groups,'" *The American Journal of Sociology,* 60 (1954), 6-14.

Garczyński, L.S. *Co To Jest Kanada?* Warsaw: Polskie Wydawnictwo Emigracyjne, 1930.

――. "Polskość Naszych Dzieci," *Związkowiec*, Toronto, No. 5, 1933.

――. *Handel, Przemysł Naszą Przyszłością.* Winnipeg: Związek Polskich Kupców, Przemysłowców i Rękodzielników, 1934.

――. "Od Atlantyku Po Ocean Spokojny," *Księga Pamiątkowa Z.P.w.K. 1906-1946.* Toronto: The Polish Alliance Press, 1946.

Gellner, John, and John Smerek. *The Czechs and Slovaks in Canada.* Toronto: The University of Toronto Press, 1968.

Gibbon, J. Murray. *The Canadian Mosaic.* Toronto: McClelland and Stewart, 1938.

Giffen, P.J. "Rates of Crime and Delinquency," in W.T. McGrath, ed., *Crime and its Treatment in Canada.* Toronto: Macmillan, 1965.

Głęborzecki, S.K. "Kanadyjskie Wilno," *Związkowiec*, Toronto, Nos. 23, 25, 27, 1957.

Glista, T. "Najpilniejsze Zadania na Przyszłość," *Związkowiec*, Toronto, No. 35, May 4, 1973.

Gocki, Rev. A.J. *Historia Osiedli Polskiej w Candiac, Saskatchewan.* Regina: n.p., 1924.

Goldlust, John, and Anthony H. Richmond. "Factors Associated with Commitment to and Identification with Canada." Paper Presented at the Conference of the Canadian Ethnic Studies Association, Toronto, October 26, 1973.

Gordon, M.M. *Assimilation in American Life.* New York: Oxford University Press, 1964.

Green, A.W. "A Re-examination of the Marginal Man Concept," *Social Forces*, 26 (1947), 2, 167-171.

Goldberg, M.M. "A Qualification of the Marginal Man Theory," *American Sociological Review*, 6 (1941), 52-58.

Grodecki, G. "Polish Language Schools in Canada," in Cornelius J. Jaenen, ed., *Slavs in Canada*, Vol. III, Inter-University Committee on Canadian Slavs. Toronto: Ukrainian Echo Pub. Co. Ltd., 1971.

Guide for New Canadians. Toronto: The Telegram, n.d.

Guillet, Edwin C. *The Great Migration.* Toronto: University of Toronto Press, 1967.

Haiman, Mieczysław. *Ślady Polskie w Ameryce.* Chicago: Dziennik Zjednoczenia, 1938.

Hamilton, L. "Foreigners in the Canadian West," *The Dalhousie Review*, XVII (1938), 448-460.

Handlin, Oscar. *The Uprooted.* New York: Grosset & Dunlap, 1951.

――, ed. *Immigration as a Factor in American History.* Englewood Cliffs, N.J.: Prentice-Hall, 1959.

Hawkins, Freda. *Canada and Immigration, Public Policy and Public Concern.* Montreal: McGill-Queen's University Press, 1972.

Helling, R. "Canadian Unity: Conformity or Diversity?" Fourth Conference on Inter-Group Relations, Port Elgin, Ontario, July 12-17, 1964.

Heydenkorn, Benedykt. "Emigracja

Polska w Kanadzie," *Kultura*, 54 (1952), 79-93.

____. "Polonia Kanadyjska," *Kultura*, 144 (1959), 85-107.

____. *'Związkowiec' - Monografia Pisma Polonijnego.* Toronto: Polish Alliance Press, 1963.

____. "Literatura Słowiańska w Kanadzie," *Kultura*, 229 (1966), 134-136.

____. "The Social Structure of Canadian Polonia," in T.W. Krychowski, ed., *Polish Canadians: Profile and Image.* Toronto: Polish Alliance Press, 1969.

____. "Polish Contribution to Canadian Culture." Toronto: The Polish Canadian Research Institute, 1970.

____. "The Immigration Policy of Canada," in J.M. Kirschbaum, B. Heydenkorn and P. Gaida, eds., *Twenty Years of the Ethnic Press Association in Ontario.* Toronto: The Ethnic Press Association in Ontario, 1971.

____. "Problemy Polonii Kanadyjskiej," in B. Heydenkorn, ed., *Sympozjum 50.* Toronto: The Polish Alliance Press, 1972.

____. *Pionierska Droga Związku Polaków w Kanadzie.* Toronto: The Polish Alliance Press, 1973.

Hill, Douglas. *The Opening of the Canadian West.* London: Heinemann, 1967.

Horn, Michiel. *The Dirty Thirties.* Toronto: Copp Clark, 1972.

Hourwich, Isaac A. *Immigration and Labour.* New York: Huebsch, 1922.

Hubicz, Edward M. *The History of Our Lady of the Lake Church, Winnipeg Beach, Manitoba, 1911-1956.* Winnipeg: n.p., 1956.

____. *Father Joe - A Manitoban Missionary.* London: Veritas Foundation Publication Centre, 1958.

____. "Early Polish Priests in Manitoba," in V. Turek, ed., *The Polish Past in Canada.* Toronto: The Polish Alliance Press, 1960.

____. *Polish Churches in Manitoba.* London: Veritas Foundation Publication Centre, 1960.

Hughes, Barry Conn. "The Seafarers' New Strongman," *The Canadian Magazine*, October 27, 1973, pp. 2-7.

Hunchak, N.J. *Population: Canadians of Ukrainian Origin.* Series No. I. Winnipeg: Ukrainian Canadian Committee, 1945.

Hurd, W. Burton. "The Case for a Quota," *Queen's Quarterly*, XXXVI (1929), 145-159.

Hutchinson, B. *The Unknown Country.* New York: Coward-McCann, 1942.

Ilustrowany Kalendarz Tygodnika Polskiego w Kanadzie na Rok 1949. Winnipeg: Polish Press, Limited, 1949.

Immigration Statistics - Canada (1956-). Ottawa: Information Canada, Manpower and Immigration, 1956.

Informator. *Polski Dorobek w Dziedzinie Handlu, Przemysłu i Wolnych Zawodów.* Toronto: Stowarzyszenie Polskich Kupców, Przemsłowców i Profesjonalistów w Toronto, 1964.

Isajiw, Wsevolod W., and Norbert J.

Hartmann. "Changes in the Occupational Structure of Ukrainians in Canada," in W.E. Mann, ed., *Social and Cultural Change in Canada*.Toronto:Copp Clark,1970.

Iwicki, John C.R. *The First One Hundred Years*. Rome: Gregorian University Press, 1966.

Jaenen, C.J. "Ruthenian Schools in Western Canada, 1897-1919," *Paedagogica Historica*, 10 (1970), 3, 517-541.

Jakimowicz, Rev. T.W. *Podręczniki Dla Użytku Polsko-Baptyjskiego Kościoła*. Buffalo: American Baptist Publication Society, 1897.

Jaworski, Adam. "Wynarodowienie Się Polaków w Kanadzie," *Kultura*, 116 (1957), 66-94.

———. "Wynarodowienie Się Polonii Kanadyjskiej," *Kultura*, (1974), 179-192.

Jaworsky, S.J. "Newspapers and Periodicals of Slavic Groups in Canada During the Period of 1965-1969," Unpublished MA Thesis, University of Ottawa, 1971.

Jenks, J.W., and W.J. Lauck. *The Immigration Problem*. New York: Funk and Wagnalls, 1912.

Jubileusz Parafii 55 Lat Św. Stanisława Kostki. Hamilton, Ontario, 55 Years Church Jubilee, 1911-1966, 1968.

Kage, J. "From 'Bohunk' to 'New Canadian,'" *Social Worker*, 29 (1961), 4.

Kalbach, W.E. *The Impact of Immigration on Canada's Population*. Ottawa: Dominion Bureau of Statistics, 1970.

Kalendarz Czasu Na 1951 Rok. Winnipeg: Polish Press Limited, 1951.

Kalendarz Polaka w Kanadzie Na Rok 1950. Winnipeg: Polish Almanac Publishers, 1950.

Kalendarz Rolnika Polskiego Na Rok 1929. Toruń (Poland): Pomorska Drukarnia Rolnicza S.A., 1929.

Kaye, V.J. "Sir Casimir Stanislaus Gzowski, A Great Canadian (1813-1898)," *Revue de l'Universite d'Ottawa*, 25 (1955), 4, 457-464.

———. "People of Polish Origin," *Encyclopedia Canadiana*, Vol. 8. Ottawa: The Canadian Company Ltd., 1965, 226-230.

———. "Problems of Research Connected with the Dictionary of Ukrainian-Canadian Biography, 1891-1900," in Cornelius J. Jaenen, ed., *Slavs in Canada*, Vol. III. Toronto: Ukrainian Echo Pub. Co., Ltd., 1971.

Kayfetz, Ben. "The Jewish Community in Toronto," in A. Rose, ed., *A People and Its Faith: Essays on Jews and Reform Judaism in a Changing Canada*. Toronto: University of Toronto Press, 1959.

Kelner, Merrijoy. "Ethnic Penetration into Toronto's Elite Structure," *Canadian Review of Sociology and Anthropology*, 7 (1970), 128-137.

Kennedy, H.A. *The Book of the West*. Toronto: Ryerson, 1925.

———. *New Canada and the New Canadians*. Toronto: Musson, 1907.

Keyfitz, Nathan. "The Growth of the Canadian Population," *Population Studies*, IV (June, 1950).

Kinastowski, S. "Dzieje Polonii w Kitchener," *Głos Polski*, 24 (June 14, 1973).

Kirkconnell, W. *The European Heritage.* Toronto: Dent, 1930.

_____. *Canadians All.* Ottawa: Minister of National War Services, 1941.

_____. *A Slice of Canada.* Toronto: University of Toronto Press, 1967.

Kirschbaum, Joseph M. *Slovaks in Canada.* Toronto: Canadian Ethnic Press Association, 1967.

Klymasz, R.B. *A Classified Dictionary of Slavic Surname Changes in Canada.* Winnipeg: Ukrainian Free Academy of Sciences Onomastica No. 22, 1961.

Kogler, R.K. "Ankieta Szkolna." Toronto: Canadian Polish Congress Mimeograph, 1965.

_____. "A Demographic Profile of the Polish Community in Canada," in T.W. Krychowski, ed., *Polish Canadians: Profile and Image.* Toronto: The Polish Alliance Press, 1969.

Kogler, R., and B. Heydenkorn. "Poles in Canada, 1971," in B. Heydenkorn, ed., *Past and Present.* Toronto: Polish-Canadian Research Institute, 1974.

Kos-Rabcewicz-Zubkowski, L., and W.E. Greening. *Sir Casimir Gzowski.* Toronto: Burns & MacEachern, 1959.

Kruszka, Wacław. *Historya Polska w Ameryce.* Milwaukee: Kuryer Press, 1905.

Krychowski, T. *The Polish Canadian Research Institute: Its Aim And Achievements.* Toronto: The Polish Canadian Research Institute, 1967.

_____. *The Register of Persons Actively Engaged in Scholarly Pursuits or Scientific Research.* Seventh Edition. Toronto: Polsko-Kanadyjski Instytut Badawczy, 1970.

Księga Pamiątkowa 20-lecia Polskiego Zboru Ew-Augburskiego w Toronto. Toronto: Rada Kościelna, 1973.

Księga Pamiątkowa z Okazji 30-lecia Istnienia Stowarzyszenia Polskich Kupców, Przemysłowców i Profesjonalistów w Toronto, Ontario, Canada, 1932-1962. Toronto: n.p., 1962.

Księga Pamiątkowa Związku Polaków w Kanadzie 1906-1946. Toronto: Polish Alliance Press Limited, 1946.

Księga Pamiątkowa Związku Narodowego Polskiego w Kanadzie, 1930-1955. Toronto: Komitet Księgi Pamiątkowej, 1955.

Landau, Herbert. *Language and Culture.* New York: Oxford University Press, 1966.

Learner, M. "People and Place," in Peter I. Rose ed., *Nation of Nations.* New York: Random House, 1972.

Lee-Whiting, Brenda B. "First Polish Settlement in Canada," *Canadian Geographical Journal*, LXXV (1967), 108-112.

L.O. *Polskie Duchowieństwo w Ameryce – Jego Zasługi, Patriotyzm i Moralność.* Toledo, Ohio: A.A. Paryski, n.d.

Lopata, Helena Znaniecki. "The Function of Voluntary Associations in an Ethnic Community: 'Polonia,'" in E.W. Burgess and D.J.

Bogue, eds., *Contributions to Urban Sociology.* Chicago: University of Chicago Press, 1964.

Lower, Arthur R.M. *Colony to Nation: A History of Canada.* Don Mills: Longman, 1971.

Lozowchuk, Y.W., and H. Radecki. "Slavs in Canada." Paper Presented to the Symposium on Race and Ethnic Relations at the Annual American Anthropological Association Meeting, Toronto, November 30-December 2, 1972.

Lubicz, Józef. *Kanada - Kraj i Ludność.* Toledo, Ohio: A.A. Paryski, 1929.

Luke, L.W. "Citizenship and Immigration." 28th Annual Meeting of the Canadian Chamber of Commerce, Victoria, B.C., October 3, 1957.

McCullough, C. "Polish Government in Exile Battles on," *The Globe and Mail,* Toronto, July 4, 1973.

McDougal, Duncan M. "Immigration into Canada, 1851-1920," *Canadian Journal of Economics and Political Science,* XXVII (1961), 162-175.

McInnis, Edgar. *Canada: A Political and Social History.* Toronto: Holt, 1969.

Magrath, C.A. *Canada's Growth.* Ottawa: The Mortimer Press, 1910.

Makowski, Bolesław. *Polska Emigracja w Kanadzie.* Linz-Salzburg: Związek Polaków w Austrii, 1951.

———. "Historia Towarzystwa Białego Orła," *Złoty Jubileusz Towarzystwa Białego Orła w Montrealu.* Toronto: Jubilee Committee, 1952.

Makowski, William B. *History and Integration of Poles in Canada.* Niagara Peninsula: The Canadian Polish Congress, 1967.

Mały Rocznik Statystyczny 1939. Warsaw: Główny Urząd Statystyczny, 1939.

Mann, W.E., ed. *Social and Cultural Change in Canada.* Vol. I. Toronto: Copp. Clark, 1970.

Markowska, D. "Family Patterns in a Polish Village," *Polish Sociological Bulletin,* 2 (1963), 8, 97-110.

Marunchak, M.H. *The Ukrainian Canadians: A History.* Winnipeg: Ukrainian Free Academy of Sciences, 1970.

Matejko, Alexander. "The New Wave of Polish Immigrants," *Migrant Echo.* II (1973), 3, 113-129.

Mazurkiewicz, Roman. *Polskie Wychodźctwo i Osadnictwo w Kanadzie.* Warsaw: Dom Książki Polskiej, 1930.

Mincer, Tadeusz. *The Agrarian Problem in Poland.* London: Polish Research Centre, 1944.

Morgan, H.J., ed. *Canadian Men and Women of the Time.* Toronto: William Briggs, 1912.

Northwest Review, 45th Anniversary Issue, Winnipeg, 1930.

O'Dea, T. *American Catholic Dilemma.* New York: Sheed and Ward, 1959.

Okołowicz, Józef. *Kanada: Garstka Wiadomości dla Wychodźców.* Kraków: Polskie Towarzystwo Emigracyjne, 1913.

Palmer, Howard. *Land of the Second Chance: A History of Ethnic Groups in Southern Alberta.* Lethbridge: The Lethbridge Herald, 1972.

Pamiętniki Emigrantów: KANADA. Warsaw: Książka i Wiedza, 1971.

Park, Robert E. *The Immigrant Press and Its Control.* New York: Harper, 1922.

Patterson, Sheila. "This New Canada," *Queen's Quarterly,* LXII (1955), 80-88.

Perkowski, J.L. "Folkways of the Canadian Kashubs," in Cornelius J. Jaenen, ed., *Slavs in Canada.* Vol. III. Toronto: Ukrainian Echo Pub. Col. Ltd., 1971.

Pielorz, Józef, OMI. *Oblaci Polscy 1920-1970.* Rome: Dom Generalny, 1970.

Pierwszy Polski Kalendarz Dla Kanady Na Rok 1915. Montreal: W.J. Ortela i Spółka, 1915.

Podoski, Wiktor. *Młodzież A My.* Ottawa: Private Edition, 1959.

Ministerstwo Spraw Zagranicznych. Wydział Polaków Zagranicą. "Korespondencja Dotycząca Prasy Polskiej w Kanadzie, 1934-1935," Mimeograph, Poland, n.d.

Polonia Zagranicą. *Powszechna Wystawa Krajowa w 1929R.* Poznań, Poland: n.p., 1929.

Polzin, Theresita. *The Polish Americans: Whence and Whither.* Pulaski, Wisc.: Franciscan Publishers, 1973.

Porter, John. *The Vertical Mosaic.* Toronto: The University of Toronto Press, 1965.

Radecki, Franciszek. "Notatki." Toronto, Mimeograph, 1973.

Radecki, Henry. "POLISH-Canadian, CANADIAN-Polish, or CANADIAN?" Toronto, York University Mimeograph, 1970.

_____. "Culture and Language Maintenance Efforts of the Polish Ethnic Group in Canada." Toronto, York University Mimeograph, 1971.

_____. "How Relevant are the Polish Part-Time Schools?" in B. Heydenkorn, ed., *Past and Present.* Toronto: Canadian-Polish Research Institute, 1974.

_____. "The Polish Voluntary Organizational Structure: Issues and Questions," in B. Heydenkorn, ed., *Past and Present.* Toronto: Canadian-Polish Research Institute, 1974.

_____. "Ethnic Organizational Dynamics: A Study of the Polish Group in Canada." York University, Unpublished Ph.D Dissertation, 1975.

Rak, Stanisław. *Agricultural Reform in Poland.* London: S.P.K., 1946.

Rakowski, Janusz. *Wczoraj i Dziś Reformy Rolnej.* Fryburg, Switzerland: Pamiętnik Literacki, 1946.

Report of the Northern Ontario Conference for Ethnic Groups and Community Development, "Harmony in Culture," School of Social Work, Laurentian University, Sudbury, Ontario, April 3-4, 1971.

Report of the Ontario Economic Council, *Immigrant Integration.* Toronto: Government of Ontario Printer, 1970.

Report of the Royal Commission on Bilingualism and Biculturalism, "The Official Languages," Book I. Ottawa: Queen's Printer, 1967.

_____, "Education," Book II. Ottawa: Queen's Printer, 1968.

_____, "The Cultural

Contribution of Other Ethnic Groups," Book IV. Ottawa: Queen's Printer, 1970.

"Report of the Select Committee on Emigration, 1860," *Journal of the Legal Association*, XVIII, Appendix 4, 1860.

Reymont, Władysław S. *Chłopi*. 4 volumes. Warsaw: Państwowy Instytut Wydawniczy, 1970.

———. *The Peasants*, trans. M.H. Dziewicki. New York: Knopf, 1925.

Richmond, Anthony H. *Post-War Immigrants in Canada*. Toronto: University of Toronto Press, 1967.

———. *Immigrants and Ethnic Groups in Metropolitan Toronto*. Toronto: York University Ethnic Research Programme, 1967.

———. "Sociology of Migration in Industrial and Post-Industrial Sociaties," in J.A. Jackson, ed., *Migration*. Cambridge: At The University Press, 1969.

———. "Immigration and Pluralism in Canada," in W.E. Mann, ed., *Social and Cultural Change in Canada*, Vol. I. Toronto: Copp Clark, 1970.

———. *Ethnic Residential Segregation in Metropolitan Toronto*. Toronto: York University Ethnic Research Programme, 1972.

———. "Language, Ethnicity and the Problem of Identity in a Canadian Metropolis," Paper Presented at the IXth International Congress of Anthropological and Ethnological Sciences, Chicago, August 28 to September 8, 1973.

Rolnik, Jacek. "Wycinanki Prasowe," *Związkowiec*, No. 8, 1935.

Rose, Arnold M. *Sociology*. New York: Knopf, 1965.

Rose, W.J. "Russian Poland in the Late Nineteenth Century," in W.F. Reddaway *et al.*, eds., *The Cambridge History of Poland*, Vol. II. Cambridge: At The University Press, 1941.

———. "Prussian Poland, 1850-1914," in W.F. Reddaway, *ibid.*, Vol. II. Cambridge: At The University Press, 1941.

Ryder, N.B. "The Interpretation of Origin Statistics," *The Canadian Journal of Economics and Political Science*, XXI (1955), 466-479.

Sajewicz, Jan, OMI. *Nasz Brat*. Prowincja Wniebowzięcia N.M.P., O.O. Oblatów w Kanadzie, 1972.

Schermerhorn, R.A. *These Our People*. Boston: D.C. Heath, 1949.

Schutz, A. "Collected Papers," *Studies in Social Theory*, Vol. II. The Hague: Martinus Nijhof, 1964.

The Senate of Canada, *Proceedings of the Standing Committee on Immigration and Labour*, Wednesday, June 18, 1947. Ottawa: King's Printer, 1947.

Sessional Papers No. 10, Vol. XXIV, Part II, "Immigration." Department of the Interior Sessional Papers 13, No. 2, Report of W.T.R. Preston, Inspector of Agencies in Europe, London, December 23, 1899, 12-19.

Seywerd, Henry. "Integration in Canada," *Migration News*, 7 (1958), 1, 1-5.

Silver Jubilee, Oblate Fathers. 1935-1960. Toronto: Assumption Province, 1960.

Skorzewski, Andrzej. *Pamiętniki*. Wrocław: Ignacy Witan, 1888.

Slavutych, Yars. "Slavic Literature in Canada," in *Slavs in Canada*, Vol. I. Proceedings of the First Conference on Canadian Slavs, Banff, June 9-12, 1966. Edmonton: Inter-University Committee on Canadian Slavs, 1966.

Smith, W.G. *A Study in Canadian Immigration*. Toronto: Ryerson, 1920.

_____. *Building the Nation*. Toronto: Ryerson, 1922.

Sobolewski, George. "Reflections on my Experiences as an Immigrant to Canada," *Migration News*, 9 (1960), 5.

"Souvenir of the Opening and Blessing of the new Holy Ghost Parish School," Winnipeg, November 23, 1958.

Statistical Year Book of Canada (1885-1904), Department of Agriculture. Ottawa: Government Printing Bureau, n.d.

Staniewski, A.J. "Do Wokandy Historyka – z Życia Polonii Toronto," Związkowiec, Jubilee Issue, April, 1935.

Stonequist, E.V. *The Marginal Man*. New York: Scribners, 1937.

Storey, M., and B. Pearson, eds. *The Canadian Family Tree*. Ottawa: Canadian Citizenship Branch, 1967.

Szczepański, Jan. *Polish Society*. New York: Random House, 1970.

Szwej, Rev. M. "Cząstka Polskiej Całości," Związkowiec, No. 14, February 20, 1973.

Tazbir, J., and F. Roztworowski. "The Commonwealth of the Gentry," in A. Gieysztor *et al.*, eds., *The History of Poland*. Warsaw: Polish Scientific Publishers, 1968.

Theodorson, G.A., and A.G. Theodorson. *Modern Dictionary of Sociology*. New York: Crowell, 1969.

Thomas, W.I., and F. Znaniecki. *The Polish Peasant in Europe and America*. 2 volumes, New York: Dover, 1958.

Timlin, Mabel F. "Canada's Immigration Policy, 1896-1910," *The Canadian Journal of Economics and Political Science*, XXVI (1960), 517-532.

The *Toronto Star* Forum, "Canada's Immigration Policy," Toronto, St. Lawrence Hall, October 17, 1972.

Trzy Prześliczne i Bardzo Skuteczne Modlitwy Przy Umierającym. Z Dodatkiem Siedmiu Pieśni Pogrzebowych i Litanie o Smierć Szczęsliwą. Drukowane Dla Pobożnego Ludu Polskiego, n.d.

Turek, V. "Poles Among the De Meuron Soldiers," *Historical and Scientific Society of Manitoba*, Series III, 9 (1954), 53-68.

_____. "Jeszcze o Polonii Kanadyjskiej," *Kultura*, 122 (1957), 85-94.

_____. *Sir Casimir Gzowski (1813-1898)*. Toronto: The Polish Alliance Press, 1957.

_____, ed. *The Polish Past in Canada*. Toronto: The Polish Alliance Press, 1960.

_____. *The Polish Language Press in Canada*. Toronto: The Polish Alliance Press, 1962.

_____. "Polacy w Manitobie: Liczba i Rozmieszczenie," *Problemy Polonii Zagranicznej*. Tom III. Warsaw: Polska Akademia Nauk. 1964.

_____. *Poles in Manitoba*. Toronto: The Polish Alliance Press, 1967.

233

Turowski, J. "Changes in the Rural Areas Under the Impact of Industrialization," *Polish Sociological Bulletin*, 1 (1966), 13, 123-131.

Turritin, A.H. "Ethnicity and Occupational Stratification in Metropolitan Toronto, 1961," York University, Department of Sociology Mimeograph, 1972.

Vallee, F.G., M. Schwartz, and F. Darknell. "Ethnic Assimilation and Differentiation in Canada," *Canadian Journal of Economics and Political Science*, XXIII (1957), 540-549.

Vernant, J. *The Refugee in the Post-War World*. London: Allen & Unwin, 1953.

Wachtl, K. *Historia Polonii w Ameryce*. Philadelphia: Polish Star Publishing Co., 1944.

Wallace, Stewart W., ed. "The Polish Group," *The Encyclopedia of Canada*, Vol. 5. Toronto: University Associates of Canada, 1937, p. 131.

Wańkowicz, Melchior. *Tworzywo*. Warsaw: Instytut Wydawniczy Pax, 1970.

____. *Three Generations*, trans. K. Cękalska. Toronto: Canadian-Polish Research Institute in Canada, 1973.

Ware, C.F. "Ethnic Communities," in E.R.A. Seligman, ed., *Encyclopedia of the Social Sciences*, Vol. v, pp. 607-613. New York: Macmillan, 1963.

Wawrów, Leszek. "Editor's Notes," *Echo*, IV (1972), No. 2.

White Paper on Immigration, "Canadian Immigration Policy." Ottawa: Queen's Printer, 1966.

Witos, Wincenty. *Jedna Wieś*. Chicago: Polskie Stronnictwo Ludowe i Związek Przyjaciół Wsi Polskiej w Ameryce, 1955.

Wojciechowski, Jerzy A. "The Future of Canada's Polish Speaking Community – Polonia's Problems and Possibilities," in T.W. Krychowski, ed., *Polish Canadians: Profile and Image*. Toronto: The Polish Alliance Press, 1969.

Wołodkiewicz, A. *Polish Contributions to Arts and Sciences in Canada*. London: White Eagle Press, 1969.

Wood, Arthur Evans. *Hamtramck: A Sociological Study of a Polish-American Community*. New Haven, Conn.: College and University Press, 1955.

Woodsworth, James S. *Strangers Within Our Gates*. N.p.: Frederick Clarke Stephenson, 1909.

____. *My Neighbour*. Toronto: The Missionary Society of the Methodist Church, 1911.

Woycenko, Ol'ha. *The Ukrainians in Canada*. Winnipeg: Trident Press, 1968.

Wskazówki Dla Uchodźców Do Kanady. Warsaw: Urząd Emigracyjny Przy Ministerstwie Pracy i Opieki Społecznej. Drukarnia Państwowa, 1927.

Wytrwal, Joseph A. *America's Polish Heritage: A Social History of the Poles in America*. Detroit: Endurance Press, 1961.

Złote Pokłosie Parafii Św. Stanisława Kostki. Toronto. 1911-1961. Toronto, 1961.

Złoty Jubileusz Towarzystwa Białego Orła w Montrealu, 1902-1952. Toronto: Jubilee Commitee, 1952.

Znaniecki, Florian. "The Poles," in H.P. Fairchild, ed., *Immigrant*

Backgrounds. New York: Wiley, 1927.

Zubrzycki, B.J. *Polacy w Kanadzie (1759-1946).* Toronto: Kongress Polonii Kanadyjskiej, 1947.

Zubrzycki, J. *Polish Immigrants in Britain.* The Hague: Martinus Nijhoff, 1956.

Związek Nauczycielstwa Polskiego w Kanadzie, "Spis Szkół w Kanadzie, Rok Szkolny 1972/73." Toronto, Mimeograph, 1973.

Zybała, Stanisław. "Foreign in Language, Canadian in Spirit, Human in Every Other Respect," in J.M. Kirschbaum *et al.,* eds, *Twenty Years of Ethnic Press Association in Ontario..* Toronto: Ethnic Press Association in Ontario, 1971.

———. "Jak Tam Na Wojęnce Ładnie . . . ," *Związkowiec,* No. 100, 1973.

OTHER SOURCES

ARCHIVES   The Canadian Polish Research Institute, Toronto
           The Mother's House. The Order of the Felician Sisters of Mary Immaculate, Mississauga, Ontario

INTERVIEWS   Mr. W. Dutkiewicz
             Mr. Peter Gzowski
             Rev. Mother Superior Mary Alexandrette, OFS
             Most Rev. Bishop Niemiński
             Mr. S.T. Orłowski
             Rev. S. Puchniak, OMI

INDEX